D1596586

CRITICAL INSIGHTS

American Creative Nonfiction

CRITICAL INSIGHTS

American Creative Nonfiction

Editor
Jay Ellis
University of Colorado at Boulder

SALEM PRESS
A Division of EBSCO Information Services, Inc.
Ipswich, Massachusetts

GREY HOUSE PUBLISHING

Publisher's Cataloging-In-Publication Data
(Prepared by The Donohue Group, Inc.)

American creative nonfiction / editor, Jay Ellis, University of Colorado
   at Boulder. -- [First edition].

   pages : illustrations ; cm. -- (Critical insights)

   Edition statement supplied by publisher.
   Includes bibliographical references and index.
   ISBN: 978-1-61925-417-6 (hardcover)

   1. Creative nonfiction, American--History and criticism. 2. Authors,
American--Biography--History and criticism. 3. Narration (Rhetoric)--History.
I. Ellis, Jay, 1963- II. Series: Critical insights.

PS366.C74 A44 2015
810
LCCN: 2015933434

First Printing

Contents _____

Resources ───────────────────────────

About This Volume

Jay Ellis

Tell all the truth but tell it slant — (Emily Dickinson) [1]

This book provides an overview of a genre of genres called "creative nonfiction," but also a look at lyric essay, which I will argue deserves consideration distinct from creative nonfiction (even though some lyric essayists use these terms interchangeably, or reject generic distinctions altogether). Simply introducing a collection of essays about creative nonfiction occasions trouble because the term remains so troubling—and compelling. Many things called "lyric essay" make good on their truth claims better than any bureaucrat's memo. Others do as well, but cross the line in their play with facts.

What line? It may be hip to deny one, but readers and writers have talked about one between the real and the fictional for at least as far back as the printing press. In the West, at least, philosophers have argued about it since Socrates (against the Greek Sophists). We keep talking about such a line for good reasons. My introductory chapter will not so much attempt to define "creative nonfiction" as to figure out why readers of American literature in particular ended up with this odd compound term—especially instead of "fiction"—for so much writing. Later, my Critical Lens chapter will attempt to make peace with some lyric essayists whose work cannot be trusted as a meaningful form of "nonfiction."

Between my chapters, Kelly Clasen provides helpful definitions in her essay on the background and history of creative nonfiction, impressively covering over a dozen of its subgenres. From captivity narratives and autobiography, Clasen traces the trail of memoir as its expectations and achievements evolve and weave. A nation on the move—sometimes through violent expansion, but also through more benign roaming of its citizens—generates an interest in narratives moving through space as much as time. Clasen thereby highlights the importance of nonfiction travel writing to much fiction. Travel, she notes, included the transport and escape of slaves, and one of the most important legacies of creative nonfiction in America has been, and will continue to be, the truths told of such heinous faults as slavery. Particularly when official accounts would elide truth, creative nonfiction can fill the historical gap, especially when this entails correcting unduly fictionalized myths of national origin. Journalism similarly needed creative slants to tell its truths. Our late capitalist dependence on narratives emphasizing choice often turn to examinations of our personal health, how we feed ourselves—even the strange dependence of some of us on pets—everything personal and once private. It seems no aspect of our daily lives remains exempt from personal reporting, yielding even more of creative nonfiction's subgenres.

Ross Griffin follows the critical responses to creative nonfiction, extending our inquiry into writing that claims truth on unstable grounds. Griffin describes three schools of definition: reality representation; the Fourth Genre school; and then a third, critical, consensus that creative nonfiction is simply a different type of fiction—a position this volume editor may agree with even as he continues to teach and support students writing "creative nonfiction." Griffin's admirable examination of the truth-claims within various types of creative nonfiction includes notice of the controversies and sometimes scandals arising from those claims, especially when a writer plays deliberately loose with facts. Despite a comparative lack of serious scholarship on our genre of genres, Griffin provides an excellent guide to critical reception, while furthering our taxonomical work on "creative nonfiction."

At this point, readers may begin to wonder if we need the term at all. Especially as I follow Griffin with my own argument for a separate category of "lyric essay"—precisely to solve some problems around truth-claims and invention—I will nonetheless argue for "creative nonfiction," if alongside that of "lyric essay."

David Bahr finishes our Critical Contexts section with a nuanced comparative analysis of Tim O'Brien's work across genres. Drawing on his own previous journalism, when he interviewed this

Vietnam veteran and writer, Bahr finds O'Brien working a spectrum between fiction and nonfiction, between autobiographical memoir to metafiction to a more fictional novel. O'Brien's distinctions between literal and emotional truth bear out the spectral argument for regarding deliberate fabrication in the service of some higher truth as a different genre (again, what I note in the growth of "lyric essay"). The degree to which O'Brien's metafictional *The Things They Carried* drew on O'Brien's actual experiences, however, leads Bahr to argue persuasively for that work's importance to creative nonfiction, as "autofiction." Difficulties of mimesis, however, lead to multiple instances where Bahr finds O'Brien bending truth—or making up details outright—to get at what he sees as the truth of his experiences. In this sense, our Critical Contexts essays avoid an untruthfully neat agreement on terms, precisely because there remain so many different perspectives on what "creative nonfiction"—and its many overlapping and alternative genres—means. In the spirit of multiple creative perspectives contributing to a collective sense of truth, our Readings chapters, therefore, were also not edited to some unnaturally enforced agreement on generic terms.

If "autofiction," therefore, works the same seam between "creative nonfiction" and fiction, as does "lyric essay," Peter Kratzke finds in Benjamin Franklin's *Autobiography* a nonfiction edge of that seam. Kratzke provides a wonderful view of his candidate for America's first creative nonfiction writer. His Franklin may be historical to us, and often historical in his own aims as a writer, but a *middle way* provides Franklin with a means of combining self-referential narratives with creative inventions that are ultimately polemical. Particularly, as Kratzke finds Franklin's various personas contradicting themselves, he ascertains, with tongue in cheek, this sometimes-elided *middle way* as a regular rhetorical goal for America's most notable writer.

Kelly Clasen's essay provides a superb example of relatively early nature writing from Susan Fenimore Cooper. This fascinating writer (whose father may have been better known—including in parody by Mark Twain), noted seasonal changes in her local environment that have proven to be historically and scientifically valuable records. Clasen places Cooper's *Rural Hours* not merely alongside, but above Henry David Thoreau's *Walden*. Reading Cooper's close adherence to nonfictional recordings of detail provides an unintended irony, as Thoreau's comparatively personal and emotional approach would fit their age's (if not ours, we hope) sexist assumptions about women writing about nature. In her extensive research, Clasen deftly finds Cooper's contributions to ecofeminist writing, while providing another example of her interdisciplinarity—weaving attention to science with ethical social concerns and presaging the work of feminist historians of science, such as Carolyn Merchant and Evelyn Fox Keller.

Christopher Allen Varlack situates Claude McKay's autobiographical writing both within his work as a novelist and within the larger tradition of African American memoir. Following the corrections of Frederick Douglass and Harriet Jacobs to romantic rationalizations of slavery, McKay's writing contributed to the concept of Negritude, while working the seam between the personal and the political that would later trouble James Baldwin. Varlack rescues the nonfiction previously ignored by scholars of McKay and of the Harlem Renaissance generally. Like Baldwin, McKay sought freedom to focus on his own aesthetic and personal concerns, and moving abroad seemed to allow this even as his experiences in London and Russia continued the political activism of his pen. Varlack provides invaluable insight to the importance of nonfiction to McKay's eventual unification of the personal and the political in his contributions to Negritude.

Shelby Foote's attempt to chronicle the war over American slavery resulted in a mammoth three-volume work of well over a million words, *The Civil War: A Narrative*. Christopher Walsh's essay focuses on the first volume, and Walsh's previous work on southern literature provides a strong backdrop for his readings of Foote's creative nonfiction. The scrupulous attention to accumulated detail compiled by Foote the military historian is carried along by the swift narrative drive of Foote the novelist. Despite the flaws Walsh rightly notes in Foote's contradictory explanations for the South's drive to war, Foote's excellent attention to anecdotal and character-driven story often supported his attempt to relate more than one side of the conflict and at more than one level. Still, Walsh finds Foote regularly struggling to tell one side of the story notably more than the other—and, in so doing, falling farther away from the nonfictional aims of his project.

G. Thomas Couser introduces us to an exemplary range of writing within the medical humanities, from the ranks of medical professionals to the more recent prominence of illness narratives. His attention to this large subgenre of creative nonfiction focuses on our need for advocacy; to speak for health care is not only timely, but fundamental. Couser highlights the inherent power differential in medical humanities, where doctors often seem to have all the power and patients none—not only in the examination room or the surgical theater, but also at the writing desk. Disability narratives then become all the more necessary to counter maladies of untruth, as they speak to normative assumptions excluding anyone who does not fit within the bulge of a statistical curve. Conditions not of disease, but of differences that cannot be erased meanwhile yield disability narratives without the happy ending of illness stories; recovery remains out of the picture, so that stories of disability demand adjustments on the part of readers in a dominant culture addicted to inspiration—especially on someone else's experiential dime.

Katherine Lashley's essay on Temple Grandin, the autistic scholar and consultant, provides us with a focused inquiry into one writer's work within medical humanities. Lashley's research on Grandin ran alongside her desire to write about her autistic sister. Grandin's writing has not received the critical attention it deserves within the academy, and Lashley remedies this well, noting the foundational status of Grandin's work to any discussion of autism spectrum disorders. Without Grandin's advocacy, it would be hard to imagine the degree to which some people with autism, and certainly more with Asperger syndrome, in some cases regard themselves as simply different from "neurotypicals." Yet Grandin remains a "supercrip," as Lashley notes, and her writing regularly respects the fact that many autistics cannot function at her level. Grandin's personal testimony to her condition, therefore, makes up only a part of her contribution to autism studies, and to a wider understanding and acceptance of the variety of experiences on the autistic end of a spectrum.

Multiple accounts of a shared experience, especially through the lens of the personal, are the focus of Shira Segal's chapter on the cinematic self. In autobiographical documentary films of family life by Sarah Polley and Jonas Mekas, Segal explores an area of creative nonfiction beyond writing. Our culture continues to become more image oriented, while more commonly *aliterate* in alphabetic texts away from screens and unaccompanied by images. The unreliable, yet irresistible power of photographs—especially those that move (whether frame by frame or digitally)—continues in their ability to convince viewers that they present a window onto something "real." Indeed, reference remains a problem in film more obviously than on the page precisely because so much mimetic work seems to be done by merely opening a camera's lens. Documentary film especially carries this burden, and Segal helpfully outlines historical problems of correspondence in nonfiction film. Segal sharply describes controversy echoing that over creative nonfiction writing, between those refusing to let go of strong objectivity goals, and those given in to relativism; of course, most valuable documentary work occurs between those poles. Segal's thorough attention to specifics, especially in Polley's film, provides both an excellent view of the difficulties of nonfiction in film, and by analogy, in writing as well.

Beth Walker's celebration of Natalie Goldberg has to attend to the multiple ways in which this well-known writer works in various media and genres. Through Zen Buddhism, Goldberg achieves a unity of purpose and accomplishment across all her activities, from teaching and studying to meditation and practice, from writing to visual art. Goldberg's workshops and her book *Writing Down the Bones* have influenced innumerable writers. In focusing on Goldberg's regard for memory as truthful experience, Walker returns us to the personal focus of much creative nonfictional memoir. Goldberg's work as a creative writer of fiction then further provides what Walker sees as an outlet protecting her nonfictional work.

Brandon Benevento finds a more complicated relation between fiction and nonfiction in the work of David Foster Wallace. Benevento finds that, under the cloud of ubiquitous consumerism, Wallace's attempts to convey the truth of personal experience through creative nonfiction unified his perspective with objectivity and social-mindedness. Contrary to what we might assume, Benevento finds evidence that one might reverse terms for Wallace's writing, regarding his literary journalism as perhaps more imagined than his fiction. But Benevento persuades us that Wallace's constant attention to ethics provides an ultimate value in full accord with, yet never overwhelming, his aesthetics.

Our final chapter brings back David Bahr, on Art Spiegelman's "Prisoner on The Hell Planet." Spiegelman's comic manipulates time through its three-dozen panels to address the author's mental illness, his mother's depression and suicide, his father's anguished reaction, the young Artie's ambivalent feelings of both guilt and anger, and the legacy of the Holocaust, which his parents barely survived. Bahr performs a deft close reading of this now foundational work of graphic creative nonfiction, while leading us through an excellent crash course in the aesthetics and rhetorics of comics, noting Spiegelman's manipulation not only of varied graphic styles, but also of the frames of his panels—all to control narrative time.

A single volume could not include even passing attention to every type of creative nonfiction, but these scholars take us on tours of writing and images that will endure. Foodways writing, sports writing, humor, prison narratives, addiction and recovery memoir, crime writing, investigative journalism, travel writing, conversion narratives (not just to religion, but political and ethical, such as vegan conversion narratives), and creative nonfiction approaches to non-medical science writing—music, art, and film criticism—the list of what we did not have room for here speaks again to the breadth of our genre of genres. Wherever writers take care with their sentences, include their eyes or their "I," or simply avail themselves of analogical and inductive reasoning instead of plopping a boilerplate deductive thesis on the head of readers, creative nonfiction techniques transform any genre of writing that seeks to do more than merely relate "information" (itself perhaps a specious word for an unstable concept). Creative nonfiction tells all the truth it can, whatever its slant.

Note

1.   Johnson, ed. #1129, from his edition of *The Complete Poems*.

Work Cited

Dickinson, Emily. *The Complete Poems of Emily Dickinson*. Ed. Thomas H. Johnson. New York: Little, Brown and Co., 1997.

On American Creative Nonfiction_____

Jay Ellis

Genres

To write about creative nonfiction entails considering its problems as a genre, both because of its relatively recent recognition as a distinct genre (or several genres recently classed together) and because of inherent difficulties with claims made by some of its authors and publishers.[1] These problems remain taxonomical: how do we define the constituent terms of its label? Some readers and certainly some writers of creative nonfiction maintain an untroubled attitude toward labeling; after all, isn't that simply what someone decides to call someone else's work? But then many writers claim the label of creative nonfiction with far less attention to the implications of its constituent words "creative" and "nonfiction" than they bring to choosing the more precise words for the rest of their writing. This volume studies creative nonfiction in several of its sub-genres, but readers will notice how regularly we encounter problems embedded in its compound term. Indeed, Ross Griffin's title for our Critical Reception chapter suggests we might adopt the better phrase "a special kind of fiction" instead. Griffin's assessment includes nuance beyond a label, however, and the label "creative nonfiction" persists in writing in and on special kinds of fiction—of all types. The Association of Writers & Writing Programs has adopted the term. Indeed, I chose our title *Creative Nonfiction*; my editor added *American*, which will help me with this argument later on.

Within academia, the properly endless growth of knowledge (but also economic pressures similar to those on toothpaste manufacturers) exerts a constant cultural-evolutionary imperative of increasing specialization. Indeed, the PhD is supposed to be an expert in something that no one else in his or her new department knows much about. This, too, creates a taxonomical pressure on the study of literature, even though, as John Gardner argued,

"Genre-crossing of one sort or another is behind most of the great literary art in the English tradition" (20). My agreement with Gardner, or my similar claim that all great works transcend their aspects of mere genre, makes it easy to ignore this problem. Unless one is endeavoring to become an expert in early Puritan creative nonfiction of the long seventeenth century, and as long as we like what we end up buying, borrowing, and reading, why worry over terms?

Because practical and ethical problems arise if we do not. Stories that claim to be true, or based on real people and places, and on verifiable events claim a different status than those deemed purely fictional. If we label them differently, we must consider those labels. Practically speaking, we need some truth in labeling. In an iTunes account, programmers have coded that system to suggest music by one artist because you listened to another with similar characteristics—some aspect of genre—that the program traces in both. (Buy a gift for someone with different tastes to warp the system's responses to you.) Late capitalism necessarily labels its products, and works of art, when sold, inevitably become—even if, as some of us believe, they only temporarily become *merely*— products hardly different from toothpaste. Before we see labeling problems in some of our following chapters, it seems fit to inquire into general problems with the label "creative nonfiction."

How does our label of "creative nonfiction" work? The philosopher Ludwig Wittgenstein described one way in which words need not have deep reference, yet work well enough within context that their meaning serves the purposes of their statement. A builder calls out to a helper for the stones he needs, "blocks, pillars, slabs and beams." Builder "A calls them out; B brings the stone which he has learnt to bring at such-and-such a call" (Wittgenstein 6e). Wittgenstein demonstrates the possibility of any two participants in language to accept the provisional aspect of that language. Indeed, Wittgenstein did not write, "blocks, pillars, slabs and beams," but rather "Würfel, Säulen, Platten und Balken" (6). In what he calls "a complete primitive language" (6), translation works well enough, we might say.

If, however, it happens often enough that writers claim pieces to be "nonfiction," yet readers of those pieces cannot find enough of what they expect when using the word "nonfiction," our language has become notably more complicated. This problem occurs often enough with the "non-" part of "creative nonfiction" that we must consider it further. Postmodernist or other unhelpfully relativist dodges about what constitutes something "true," and what details are purely invented or intentionally altered, don't keep us from at least trying to clarify the "non-" when possible.

For this chapter, we will rely provisionally on a definition of "non-" related to what the philosopher John Searle calls "*observer independent*" matter and events. Searle uses this and related terms to refer to things that exist without need of our perception of them: "This class includes mountains, molecules, and tectonic plates" (original emphasis, 52). Searle notes that part of what happens in our brains when we perceive something is also observer-independent, such as our neurons firing; even if we struggle with imperfect means of "observing" that phenomenon, two observers using the same apparatus can observe that firing and measure the same things. Consciousness, however—our awareness of what we have perceived after our neurons fire in perception of something observer-independent—remains subjective. Searle claims consciousness is nonetheless "psychologically real, observer-independent phenomena" (52). Only each individual consciousness may experience that firing in exactly that way, or in any case, we cannot objectively capture or measure—at least yet—the epiphenomena of that conscious experience the way we can detect neural firing itself.

Consciousness is therefore an experience, inherently subjective, but this does not mean we should give up on shared standards of agreement on what we observe. These distinctions will be helpful, ironically so, because Searle's statements directly about creative nonfiction remain perhaps less useful when troubles arise over whether a writer's claim of "nonfiction" should be trusted. On fiction and truth, this speech-act theorist respects the writer's intentions without trouble over whether they are genuine. M. H. Abrams describes this view:

> [F]ictive sentences are meaningful according to the rules of ordinary, nonfictional discourse, but [. . .] in accordance with conventions implicitly shared by the author and reader of a work of fiction, they are not put forward as assertions of fact, and therefore are not subject to the criterion of truth or falsity that applies to sentences in nonfictional discourse. (95)

Abrams then cites Searle's "The Logical Status of Fictional Discourse:" even a claim of truth within fiction is made in awareness that readers know "a writer of fiction only 'pretends' to make assertions" (Abrams 95).

This, of course, works better within fiction than within, or about, nonfiction. Some creative nonfiction writers claim to be relating facts, nonetheless claiming that the "creative" part of their genre allows deliberate manipulation of those facts. We will tackle this problem in our Critical Lens chapter, where we will see John D'Agata attempting to change the location of a Tabasco-sauce bottle in a story about suicide. Such a situation deliberately refutes not only distinctions between observer-independent facts (say, a Tabasco-sauce bottle's location) and our necessarily subjective experience, or creative remembering, of our observer-relative perception of those facts (say, where we think it was found)—but also a distinction between the bottle's location and where we want it to have been found in order to achieve a supposed poetic resonance. In that chapter, I will argue that the label "lyric essay" ought to be used instead of "creative nonfiction," rather than loosely synonymous with it, when a writer wants that much creative freedom. My argument certainly won't result in "Creative Nonfiction" programs and departments across the country changing their names to "Lyric Writing" or some other alternative. But in writing carefully, one has to choose words carefully—especially on a subject where many do not—and all the more so when claiming at least to introduce, if not wholly to cover, that subject.

Apart from constant institutional pressures to split academic study into increasingly specialized programs and continual economic pressures on writers (temporarily, we may include scholars here) to claim they are writing in some fundamentally new way (see "postmodernism"), such problems merit the question, *why not simply call all creative works "fiction?"* Here, I will suggest two answers: one reason some writers claim the "non-" when they might more helpfully label their writing "fiction based on facts" (a different claim than "nonfiction") is an abiding anxiety, particularly American, over the word "creative;" another reason is a parallel abiding American obsession with "facts" or writing "truth."

Creative American Anxieties

"[T]he first book printed in English America" was *The Bay Psalm Book* (Eames v). From the beginning, New England literary history planted by Europeans expresses anxiety over fidelity to observer-independent truth. For as difficult as it may seem to most contemporary readers, the Puritans regarded everything in the world as fundamentally connected, indeed presaged, in their Bible—purely true. Typological hermeneutics, a theoretical means of one thing (or type) predicted, or foreshadowed, by another thing (or type) was not a science of interpretation (or hermeneutics) for the Puritans, but rather a living factual relation in human time. For the Puritans, only a lack of full "grace" and the quotidian human experience of temporality could account for distinctions between subjective, observer-dependent thoughts and feelings, and the observer-independent reality of God's creation, which, "in the eye of eternity," existed in "an everlasting present" (Berkovitch 36).

Outside of time, God would certainly deliver the perfectly organized book of his truth, with every detail reliably connected to every other; therefore, "much of the Old Testament is read as a *type* of the revelation to come in the New Testament. Both Jonah and Solomon are *types* of Christ, [. . .]" (Harmon & Holman 530, original emphasis). The inheritance for New England writers from this includes a sense of required correspondence between writing and its proper subject, the Truth of God. Put another way, one should only be writing about the Truth, and one should do so as plainly—as truthfully—as possible.

Richard Mather's 1640 "Preface" stands as one of the first arguments in New England Puritan theology against adornment, if not against invention and imagination altogether. As such, it enjoins word choice that is truthful because it supposedly lacks artifice. Here, he frames the translated hymns to follow:

> If therefore the verses are not always so smooth and elegant as some may desire or expect; let them consider that *God's Altar needs not our polishings* [. . .] for we have respected rather a plain translation, [than] to smooth our verses with the sweetness of any paragraph, and so have attended Conscience rather than Elegance, fidelity rather than poetry, in translating the hebrew words into [the] english language [. . .]. (Mather [xxxii], my emphasis)[2]

The foundationalist attempt to convey literal truth always swerves under the unavoidably creative hand, however, whether writing something putatively original, yet divinely inspired, on the page, or in translating words deemed already holy and infallible. In "The Bay Psalm Book and the 'Halfway' Poetics of Worship," Amy Morris notes the ironic result of the translators' attempt: by seemingly avoiding aesthetics, "the New England compilers inevitably fashioned an alternative aesthetic and promoted a different kind of poetic effect" (76). Creativity, however meager, remains unavoidably inherent in writing, including translation.

America's first great New England poet in print, Anne Bradstreet, published in her lifetime only what we would call creative nonfiction poetry: nonfiction poems, as they referred to seasons, politics—subjects of "genuine erudition" (Westbrook 39). Published in 1650 (without her knowledge by her brother-in-law in England), she was hailed as no less than a *"Tenth Muse,"* a wonder first as a celebrated poet from America—and second as a woman (Westbrook 38, italics from title). No one except literary historians, however, would read those poems now. The private and personal poems unpublished in her lifetime now speak to us as poetic memoir, but she agonized over them and in them, worrying that undue attention to anything other than the plain fact of god, and devotion to him, occasioned the terrible hardships they often describe. The burning of her beloved library, the death of several of her children, horrible fevers she suffered—all could be God's judgment on her for turning her attention to the wonders of nature, and—most importantly to us here—language.

Many critics of our confessional age (such as Adrienne Rich) have fixed upon her rebellious modes, but have done so within a political context that hardly existed in Bradstreet's time. Bradstreet's dynamic of a guilty faith becomes her ultimate proof of God's existence, even as Morris points out, we see these constraining her poetic meter (Morris 92–94). Her ambivalence about creative expression parallels a tension between subjects: the truth of God and the potentially distracting inventions of verse attending to anything else, including its own aesthetic achievement. Faith distrusts creativity as much as it does non-religious subjects.

So too does business, and the business of democratic rhetoric, distrust creativity by the mid-eighteenth century. As truth becomes scientific, in a world without divine correspondence, no matter: the importance of fidelity over invention continues. Even in Benjamin Franklin's ironic expressions of creativity (as Peter Kratzke traces them later in this volume), we see the ongoing ambivalence about invention. Franklin may write from the point of view of a woman, or deliver an almanac full of partially tongue-in-cheek contradictory advice. But verse remains simultaneously too creative and unremunerative. After his brother prints some of Ben's poems, the "first sold wonderfully [. . .]."

> This flattered my Vanity. But my Father discourag'd me, by ridiculing my Performance, and telling me *Verse-makers were generally Beggars*; so I escap'd being a poet, most probably a very bad one. But my Prose Writing has been of great *Use* to me in the Course of my Life, and was a principal Means of my Advancement. (Franklin 1138, my emphasis)

Creativity simply doesn't pay, but it also precedes his turn not only to prose, but to writing what is "*Use[ful]*" to "Advancement."

What continues here is the call on writing not to stray creatively too far from necessity, here the necessities of advancement on numerous fronts: social, political, and financial. Indeed, Franklin's lexicon suggests a stark ledger (for a frugal man fond of lists) with negative words opposite the positive. Franklin's *Autobiography* much prefers "useful" (twenty-five times) and "business" (ninety-two times) to "idle" (eight times, all negative in tone). To "scribble," if it meant to "handle a Pen" (1365) in a just cause or successful business is encouraged, but "scribbling" in verse wastes time. When a bohemian friend, James Ralph, persuades Franklin to submit one of Ralph's poems as his own and this meets with success, Franklin worries at first. "This Transaction fix'd Ralph in his Resolution of becoming a Poet. I did all I could to dissuade him from it, but He continu'd scribbling verses, till *Pope* cur'd him.—He became however a pretty good Prose Writer" (1342, original emphasis). The danger averted, the country whose business is business gains a "pretty good" pen back from the malady of creativity.

By 1809, Washington Irving creatively attributed his tall tales to fictional authors. Not just Diedrich Knickerbocker, but Jonathan Oldstyle, Geoffrey Crayon, and Fray Antonia Agapida stood in the docket for Irving's fictions. The true author even concocted a hoax, posting advertisements for Knickerbocker's whereabouts after the fictional historian skips his hotel bill (Jones 92–95). Here, creativity runs free while obscuring creative authority. Irving's hoax "generated the kind of response a modern marketing firm could only dream of" (Jones 94). It also extended Franklin's play with truth in nonfiction; as he pulled off this hoax for his *History of New York*, "Irving played fair" in the nonfiction, remaining "accurate as far as names and events" in the book (Jones 96). At this point, what was anxiety adds a creative dodge that nonetheless plays on the abiding need of the public for correspondence to truth. In this case, Irving presents a work of "history" substantiated by notable accuracy, but does so through a fictional author for whom the real author convinces New Yorkers to search—a fictional joke on their need for truth in writing.

Nathaniel Hawthorne's "Custom-House" introduction to *The Scarlet Letter* in 1850 then claims to have found the cloth letter

"A" itself (factual evidence for a nonfiction story), along with the rough outline of that story, left behind by a "Surveyor Pue" (145–146). His narrator rejects possible assumptions that "the dressing up of the tale, and imagining the motives and modes of passion that influenced the characters" were either constrained or suggested by the original manuscript. Hawthorne therefore claims the creativity of detail, while continuing the fictional claim of "the authenticity of the outline" (146). Creativity here asserts itself, while simultaneously claiming potato-like roots in the real soil of the author's Puritan heritage, with a scarlet letter as real as a Tabasco bottle speaking from the past. Hawthorne knows that his readers know the entire story is fiction, but the play with the found-manuscript-conceit nonetheless signals the American need for connection to the factual, even within a fiction. In comic prosopopeia, Hawthorne conjures up the ghost of Pue to charge him with artistic license for telling the truth about Hester Prynne, to "give to your predecessor's memory the credit which will be rightly its due!" (147). This "predecessor" is not so much Prynne as it is the first author, Pue. Hawthorne thus concocts a limited liability holding company for his creative endeavor. Spread out the risk, but take all creative credit.

This occurs against its own local historical anxieties about making things up, as opposed to telling the social truths of Hawthorne's time through moral suasion.[3] The following year, he published *The House of the Seven Gables*, again including a rhetorical frame even while arguing for creative freedom. The "Preface" makes an "even if" argument, first claiming that he has not made up too much, and then that even if he has, he claims the right to do so. This is all against a presumed counter-argument of straw: "Many writers" who make their morals obvious, "as by sticking a pin through a butterfly." Instead, "[a] high truth, indeed, fairly, finely, and skilfully wrought out, brightening at every step, and crowning the final development of a work of fiction, may add an artistic glory, but is never any truer, and seldom any more evident, at the last page than at the first" (Hawthorne 352). It also earns more subtle metaphorical word choice. The force of Hawthorne's language points to many concerns, but one remains the anxiety over creativity.

Clumsy Separations—and Combinations

We can see Hawthorne insists on artistic freedom to imaginatively create details, nonetheless claiming a moral purpose. Eventually, he moved away from the term "romance" (McWilliams 79–81), but he never earnestly claimed he was not making things up as much as he was (unless we believe in the ghost of Surveyor Pue). By our time, canon-making and unmaking has lumped the work of both Hawthorne and his moral suasion contemporaries (Harriet Beecher Stowe, for instance) under the single term "novel." The word grew big enough to include both, even as arguments in book reviews, book clubs, and some academic circles continue to play tug-of-war with the proper purpose of fiction writing. Long fiction of all types, with varying priorities for creativity and aesthetics on the one hand, and attention (however obvious) to social and moral concerns on the other, fits under the term now.

Indeed, generic terms remained up for grabs during Hawthorne's time. John McWilliams notes that, "Nina Baym's detailed study of the language of American periodicals from 1820 to 1860 shows that the terms 'novel' and 'romance' were so regularly interchangeable among reviewers that their usage amounts to a 'definitional chaos' (426–443)" (75). Henry James referred to these distinctions as "clumsy separations" (17). Why do we now seem to need the separate category of creative nonfiction? Partly because of the creativity anxiety traced above and partly because of the culture's parallel abiding pressure to adhere to facts, and its appetite for what at least seems a true story (think of New Yorkers searching for the incorporeal Knickerbocker).

A hundred years after Hawthorne's positions, Dwight Macdonald called out a failure of Americans to care as much about imagination and ideas, as about facts:

> Our mass culture—and a good deal of our high, or serious, culture as well—is dominated by an emphasis on data and a corresponding lack of interest in theory, by a frank admiration of the factual and an uneasy contempt for imagination, sensibility, and speculation. We are obsessed with technique, hagridden by Facts, in love with information. Our *popular* novelists must tell us all about the historical and professional backgrounds of their puppets; our press lords make

millions by giving us this day our daily Fact; our scholars—or, more accurately, our research administrators—erect pyramids of data to cover the corpse of a stillborn idea; [. . .]. (201, my emphasis)

Macdonald's complaint against "The Triumph of the Fact" was voiced in 1957; he died in 1982, two years before Apple launched its Macintosh computer and twenty-two years before Facebook. One wonders what he would have made of Big Data (or panegyric rhetoric about it), or of people reporting what they ate for breakfast via Twitter, let alone of so-called "reality" television.

Ironically, one form of creative nonfiction—careful literary journalism, the type whose facts are checked—evolved, in part, to satisfy a desire for more than mere facts. But in some writing that looks like careful literary journalism—seemingly relying on facts, yet claiming the freedom to manipulate them—we will find creative nonfiction at the edges (specifically, refer to our chapter on the lyric essay). The American appetite for things labeled as factual seems only to have grown since Macdonald's complaint, perhaps particularly as the internet makes it quite easy not only to choose one's interpretation of the facts, but rather seemingly to choose the facts themselves. That is, the reliability of supposed facts—when their traditional sources have fallen and scattered into millions of Twitter feeds and blog posts, with little to no sense of the ethos behind them—has become something mythical itself (and a reason this writer teaches information literacy as necessary for strong nonfiction composition). Macdonald's complaint holds up with ironic depth accrued through the internet, so that now we have a wholly ambivalent regard for both creativity and nonfiction (our term, which ought meaningfully to entail "fact" and "truth"). We hunger for and yet distrust both. So who used these terms together first?

Lee Gutkind may have first combined them in the late 1970s. The National Endowment for the Arts adopted "creative nonfiction" as a category in 1983 to include nonfiction authors in consideration for creative writing fellowships. Gutkind then founded *Creative Nonfiction* magazine in 1993, and since then, the term crowds out others in the proliferation of writing programs teaching everything from literary journalism to lyric essay. Gutkind's definitions help, particularly when we later consider forms of the lyric essay bordering on what Macdonald called "parajournalism," because Gutkind champions the creativity of this genre of genres without playing deliberately loose with fact—difficult as that may be. Gutkind even titles his latest book *You Can't Make This Stuff Up*, a phrase usually uttered in appreciation of a particular story's truth being stranger than any possible fiction. For a guide to writing as well as reading in the genre, however, this title serves as a command: do not make up too much in creative nonfiction.

Making Things Up—But Not Too Much

> The use of imagination is not what lands creative nonfiction writers in trouble; it is the *misuse* of imagination.
> Certainly, we are—or should be—limited to only what is true when writing nonfiction, but what we imagine about something, someone, or some event is true in itself. It is true that we imagined it.
> The important distinction here: truth in labeling.
>
> (Gutkind, *Keep* 150, original emphasis)

Like Searle, then, Gutkind is falling back on genre as labeling; by calling something "creative nonfiction," the "creative" part allows for something we might call the truth of an observer-relative experience. We may be able to map the synaptic firing of a brain imagining something, but we may never be able to determine whether the truthfulness of that something has any correlation with observer-independent truth—blessedly so, as each individual consciousness necessarily perceives the same observer-independent truth with unavoidable creative variation. To argue that this creativity opens the gate for deliberately—consciously—altering an account of something is no more logical than arguing that the ease with which one may steal art on the internet makes it ethical to do so. (It only makes it quicker, easier, and more prevalent, all of which tempts the ethics of people less interested in supporting art than in consuming it.) Similarly, weak appeals to our condition as one overloaded with information—as if that fundamentally changes the ethics behind how we think—merely make it easier amongst a proliferation of facticity to stake out indefensible positions as if they were not logical dodges.

There are hoaxes, however, and there are disingenuous or simply ill-reasoned positions on these problems. Gutkind attempts to guard the edges of the cliff and admirably attends to good intentions. Creative nonfiction publishing abounds in stories where the writer honestly remembers an event in an entirely different way than others who experienced the same event. Lie detector tests, even when they work, only catch people who, on some level, know they are lying. But we know how well our memories truthfully lie to us, as it were; they "make up the gaps" in our incomplete perception of observer-independent phenomena by filling those gaps with entirely subjective and quite possibly inaccurate details, in order to form a coherent narrative of past events even when no such coherence is possible.

Gutkind provides an example of how to handle "truth in labeling" for such situations. "For example, the writer of a childhood memoir should feel free to employ this (properly signaled) foray into invention [. . .]." "[P]roperly signaled" seems to me quite helpful, though it requires a generous sense of trust on the part of readers. Again, we can only recall the culturally-anxious history of preference for "plain truth" and its distrust of art, to understand why some artists of obvious talent do not simply label their work as fiction. Searle's "intention" and Gutkind's "labeling" and "signal[ling]" are observer-relative and obtain meaning only from a transaction within the marketplace of publishing and reading various genres of writing—one that has often and seems inevitably often to prefer the "non-" before the "fiction."

Gutkind calls the honest signal to the reader that some details may be imaginatively true to the writer, without necessarily being factual, an "imaginative brush" (*Keep* 151). A good metaphor, as brushes come in different sizes. The bigger the brush (i.e., the more that is made up), the more overt the signal needs to be from the writer. Gutkind cites Judith Ortiz Cofer's switch to italics for a cousin's point of view; not only is the switch away from the writer's conscious memories (or even imaginative recreations we call "memory"), but it is furthermore a point of view delivered through dreams of that cousin. Italics provide the reader with a clear shift in what Searle calls intention, as if to say, *bear with me here as I make some things up to get at the larger truth of this story.* This example serves perfectly in an argument that we actually find ourselves always along a spectrum between the untenably opposite labels of intention called "fiction" and "nonfiction." We may ask, for instance, how many italics are too many before we simply call the work "autobiographical fiction." If readers must remain on their guard, and writers careful to fairly indicate when they are blurring a boundary between genres so problematically and provocatively labeled "non-," then why not at least agree to call all writing that contains anything but the most objective and fact-checked adherence to observer-independent objects and events "made-up" writing?

My term "made-up" writing can't solve the problem of the gap for several reasons. It's clunky, for one, and its very usefulness for describing any form of writing renders it tautological; of what use is a term that applies to everything? All writing is the result of a writer making things up, if one checks the richly various definitions of the phrase "make up" under the heading of the word "make" in the *American Heritage Dictionary.* "1. To put together; construct or compose: *make up a prescription*" does not seem to suggest a pharmacist who is also an alchemist, but rather one working with readily-available drugs even if they will be compounded into a prescription never used before. So too, "2. To constitute; form: *One hundred years make up a century*" appeals to a collective and agreed-upon fact, even if it is one that remains entirely dependent on collective observers who happen to have evolved with ten fingers and ten toes each. (If we had twelve, we would not demarcate time— not at all an observer-independent phenomenon—with a base-ten system of counting.)

But then the *American Heritage* definitions take an interesting turn. "3. To alter one's appearance for a role on the stage, as with a costume or cosmetics," points directly to the mimesis problem, such as troubled Socrates. He distrusted "mimetic forms," or "dramatic enactments of comic, satiric, or tragic incidents by actors wearing masks" as corrosive, "and he bars such poetry from his ideal state" ("Imitation"). From masks to cosmetics, I would also add that this definition connotes not only a distrust of actors pretending to be something they are not, but also a distrust of women, in "or cosmetics," as our dictionary then adds, "4. To apply cosmetics." The burden of pretense that is supposedly the realm of the feminine is, of course, a patriarchal construction. Against that linguistic history, "to make up" now seems to falsify, or if not yet for some readers, the next definition avoids ambiguity: "5. To devise as a fiction or *falsehood*; invent: *made up an excuse*" (first italics added).

Ambiguity returns, however, as the phrase continues to serve us wherever we need it: "6. To make good" or make up "the difference in the bill" and "7. To compensate for" what can only be a lack—such as our lack of sufficient objective, fact-checkable details corroborated by multiple sources, or by the limited accessibility of an observation-independent object or event for corroboration. My favorite is "8. To resolve a quarrel: *kissed and made up*," but there's also, "9. To make ingratiating or fawning overtures"—which comes to mind when recalling that James Frye relabeled his *Million Little Pieces* as memoir after its rejection as a novel (Peretz), surely a "fawning overture" to a public hungrier for "true" than for "fictional" stories. In 10., we simply have the sense of taking or retaking "an examination of course" because it was missed—or failed. (Ah, revision, and the errors that Franklin discounted as mere "errata.") "11. To set in order: *make up a room*" signals the way that writers all desperately attempt to relay, in some ordered fashion, experience in a universe that may not actually provide us with much order at all. And our dictionary's last definition gets us firmly on the page, as "12. *Printing*: To select and arrange material for: *made up the front page*." I love that we end with journalism, making up the front page of a newspaper (and now just as importantly, its website's "home page"), even as editors and compositors know that printed publications of any type require similar activity.

We make things up in every sense of our definitions for that activity. The best we can do with "creative nonfiction" is, in the writing, to label it fairly, without bowing to the marketplace when our culture's obsessions with so-called "reality-" (a term now utterly opposite its originally-intended meaning on television) and its historical fear of creativity exert pressure on writers to claim the "non-" when they should not. Indeed, we will see the value of adding to this book the term "lyric essay" as a label distinct from "creative nonfiction," even if it overlaps with it.

The best we can do as readers of creative nonfiction is to demand honest attempts at fair labeling. Inevitably, writers will continue to be caught "making things up" more than Gutkind and most of the rest of us readers of creative nonfiction prefer. Many of the excellent writers you will read about in the rest of this volume will be caught "making things up" in ways that again raise questions about this genre called "creative nonfiction." What those writers have to say about our shared realities, however, especially when they report from dark corners of epistemological experience that we may be lucky enough not to have inhabited, remains important enough to warrant this genre. But perhaps only as long as we remember the importance of making things up in fiction—or lyric essays—as well, can we honestly celebrate creative nonfiction as a worthy way to make up the gaps in stories making a special claim to truth.

Notes

1. Serious study of genre can always begin with Miller's "Genre as Social Action."

2. I have normalized the spelling from this facsimile edition but left capitalization as is.

3. McWilliams provides an excellent overview of the "novel" vs. "romance" tension over moral suasion vs. aesthetic freedom, as well as various critical positions on this unstable, yet persistent American literary legacy.

Works Cited

Abrams, M. H. *A Glossary of Literary Terms*. 7th ed. New York: Harcourt Brace, 1999.

Association of Writers & Writing Programs. "Guide to Writing Programs."
Association of Writers & Writing Programs. n.d. Web. 2 Oct. 2014.

Baym, Nina. "Concepts of the Romance in Hawthorne's America."
Nineteenth-Century Fiction, Special Issue Dedicated to Blake Nevius
38.4 (Mar. 1984): 426–443. JSTOR. Web. 2 Nov. 2014.

Berkovitch, Sacvan. *The Puritan Origins of the American Self.* New
Haven, CT: Yale UP, 1975.

Bradstreet, Anne. *The Works of Anne Bradstreet.* Ed. Jeannine Hensley.
Cambridge, MA: Belknap P of Harvard UP, 1967.

Eames, Wilberforce. "Introduction." *The Bay Psalm Book: Being a*
Facsimile *Reprint of the* First Edition, *Printed by Stephen Daye*
At Cambridge, in New England in 1640. NY: New Dodd, Mead &
Company, 1903. v–xvii.

Franklin, Benjamin. *Benjamin Franklin: Writings.* Ed. J. A. Leo Lemay.
New York: Library of America, 1987.

Gardner, John. *The Art of Fiction.* New York: Vintage, 1991.

Gutkind, Lee. *You Can't Make This Stuff Up: The Complete Guide to*
Creative Nonfiction—from Memoir to Literary Journalism and
Everything in Between. Boston: Da Capo, 2012.

_____. *Keep It Real: Everything You Need to Know About*
Researching and Writing Creative Nonfiction. New York: Norton,
2008.

Harmon, William & C. Hugh Holman. "Typology." *A Handbook to*
Literature. 7th ed. Upper Saddle River, NJ: Prentice Hall, 1996. 530.

Hawthorne, Nathaniel. *Hawthorne: Collected Novels: Fanshawe, The*
Scarlet Letter, The House of the Seven Gables, The Blithedale
Romance, The Marble Faun. New York: Library of America, 1983.

"Imitation." *Encyclopedia of Rhetoric.* Ed. Thomas O. Sloane. Oxford UP,
2001. Published online 2006. Web. 14 Oct. 2014.

James, Henry. "The Art of Fiction." *Essentials of the Theory of Fiction.*
3rd ed. Ed. Michael J. Hoffman & Patrick D. Murphy. Durham, NC:
Duke UP, 2005. 13–19.

Jones, Brian Jay. *Washington Irving: An American Original.* New York:
Arcade, 2008.

Macdonald, Dwight. "The Triumph of the Fact." *Masscult and Midcult: Essays Against the American Grain*. New York: NY Review of Books, 2011. 201–233. Kindle Edition.

"Make." *The American Heritage Dictionary*. 3rd ed. 1992.

Mather, Richard. *The Bay Psalm Book: Being a* Facsimile *Reprint of the* First Edition, *Printed by Stephen Daye At Cambridge, in New England in 1640*. New York: New Dodd, Mead & Company, 1903. xvii.

McWilliams, John. "The Rationale for 'The American Romance'." *boundary 2*, New Americanists: Revisionist Interventions into the Canon 17.1 (Spring, 1990): 71–82. JSTOR. Web. 24 Oct. 2014.

Miller, Carolyn. "Genre as Social Action." *Quarterly Journal of Speech*. 70 (1984): 151–167.

Morris, Amy M. E. "The Bay Psalm Book and the 'Halfway' Poetics of Worship." *Popular Measures: Poetry and Church Order in Seventeenth-Century Massachusetts*. Newark, NJ: U of Delaware P, 2005. 76–113.

Rich, Adrienne. "Anne Bradstreet and Her Poetry." *The Works of Anne Bradstreet*. Ed. Jeannine Hensley. Cambridge, MA: Belknap P of Harvard UP, 1967. ix–xx.

Searle, John. "What Your Computer Can't Know." *The New York Review of Books*. 61.15 9 Oct. 2014: 52–55.

Westbrook, Perry D. *A Literary History of New England*. Bethlehem, PA: Lehigh UP, 1988.

Wittgenstein, Ludwig. *Philosophical Investigations: The German text, with an English Translation*. Trans. G. E. M. Anscombe, P. M. S. Hacker, & Joachim Schulte. Ed. Hacker & Schulte. Rev. 4th ed. Chichester, West Sussex: Wiley Blackwell, 2009.

CRITICAL
CONTEXTS

American Creative Nonfiction: Background and History

Kelly Clasen

Since the colonial era, written records of authentic experiences have been instrumental in the development of the nation's literary identity. Although it is often difficult to discern the extent to which an author's attention to the potential literary artistry of truth-telling has influenced his or her writing, some of the most uniquely American texts fall into the category of creative nonfiction. Mark Twain's remembrances of his Mississippi River travels, John Muir's celebration of California's mountain ranges, Truman Capote's reconstruction of small-town Kansas murders—such accounts, and countless more, span generations and have been essential in defining and preserving the cultural character of the country. They inspire readers to delve into the distant and more recent past to become immersed in the events, landscapes, conflicts, and customs of the United States and its diverse communities.

As early as the seventeenth century, colonists demonstrated their appreciation for creative nonfiction by popularizing captivity narratives, accounts of seizure and escape that often dramatized the savagery of Native American captors and highlighted the Puritan principles of their hostages. *A Narrative of the Captivity and Restoration of Mrs. Mary Rowlandson,* published in 1682, exemplifies such characteristics. Rowlandson identifies "the dolefulest day" of her life as February 10, 1675, during which Wampanoag Indians attacked Lancaster, a settlement in the Massachusetts Bay Colony (310). They set homes on fire, murdered several residents, and took Rowlandson and her three children, among others, captive. Rowlandson, the wife of a Lancaster minister, spent eleven weeks traveling around with the Wampanoag, and her youngest daughter Sarah died about a week into captivity. Despite such horrors, Rowlandson drew strength from her spirituality, and her inspirational account of her family's ordeal was widely circulated.

Other captivity narratives of the era also were well publicized, such as *The Captivity of Hannah Dustin* (1696–97) by Cotton Mather and *The Redeemed Captive, Returning to Zion* by John Williams (1707), and similarly promoted piety in the face of calamity. This rhetoric helps situate the works within the category of creative nonfiction because authorial ideology, creatively expressed within the context of historically accurate storytelling, exerts its influence upon the accounts and shapes their development. Unlike other forms of nonfiction, creative nonfiction, according to Lee Gutkind, does not require "balance and objectivity" (11). The genre allows for a quantity of dramatic license that facilitates impassioned accounts of events, helping distinguish such accounts from nonfiction. The questions of authorship and authenticity surrounding some captivity narratives further encourage this literary categorization. According to Kathryn Derounian-Stodala and James Levernier, "More often than not the individual captivity narrative constitutes an amalgamation of voices and input, each with its own agenda and design" (11). It seems clear that, while some authors who lived to tell of Native American captivity relayed the drama of the experience through direct reportage, others may have employed literary devices to capitalize on the reading public's voracity for these tales. Like slave narratives, another important form of captivity narrative, each text must to be evaluated according to its own merits—its origins, reliance upon literary devices, and message—before it is categorized.

Colonial-era writers also enriched the country's literature through autobiography, which, along with memoir, remains a popular form of creative nonfiction today, although writers from every era in American history have produced culturally significant autobiographical works. Influential men of letters like Thomas Jefferson, John Adams, and Benjamin Franklin wrote prolifically and well outside of the realm of political texts to include works that are considered essential to the early American canon. Franklin's well-known autobiography has been characterized by Jay Parini as the "first major autobiography by an American" and the book with which "American literature begins" (11, 13). Parini notes that the term "autobiography" was not yet in circulation when Franklin was writing, but that the chronicle of his life from 1771 to 1788 "broke the generic boundaries suggested by 'memoir' and 'confession,' combining both and moving beyond both" in what emerged as an "exemplary life" of the author (12). Certainly, as Ben Yagoda explains, the expectations for memoir and autobiography have evolved significantly over time, with the most recent incarnation of memoir allowing for "a certain leeway" with content that is no longer expected of the autobiography (2–3). Today, memoir is generally considered a subcategory of autobiography that offers a glimpse into a particular period of the author/subject's life, while an autobiography offers a more encompassing picture. For example, Maya Angelou's *I Know Why the Caged Bird Sings* (1969)—a memoir that draws on literary devices such as metaphor and addresses her early experiences with racism, insecurity, abuse, and teenage pregnancy—is also the first of six volumes in her autobiography.

Of course, many forms of creative nonfiction are auto-biographical in nature and are associated with various subgenres, such as travel writing, which has a rich and varied history in this country. Since the late-seventeenth century, such works have encouraged readers to consider the ever-evolving sense of American identity as it is reflected in the writings of travelers on both American soil and abroad. Rowlandson's captivity narrative is often also associated with travel writing because it describes her journey into the New England wilderness. Philip Gould notes that other forms of early travel writing, such as William Penn's "Some Account of the Providence of Pennsylvania in America" (1681), were produced to help attract British emigrants and, therefore, offer an idealized version of the New World (13). In the eighteenth century, British American travel writing continued to develop "in the context of other genres like nature writing, promotional writing about settling the American frontier, spiritual autobiography, and military history" (Gould 13). Despite the topical variety in travel writing from this era, all forms were, to some extent, "promotional writings" that cast British America as a land of abundance for readers (Gould 25). In 1819, Washington Irving exerted his profound influence on the genre with the first serial installments of *The Sketch Book of Geoffrey Crayon, Gent.*, a work that interposes pseudonymous autobiographical sketches with some of his most renowned stories, including "The Legend of Sleepy Hollow," and which delighted both American and British readers. Early in *The Sketch Book*, Irving emphasizes the allure of travel for him and admits to having a "rambling propensity" (7), and this theme helps link the book's varied chapters, a handful of which are set in America, but most of which describe English scenes. Irving notes that "it is the fashion for modern tourists to travel pencil in hand, and bring home their portfolios filled with sketches" (9).

Certainly, records of expeditions abroad also dominate early American letters. Thomas Jefferson recorded his experiences in France, Holland, and Germany from 1784 to 1789. In 1804, John Quincy Adams published an account of his tour of the Silesia region of Central Europe. Many influential novelists of the nineteenth century also kept records of their expeditions, whether for the creative fulfillment that comes from ordering new experiences, or for potential publication—or both. James Fenimore Cooper wrote books about his European travels during the 1830s, and although they are generally considered novels, Herman Melville's *Typee: A Peep at Polynesian Life* (1846) and *Omoo: A Narrative of Adventures in the South Seas* (1847) were inspired by his experiences as a seaman. Two decades later, Mark Twain would draw upon this tradition in *The Innocents Abroad* (1869) and *A Tramp Abroad* (1880); although both chronicle his experiences in Europe, the latter text includes many fictional elements.

Of course, Twain is better known for his American travelogues, particularly *Roughing It* (1872)—in which he describes, with characteristic humor, his stagecoach journey out West and excursion to the Sandwich Islands—and *Life on the Mississippi* (1883), a memoir about his days as a steamboat pilot. Other prominent figures in the regional literary movement also wrote travel sketches around the end of the century, in addition to widely-read fiction. Sarah Orne Jewett composed first-person accounts of her frequent outings around coastal Maine for publication in periodicals of the era and for inclusion, alongside her stories, in various collections. Sioux author and activist Zitkala-Ša, also known as Gertrude Simmons Bonnin, published eye-opening autobiographical articles about being recruited by Quaker missionaries to leave the Yankton Reservation to attend a school in Indiana designed to teach Native American children manual skills and assimilate them into the dominant culture. Yet other fiction writers were inspired by their respective regional affiliations to produce other types of nonfiction. Hamlin Garland, whose short stories and novels feature the hard-working people of the upper Midwest, found success with his 1917 autobiography, *A Son of the Middle Border*, and its 1921 sequel, *A Daughter of the Middle Border*, which won a Pulitzer Prize.

Travel writing continued to adopt diverse forms in the twentieth century. In the first decade, William Dean Howells and Henry James, both known for their contributions to the realist movement in American fiction, published nonfiction accounts of their travels in Europe. Although it was not printed until three years after his death, Nobel Prize-winning modernist Ernest Hemingway enriched the travel-writing canon with *A Moveable Feast* (1964), a memoir about the expatriate experience in 1920s Paris that featured many socialites with whom he hobnobbed (including Gertrude Stein— also an innovator of creative nonfiction with her 1933 book *The Autobiography of Alice B. Toklas*, in which she describes her own life through the narrative voice of her longtime partner). Like Melville's work, the travel narratives of Beat writer Jack Kerouac are classified as fiction, yet his seminal work *On the Road* (1957) offers only thinly veiled accounts of his road-trip escapades with fellow Beats Neal Cassady, William S. Burroughs, and Allen Ginsberg. A few years later, John Steinbeck would produce a more innocuous road narrative in *Travels with Charley* (1962), which chronicles the aging author's cross-country journey with his poodle—a work that perhaps foreshadowed the recent popularity of dog-themed nonfiction. Adventure literature—the creative aftermath of shipwrecks, hiking expeditions gone awry, dangerous military operations, and the like—has also long enjoyed popularity in this country and remains a prevalent subcategory of both biography and travel writing. Some works, like Alfred Lansing's *Endurance: Shackleton's Incredible*

Voyage (1959), recount others' travails, while others, like Jon Krakauer's *Into Thin Air: A Personal Account of the Mount Everest Disaster* (1997), offer first-person accounts of survival.

While the term "travel" may, for contemporary readers, conjure a pleasant association with the term "vacation," it is important to note that not all travel writing chronicles leisurely—or even voluntary—mobility. As Virginia Whatley Smith has demonstrated, captivity and forced relocation are inherent to the records of many former slaves, and "[t]he slave narrative thus generated its own sub-genre of travel writing" (197). Smith identifies *The Interesting Narrative of Olaudah Equiano, a Slave, Written by Himself* (1789) as "the seminal model for the slave narrative" (198) in its first-person testimony of the brutalities of slavery and the story of his subsequent freedom. Around the middle of the nineteenth century, narratives by former slaves including Frederick Douglass, William Wells Brown, and Harriet Jacobs became popular, forcing readers to confront the dehumanizing effects of legally sanctioned racial oppression and helping fuel the abolitionist movement. After the Civil War, Booker T. Washington and other former slaves continued to record their experiences, further developing the genre. The prominence of slave narratives in academic curricula today and the 2013 adaptation of Solomon Northrup's *Twelve Years a Slave* (1853) into a critically acclaimed film speak to the resonance of the form. However, the extent to which any particular slave narrative fits into the category of creative nonfiction varies greatly, with some, more than others, exhibiting the attention to literary technique that typifies the genre. Other works, like Hannah Bond's *The Bondwoman's Narrative*, which was likely written in the 1850s, but published for the first time in 2002 under the pen name Hannah Crafts, are considered novels, but have been deemed largely autobiographical by scholars. Like with Native American captivity narratives, questions of authorship shroud some accounts, as it was common for white sympathizers to record the stories of freed or escaped slaves and to potentially take some literary license. Regardless of an individual account's accuracy, slave narratives are significant as the first major movement in a rich legacy of African American literature. Moreover, the texts were essential to the development during the mid-twentieth century of other influential autobiographical writings that advocated for increased civil rights, such as those by Malcolm X and Richard Wright.

National conflicts over race, equality, individuality, and capitalism were also catalysts for intellectual radicalism and literary experimentalism in the decades leading up to the Civil War. In the early 1840s, a group of reformists that included Ralph Waldo Emerson, Margaret Fuller, Henry David Thoreau, and Bronson Alcott, among others, introduced their transcendentalist philosophy, which celebrated independence and individualism and challenged racial and gender inequality, and wrote about their experiments in transcendental living. *Walden* (1854), in which Thoreau investigates an existence characterized by solitude and asceticism as an alternative to the "lives of quiet desperation" (8) plaguing most Americans, remains one of the most influential books to emerge from this intellectual movement—and from this country. Despite his keen attention to accurately recording the natural features of his setting, Thoreau fictionalizes key aspects of his experiences at Walden Pond, including the length of his stay, and he provides his readers with a conclusion (Parini 13). Such moves align it with other works of creative nonfiction, and it remains an inspirational force in many other genres, including nature writing.

Other writers of the mid-1800s, including Susan Fenimore Cooper, were also drawing upon nonfiction forms, such as the diary and natural history, to create texts that helped establish a foundation for modern nature writing, but *Walden* has achieved the most celebrated status. Indeed, influential ecocritic Lawrence Buell has dubbed Thoreau the "patron saint of environmental writing" (115). Along with Emerson, Thoreau helped inspire writers of the late nineteenth century, such as John Muir and John Burroughs, to encourage protection for natural spaces through their nonfiction, which frequently included a combination of scientific facts, accurate observations of the natural world, and personal or philosophical reflections. In 1903, Mary Austin made a significant contribution to creative nonfiction when she combined elements of regional fiction and environmental nonfiction in *The Land of Little Rain* to promote an ethic of stewardship toward the American Southwest, its land and its life forms. The last half of the twentieth century saw the continued growth of American nature writing, led by authors such as Edward Abbey, Aldo Leopold, Rachel Carson, and Annie Dillard, all of whom have been instrumental to the genre's development. Carson's *Silent Spring* (1962), an indictment of the chemical industry and its effects upon living things, which she famously introduces with her "Fable for Tomorrow" featuring a once-vibrant community beset with a "strange blight" (1), is often associated with the beginning of the modern environmental movement.

The second half of the twentieth century witnessed the birth of additional creative nonfiction forms, including the literary journalism pioneered by Tom Wolfe, Gay Talese, Hunter S. Thompson, Joan Didion, and others who challenged the status quo by infusing their reporting with literary techniques that are traditionally associated with fiction. According to Marc Weingarten, "Wolfe and many of his contemporaries recognized [...] one salient fact of life in the sixties: the traditional tools of reporting would be inadequate to chronicle the tremendous cultural and social changes of the era" (6). Also called "the New Journalism" because of a 1973 anthology of representative writings co-edited by Wolfe with that title, the genre's roots can nevertheless be traced to the literary naturalism movement of the late-nineteenth and early twentieth century, during which journalists such as Stephen Crane, Jack London, and Upton Sinclair wrote realistic novels that critiqued various aspects of modern society. Truman Capote's groundbreaking *In Cold Blood* (1965)—a meticulously researched examination of the 1959 Clutter family murders in Holcomb, Kansas, that is written in a novelistic style and that was first serialized in *The New Yorker*—was also highly influential on the genre's development.

In Cold Blood, which Capote classified as a "nonfiction novel" (Weingarten 33), is also considered a seminal work of true crime, a genre in which writers research criminal acts, usually murders, and which often necessitates a degree of speculation in the author's establishment of a cohesive, engaging narrative. It remains a popular form of nonfiction today although, according to Harold Schechter, "America was from the beginning fertile ground for true narratives of crime" like the Puritan execution sermon (xii). Suggesting that real life is, in fact, often more fascinating than fiction, many prominent fiction writers have experimented with true crime; Nathaniel Hawthorne, Ambrose Bierce, Frank Norris, Theodore Dreiser, and Zora Neale Hurston are among them. Some more recent, widely read examples include John Berendt's *Midnight in the Garden of Good and Evil* (1994) and Erik Larson's *The Devil in the White City: Murder, Magic, and Madness at the Fair That Changed Everything* (2003).

Like those authors who attempt to understand criminal acts by writing about them, others turn to creative nonfiction to try to make sense of illnesses and disabilities. Such narratives benefit their writers, who often increase their self-awareness during the therapeutic composition process, as well as their readers, who may take comfort in identifying with others who have faced similar health-related challenges. Illness narratives gained prominence toward the end of the nineteenth century in response to what Arthur Kleinman describes as "the alienation of the chronically ill from their professional care givers and, paradoxically, to the relinquishment by the practitioner of that aspect of the healer's art that is most ancient" (xiv). The resultant texts often recount the highly personal trials of the authors, as does William Styron's *Darkness Visible* (1990), a raw account of crippling depression. Nevertheless, other works, like Philip Roth's *Patrimony: A True Story* (1991), a memoir that recalls his father's experiences with a terminal brain tumor and its effect upon his family, give voice to the suffering of others.

Americans' health concerns have also contributed to the skyrocketing popularity of food writing. Indeed, since the late twentieth century, public ideologies have been increasingly linked to an understanding of how the production and consumption of food impacts people's health, the economy, and the environment. Moreover, what a person chooses to consume—locally grown produce or Green Giant vegetables, a vegan diet or a traditional

Mexican one—often provides a carefully constructed, complex reflection of one's sociocultural background and beliefs. A diverse group of writers' attention to what we heap on our plates has created a loosely defined category with examples that run the gamut from environmentally minded critiques of industrial food systems, like Michael Pollan's 2007 bestseller *The Omnivore's Dilemma*, to cheerily narrated kitchen narratives, like those permeating the increasingly influential blogosphere. Despite the recent outpouring of food writing, its roots are deep and far-reaching in this country. According to Molly O'Neill, there are "foreshadowings of the more specialized food writing of our day in a variety of sources and in every phase of American history: journals, letters, novels, poems, travel accounts, autobiographies, histories, ethnographic studies," but "an explosion of lively, diverse, mouth-watering food prose" occurred during the mid-twentieth century (xx). Today, food writing can be broken down into many categories that frequently overlap with other nonfiction genres, yet it is common for authors across the field to embrace descriptive writing that evokes sensory reactions. When celebrity TV chef Anthony Bourdain describes his first childhood spoonful of vichyssoise—"the crunch of tiny chopped chives […], the rich, creamy taste of leek and potato, the pleasurable shock, the surprise that it was cold" (9–10)—the reader's experience is almost visceral. Such writing and readers' responses to it often reveal as much about Americans' gastric indulgences as they do about the human condition.

The dawn of this century saw a yet another form of creative nonfiction gain prominence: the dog memoir. After the success of John Grogan's *Marley and Me* in 2005, which spawned a box-office hit in 2008, publishers lapped up the sometimes-funny, usually moving stories of human-canine relationships, and the American reading public responded by sending many onto bestseller lists and creating a genre that some have dubbed the "dogoir." Like other forms of creative nonfiction, the dogoir frequently straddles various categories. For example, the popular 2012 book by Teresa Rhyne, *The Dog Lived (and So Will I)*, features characteristics of the illness narrative, humor writing, the dogoir, and the memoir—all wrapped up in a true-life tale about one beagle and his owner fighting cancer together.

More traditional memoirs have continued to grow in popularity in the early twenty-first century as well, despite the "seemingly endless stream of memoir scandals" following the infamous exposure of James Frey's 2003 book *A Million Little Pieces: A Memoir* as largely fictional (Yagoda 7). Public figures—from reality TV stars and athletes to politicians and celebrated authors—have found memoir to be an effective platform for disseminating their anecdotes. In 2014 alone, bookstores cleared off shelf space for memoirists as diverse as Hillary Clinton, Oprah Winfrey, and Rob Lowe, while the gut-busting prose of numerous well-known American comedians—Ellen DeGeneres, Tina Fey, Jon Stewart, Mindy Kaling, and Chelsea Handler, to name a handful—was also on prominent display. Of course, in the past decade, many people outside of the public eye have written well-received accounts of their far-from-average trials and triumphs. Jeannette Walls' *The Glass Castle* (2005), the story of an unconventional upbringing; Elizabeth Gilbert's *Eat, Pray, Love* (2006), a chronicle of international travel and self-discovery; and Piper Kerman's *Orange Is the New Black: My Year in a Women's Prison* (2010), an immersion in correctional-facility culture, are among the extraordinary true stories that have gripped readers' imaginations since the dawn of the new century.

Kerman's book might be classified as yet another form of American captivity narrative—one that has yet to fully develop, but that highlights the importance of a literary tradition that extends back to the colonial era. Acknowledging this entrenched, varied wealth of creative nonfiction in American literary history deepens one's understanding of how people across time and across the nation have found fulfillment in recording their most significant experiences and those of others. These true stories—beautifully, comically, grippingly told—are one of the country's natural treasures.

Works Cited

Bourdain, Anthony. *Kitchen Confidential: Adventures in the Culinary Underbelly*. New York: Bloomsbury, 2000.

Buell, Lawrence. *The Environmental Imagination: Thoreau, Nature Writing, and the Formation of American Culture.* Cambridge: Harvard UP, 1995.

Carson, Rachel. *Silent Spring.* 1962. New York: Houghton Mifflin, 2002.

Derounian-Stodola, Kathryn Z. & James A. Levernier. *The Indian Captivity Narrative: 1550–900.* New York: Twayne, 1993.

Gould, Philip. "Beginnings: The Origins of American Travel Writing in the Pre-Revolutionary

Period." *The Cambridge Companion to American Travel Writing.* Ed. Alfred Bendixen & Judith Hamera. Cambridge: Cambridge UP, 2009. 13–25.

Gutkind, Lee. *The Art of Creative Nonfiction: Writing and Selling the Literature of Reality.* New York: Wiley, 1997.

Irving, Washington. *The Works of Washington Irving*, Volume 1. New York: Nottingham Society, 1856.

Kleinman, Arthur. *The Illness Narratives: Suffering, Healing, and the Human Condition.* New York: Basic Books, 1988.

O'Neill, Molly. *American Food Writing: An Anthology with Classic Recipes.* New York: Library of America, 2009.

Parini, Jay, ed. *The Norton Book of American Autobiography.* New York: Norton, 1999.

Rowlandson, Mary. "A Narrative of the Captivity and Restoration of Mrs. Mary Rowlandson." *The Norton Anthology of American Literature, Volume A.* 6th ed. Ed. Nina Baym. New York: Norton, 2003. 309–340.

Schechter, Harold, ed. *True Crime: An American Anthology.* New York: Library of America, 2008.

Smith, Virginia Whatley. "African American Travel Literature." *The Cambridge Companion to American Travel Writing.* Ed. Alfred Bendixen & Judith Hamera. Cambridge: Cambridge UP, 2009. 197–213.

Thoreau, Henry David. *Walden.* 1854. Ed. William Rossi. New York: Norton, 2008.

Weingarten, Marc. *The Gang That Wouldn't Write Straight.* New York: Three Rivers Press, 2005.

Yagoda, Ben. *Memoir: A History.* New York: Riverhead Books, 2010.

Critical Reception of "A Special Kind of Fiction"

Ross Griffin

The phrase "a special kind of fiction" (*Touching* 25) is one frequently used by Paul John Eakin to describe autobiography. When one reads an autobiography, they are exposed to a different kind of reading experience than if they were reading a work of fiction. What the author says about their lives and the lives of those around them, what he or she says about their views and beliefs, suddenly these things begin to really matter. Why is this? We know that the author is telling us the story of his or her own life. But why do we read this story in the same light as history or newspaper reportage? One of the reasons is that autobiography can be considered just one of many manifestations of what has become known in recent times as creative nonfiction, a genre whose blend of referential fact and authorial ingenuity had resulted in what Eakin quite correctly calls "a special kind of fiction."

What Is Creative Nonfiction?

But what is considered today to be creative nonfiction has existed in several other guises over the centuries. In addition to autobiography, literary journalism, long-form journalism, new journalism, the nonfiction novel, the nonfiction narrative, the personal essay, life-writing, and memoir have all been correctly used at some point to describe the literary form that deliberately uses the strategies of fiction to present fact-based accounts. Consequently, definitions of the genre are many. Each invariably states that creative nonfiction is a literary form, which somehow presents a factual narrative using the techniques of fiction. But none, however, offer any conclusive insight into its ontology or make-up.

So what exactly is creative nonfiction? A closer examination of the genre's current title does nothing to shed any further light on this description. 'Creative' suggests something imaginative, new, and previously unseen. Yet 'nonfiction' would seem to be the binary opposite. It implies a narrative derived from a pre-existing series of facts that can be referentially verified. Thus, rather than definitively indicating the nature of the genre, the term 'creative nonfiction' would appear to perpetuate the confusion within the form, which allows it to be interpreted as either fact or fiction. At various intervals over the centuries, creative nonfiction has come to prominence, only to cede once more into the background as other forms emerged. However, in the last thirty-five years or so, critical interest in the genre has greatly increased to form a body of theoretical material much larger and more considered than what had ever previously existed. While critics continue to disagree over its exact definition, three separate schools of thought have come to the fore.

The first was found in Mas'ud Zavarzadeh's *The Mythopoeic Reality*. Published in 1976, Zavarzadeh's was the first extended study of creative nonfiction. He saw the form as one that represented reality exactly as it was, so much so, that the nonfictional narrative was actuality transcribed, not interpreted. Its author was "the 'midwife' of experiential reality" (Zavarzadeh 123), and the variety of literary devices he or she used in this birthing process, the various acts of selection and omission, the subtle nuances of language, and the subjectivity of the author, were not to be mistaken for fictionalizing agents. Rather they were simply the most 'appropriate means to assist the verbal birth of a segment of reality' (123). The only factor Zavarzadeh saw as preventing creative nonfiction from providing an absolute account of actuality was the physical limitation of the written page. But regardless of this shortcoming, creative nonfiction still represented "a zero degree of interpretation of man's situation" (Zavarzadeh 41). Such a highly referential view of the genre obviously presents one of the most radical understandings of the form and, as a consequence, is often disregarded by critics.

Rivalling this view of creative nonfiction is what I call the 'Fourth Genre School.' The moniker is derived directly from critical works by a group of theorists who specifically posit creative nonfiction as a new, standalone genre distinct from the pre-existing generic categories of poetry, drama, and fiction previously identified by Northrop Frye. The most prominent of these theorists include, among others, Lee Gutkind; Stephen Minot; Robert Root, Jr; Barbara Lounsberry; Mimi Schwartz; and Sondra Perl. Unlike its peers, this definition of creative nonfiction is based on a generic hybridity, which allows the form to accord equal status to both the empirical *and* creative elements of its narrative. Although realizing that the intent of the author is still to reproduce reality as precisely as possible, theorists of the Fourth Genre School also "assume that the readers understand that any true story [...] is based on a mix of memory and imagination" (Perl 171).

They thus advocate a strict adherence to creative nonfiction's strict code of ethics to ensure that the people, places, and events portrayed in the accounts are a faithful reproduction of their actual occurrence. Yet paradoxically, the Fourth Genre School also actively encourages the use of poetic license. As their primary concern is the accurate representation *of the experience of the events* more so than the events themselves, they view poesis as an essential part of a literary practice, which seeks to emphasise the 'literariness' of the author's personal view of the world. For theorists such as Sondra Perl, this was still "writing true" (xii), but "in an individual voice that openly says, 'See this world my way'" (5). Furthermore, while the Fourth Genre School posits creative nonfiction as a factual genre whose narrative was "limited to only what is true" (Gutkind, *Keep* 150), its understanding of the genre is often undone by the paradoxical nature of what it sees as creative nonfiction's intrinsic duality; it considers that "what we imagine about something, someone, or some event [to be] true" also because "It is true that we imagined it" (Gutkind, *Keep* 150). While other concerns exist, the insights offered by the Fourth Genre School are still valuable and emphasize a duality within the form separating it from the three other traditional literary genres.

In addition to these interpretations of creative nonfiction, there exists a third dominant understanding of the genre. Citing the dependence on a number of poetic literary techniques for the construction of its narrative, the majority of critics insist on viewing creative nonfiction as "a species of fiction" (Foley 41).[1] However, characterized by a verisimilitude amplified beyond that of traditional realistic or historical novels, each also agrees that works of creative nonfiction are quite unlike traditional works of fiction. I see this view of the genre as offering the most logically appropriate view and one that can be rationalized quite easily.

John Searle attempts to differentiate between fiction and traditional nonfiction using a model of vertical and horizontal rules (The term 'traditional nonfiction' refers to works of newspaper reportage, documented histories, educational texts, and so forth). These indicate whether a work should be interpreted as fact or fiction. Although Searle applies them to a piece of 'straight' journalism and an obviously fictional text respectively, they can also be brought to bear on the ontologically uncertain creative nonfiction. The vertical rules "establish connections between language and reality" (Searle 326). They are literal and empirical and encourage the referential reading of an account. Such precise, unambiguous constructs are at the core of creative nonfiction's narrative. However, Searle accompanies these vertical rules underscoring the referentiality of an assertion with a set of horizontal rules. Defined as "a set of extralinguistic, nonsemantic conventions that break the connection between words and the world" (326), they allow the author to use words "without undertaking the commitments that are normally required by [their literal] meanings" (326). More concisely phrased, these horizontal rules refer to any method of poetic description, such as metaphor, omniscient narration, or free indirect discourse, available to an author. These literary devices are rarely found in conventional referential texts. But as a form that emphasizes the craft of its narrative as much as the content, they are common in creative nonfiction. Therefore, although describing empirically legitimate entities, the expressive language used within the genre to represent the experiences of the author transform the nonfictional narrative into the "non-deceptive pseudo-performance" (325), which Searle views as the identifying trait of fiction despite the illocutionary intentions of the creative nonfiction author to the portrayal of a referential truth.

Critical Insights

Because, as Weber states in *The Literature of Fact*, "all forms of writing offer models or versions of reality rather than actual descriptions of it" (14), the world portrayed by creative nonfiction should, therefore, be viewed as one *analogous* to the actual world rather than an identical reproduction. The goal of the creative nonfictional author is that his or her work be read as an empirically viable text. Yet for it to exist, the narrative must first pass through the interpretive lens of both memory and the mind's eye. Such an interpretation is ideally suited to the generic idiosyncrasies of creative nonfiction, highlighting quite clearly the tension between fact and fiction, which is intrinsically part of the form. But while the narrative is posited to the reader as being empirically legitimate, the manner of its construction means that the discourse can only ever be described as being closely similar to, or derived from, accepted fact.

Characteristics

However, viewing creative nonfiction as a type of fiction does give rise to further questions, and the primary of these are at the core of this chapter; what distinguishes creative nonfiction from other fictional discourses, and what is it about the genre that encourages its readers to believe that the form possesses a 'truth' lacking in other fictional forms? Perhaps creative nonfiction's most noticeable feature as a fictional genre is that the trope of suspense within its narrative differs significantly from that found in traditional forms of fiction. Committed to representing only people, places, and historical events that have actually occurred, its narrative structure is generally one that reveals *how* and *why* certain events occurred more so than documenting a dramatic account of events. This commitment means that the 'textual elements' of creative nonfiction can be subsequently understood as "possessing referents in the world of the reader" (Foley 26). As many of these entities can be verified by the general public, they can be interpreted as a mechanism used to advance the narrative in addition to amplifying its verisimilitude.

However, as quite often occurs in creative nonfiction, these historical elements are frequently located in "dark areas" of history, that is, "the aspects [of history] about which the 'official' record has nothing to report" (McHale 87). This characteristic of the genre means that often less tangible 'facts,' such as the inner thoughts of characters or private conversations, are presented in the text. This characteristic of creative nonfiction makes generic clarity an issue. However, this problem can be resolved by adapting a model posited by Scholes, which outlines the primary plot structures of empirical narrative. While I have already stated that creative nonfiction should *not* be interpreted as an empirical form, the model suggested by Scholes, which divides the genre into two constitutive parts according to narrative approach, can still be applied to the fictional genre.

The first of these is labelled "the biological form" (Scholes 214). Describing a pattern of plot which "[takes] its shape from the birth, life and death of an actual individual" (Scholes 214), this narrative structure lends itself to the type of creative nonfiction that prioritizes the private musings of personal affairs previously unknown to the reader. It generally consists of a "retrospective prose narrative written by a real person concerning his own existence, where the focus is his individual life" (Lejeune 4). Because it is primarily based on the conveyance of emotional experience, it can be considered as historically 'soft' and epitomized largely by self-referential texts. Notable examples of this type are autobiographies/memoirs such as Harriet Jacob's *Incidents in the Life of a Slave Girl*, Henry Adams' *The Education of Henry Adams,* and Tim O'Brien's *If I Die in a Combat Zone.*

The second grouping is characterized by incident-inspired narratives that frequently proclaim an unknown, but factually-accurate and rigorously-researched insight into an accepted historical truth. Described as "the historical form" (214) by Scholes, it mirrors the highly referential kinds of creative nonfiction. It is exemplified most famously by Truman Capote, who famously spent six years researching and writing his "nonfiction novel," *In Cold Blood*, and later by the literary journalism of authors such as Neil Sheehan (*A Bright Shining Lie*) and Dee Brown (*Bury My Heart at Wounded Knee*).

But it must be stated that regardless of whether their narratives are referentially 'hard' or 'soft,' portraying the trivial details of an old friendship or the revised version of a widely-known event with potentially widespread consequences, the respective authors in each sub-category of creative nonfiction considered their respective accounts to be as accurate as that found in any piece of newspaper journalism or historical text. Both adhere to the tenets of the "implicit or explicit contract" that Paul John Eakin refers to in the Foreword to Lejeune's *The Autobiographical Pact.* This pre-established arrangement between author and reader "determines the mode of reading of the text" (xi). More clearly phrased, this contract implies that the reader subconsciously agrees that the events documented in the narrative occurred as they have been portrayed in the text. This empiricism is primarily derived from creative nonfiction's status as an experiential genre. As noted by Linda Hutcheon in *The Poetics of Postmodernism,* it is this assertion of personal testimony within creative nonfiction that provides the basis of the genre's claim that its narrative is a replication of truth or historical fact. It is important to note that, while this trope traditionally describes the author's own involvement in an event as per the "biological form" (214) put forth by Scholes, it can also encompass one's experiences of researching an event that has passed.

A consequence of this trait is that authorial subjectivity is thus an intrinsic part of the narrative's composition. Sondra Perl considers this aspect of creative nonfiction to be as important as the "factual truth" of the narrative. Incidents are portrayed as they would be in referentially-assured texts, but for Perl, the goal of the creative nonfictional author is *to represent his or her own personal responses* to these events as much as represent the events themselves. The "who, what and where that most people agree upon" is counterpointed against "the experience seen through the writer's eyes" (81). Daniel Lehman summarizes this idea quite clearly by stating that "the writer of nonfiction produces a document for an audience that reads history as both text and experience" (*Matters* 2–3).

Significantly however, while Lehman's statement reiterates the genre's refusal to prioritize between the rival elements of its narrative, it also offers an alternate means of understanding how the portrayal of authorial experience reinforces the empirical viability of the text. The accuracy of the events documented within the nonfiction novel is assured to the reader in what can be understood as an outward exertion of referential pressure. As the places, people, and events experienced by the author exist in actuality, bar the most extreme instances of violence or war, it is not outside the bounds of possibility for the reader to engage with these elements of the text on their own terms. A corollary to this potential for a shared narrative experience external to the text is that the 'characters' of creative nonfiction also have the power of reply. Should the account drastically differ from the accepted version of events, as most infamously was the case in 2003 with James Frey's addiction memoir, *A Million Little Pieces*, those documented in the narrative "can talk back to their authors," enabling them to either "endorse [...] or undercut" (Lehman, "Proper Name" 68) the integrity of the account. Thus creative nonfiction can be said to exist on what Lehman calls "a multi-referential plane" (*Matters* 4), one which occupies a common realm between the narrative and the experiential world. By presenting a series of experiences in which the depicted "phenomena [...] are also available to and experienced by the reader outside the written artifact" (4), the sense of veracity underscoring the fictional narrative which the author desires to convey to the reader is bolstered.

With any discourse claiming to represent reality, there is controversy surrounding the manner in which it portrays both the verifiably historical and the unquantifiable personal parts of its narrative. By deliberately using methods drawn from fiction to construct its narrative, creative nonfiction's claim that its narrative is a mimetic representation of historical reality means that is one of the genres most susceptible to these criticisms. The artifice begot by the use of these techniques is most commonly demonstrated by extended periods of authorial reflection and a *belles-lettres* style of prose, both of which emphasize the sensory details of the documented events.

Some of the finest examples can be found in James Agee's *Let Us Now Praise Famous Men,* where something as routine as farmland is portrayed as follows:

> Fields are workrooms, or fragrant but mainly sterile work-floors without walls and with a roof of uncontrollable chance, fear, rumination, and propitiative prayer, and are as the spread and broken petals of a flower whose bisexual centre is the house. (124)

Emotion is conveyed with a similar poesis. In *The White Album*, Joan Didion describes her reaction to the moment in 1968 that she was told that she was suffering from the early stages of multiple sclerosis:

> The condition had a name, the kind of name usually associated with telethons, but the name meant nothing and the neurologist did not like to use it. [...] I had at this time, a sharp apprehension [...] of what it was like to open the door to the stranger and find that the stranger did indeed have the knife [...] the improbable had become probable, the norm: things that happen to other people could in fact happen to me. (46–47)

Even an event as terrible as war was related with literary finesse by Michael Herr in *Dispatches*:

> Every fifth round fired was a tracer [...] everything stopped while that solid stream of violent red poured down out of the black sky. If you watched from a great distance, the stream would seem to dry up between bursts, vanishing slowly from air to ground like a comet tail [...] It was awesome, worse than anything the Lord had ever put down on Egypt, and at night, you'd hear the Marines watching it, yelling, "Get some!" [...] The nights were very beautiful. (132–133)

While most commonly a poetic description of the author's reactions and experiences, these literary devices can also include the selection, omission, and manipulation of certain scenes by the author, omniscient and anterior forms of narration, free indirect discourse, the inclusion of unverifiable interior monologues, and an inconsistent movement of time throughout the narrative. By no means a definitive list, these techniques demonstrate why many critics of creative nonfiction cast doubt on the accuracy of events portrayed in the form.[2] Described as "strategies of dramatic immediacy" (323) by Eric Heyne, these methods are crucial to creative nonfiction, distinguishing its narrative from traditional nonfictional discourses as well as providing the ontological bedrock upon which creative nonfiction is based.

Such artifice is also demonstrated by a host of other poetic approaches. This was done with the unorthodox use of a host of grammatical constructs. In his anthology of New Journalism, Wolfe describes these literary pyrotechnics as "the lavish use of dots, dashes, exclamation points, italics, and occasionally punctuation that never existed before" (21). The presence of multiple accounts of the same event in a narrative was also very much a characteristic approach of creative nonfiction's underlying poesis. Authors such as Truman Capote and C. D. B Bryan sought to make their readers aware that they were only viewing a partial, and by no means absolute, account of specific events. This trope is re-enacted by an authorial switching of the narrative stance from first to second to third person. A practice that also extended to the switching of narrative *voice*, this strategy subtly encouraged the reader to integrate their own opinions and beliefs into the nonfiction text by inferring the malleability of written fact. Such meta-narrative tendencies are exemplified by Joan Didion's *The White Album,* Ron Kovic's *Born on the Fourth of July*, and Norman Mailer's *The Armies of the Night*.

Often found counterpointing such obvious poesis in creative nonfiction, however, is a multitude of extraneous literary and non-literary material. Integrated into the body of the text, these entities are unessential to the narrative. Yet they create a referential frame which associates the details of the account with independent sources of "empirical validation" (Foley 26), thus encouraging the reader into interpreting the narrative's truth-claims as real. Most commonly found in the guise of fore- and after-words, these literary devices have two primary purposes in creative nonfiction. They allow the author to personally reassure the reader of the verity of the account. Secondly, they reiterate the referential integrity of the text by outlining the lengths undertaken by the author to adequately research the chosen subject, while also revealing certain unusual sacrifices made by the author in order to authentically represent actual events.

Such devices can also include a number of other literary materials such as author's notes, bibliographies, and personal dedications more commonly found in conventional empirical texts. These are, in turn, often complemented by a host of non-literary materials, such as photographs, maps, and newspaper articles. Instilling legitimacy into the retelling of events, unlike any other fictional discourses, these nonessential entities allow creative nonfiction to present a "narrative that intersects with actual lives" (Lehman, *Matters* 153). Deliberately inserted, the cumulative effect of any, or all, of these entities is a realignment of the reader's perceptions of the narrative from that of an apocryphal recollection of events to one which could be considered as referentially viable as an empirical text. Acting as a "connector" (Hunter 237) between the world of the reader and the author, their abundance in the narrative actively encourages the former to interpret the work as factual.

The presence of such historical elements, combined with an authorial commitment to only represent that which could occur in actuality, means that creative nonfiction is intrinsically designed to educate its reader. This attribute is remarked upon by Lee Gutkind, who states that the "information derived from mundane legwork, research, and scholarship are the roots of creative nonfiction; they constitute the important teaching element, the informational content" (53) of the form. Dating back as far as the 1700s, creative nonfiction's desire to educate and teach its readers about the world around them is apparent as an integral part of its portrayal of reality. In *History and the Early English Novel*, Robert Mayer notes how, for centuries, a number of periodicals and journals argued that Defoe's *A Journal of a Plague Year* should be interpreted referentially because of the abundance of historically verifiable, real-world details contained within it. This didacticism was also an attribute of American nineteenth-century slave narratives, which sought to heighten public awareness of the barbarity of the slave trade still existing in the United States at the time.

In the opening pages of *Matter of Fact*, Daniel Lehman describes how a newspaper report he wrote detailing the personal problems and ultimate suicide of a prominent towns-figure had resulted in a late-night phone call from the gentleman's daughter seeking redress from Lehman for many of the previously unknown revelations he had made public. In Lehman's own words," I as a writer, the woman as a reader, her father as the subject of the narrative—each one of us was implicated materially and historically by the words on the page" (2). The key word here for Lehman, and for all readers of creative nonfiction, is 'implicated.' No longer confined in terms of significance by the boundaries of the written page, no longer just arbitrary signifiers, they seep out into reality and seek out their respective signified. Deliberately constructed by the author, the words take on a newfound importance. They affect the lives of real people; they suddenly matter.

Notes

1. Barbara Foley's *Telling the Truth: The Theory and Practise of Documentary Fiction*, Ronald Weber's *The Literature of Fact: Literary Nonfiction in American Writing*, and John Hellman's *Fables of Fact: The New Journalism as New Fiction* endorse this view more capably than many other comparable texts on creative nonfiction.
2. The most comprehensive analysis of these methods I have found is in Gay Talese and Barbara Lounsberry's anthology of the form, *Writing Creative Nonfiction: The Literature of Reality*.

Works Cited

Adams, Henry. *The Education of Henry Adams*. New York: Penguin Books, 1995.

Agee, James & Walker Evans. *Let Us Now Praise Famous Men: Three Tenant Families*. London: Violette, 2001.

Brown, Dee Alexander. *Bury My Heart at Wounded Knee: An Indian History of the American West*. London: Vintage, 1991.

Bryan, C. D. B. *Friendly Fire*. New York: Putnam, 1976.

Capote, Truman. *In Cold Blood: A True Account of a Multiple Murder and Its Consequences*. London: Abacus, 1984.

_____. Interview by George Plimpton. *New York Times* 16 Jan 1966: Books. Web. 14 Feb 2012.

Defoe, Daniel & Paula R Backscheider. *A Journal of the Plague Year: Authoritative Text,Backgrounds, Contexts, Criticism*. New York: Norton, 1992.

Didion, Joan. *The White Album*. Harmondsworth: Penguin, 1984.

Eakin, Paul John. "Foreword." *On Autobiography*. By Philippe Lejeune. Minneapolis: U of Minnesota P, 1989.

_____. *Touching the World: Reference in Autobiography*. Princeton: Princeton UP, 1992.

Foley, Barbara. *Telling the Truth: The Theory and Practice of Documentary Fiction*. Ithaca, NY: Cornell UP, 1986.

Frey, James. *A Million Little Pieces*. New York: Random, 2003.

Gutkind, Lee & Hattie Fletcher Buck. *Keep It Real: Everything You Need To Know About Researching and Writing Creative Nonfiction*. New York: Norton, 2009.

Hellmann, John. *Fables of Fact : The New Journalism as New Fiction*. Urbana, IL: U of Illinois P, 1981.

Herr, Michael. *Dispatches*. London: Picador, 2002.

Heyne, Eric. "Where Fiction Meets Nonfiction: Mapping a Rough Terrain." *Narrative* 9.3 (2001): 322–333.

Hunter, J. Paul. *Before Novels: Cultural Contexts of Eighteenth-Century English Fiction*. London: Norton, 1992.

Hutcheon, Linda. *A Poetics of Postmodernism: History, Theory, Fiction*. New York: Routledge, 1988.

Jacobs, Harriet A. *Incidents in the Life of a Slave Girl*. New York: Harcourt, 1973.

Kovic, Ron. *Born on the Fourth of July*. London: Corgi, 1990.

Lehman, Daniel W. *Matters of Fact: Reading Nonfiction over the Edge*. Columbus: Ohio State UP, 1997.

_____. "Proper Names Are Poetry in the Raw': Character Formation in Traumatic Nonfiction." *River Teeth: A Journal of Nonfiction Narrative*. 15.1. (Fall 2013): 57–71. *Project Muse*. Web. 23 Sept 2013.

Lejeune, Philippe. *On Autobiography*. Minneapolis: U of Minnesota P, 1989. Theory and History of Literature v. 52.

Mailer, Norman. *The Armies of the Night*. London: Pen, 1970.

Mayer, Robert. *History and the Early English Novel: Matters of Fact from Bacon to Defoe*. ACLS Humanities E-Book, 1997. Web. 27 Aug. 2012.

McHale, Brian. *Postmodernist Fiction*. New York: Methuen, 1987.

O'Brien, Tim. *If I Die in a Combat Zone*. London: Grafton, 1989.

Perl, Sondra & Mimi Schwartz. *Writing True: The Art and Craft of Creative Nonfiction*. Boston: Houghton, 2006.

Scholes, Robert. *The Nature of Narrative*. London: Oxford UP, 1966.

Searle, John. "The Logical Status of Fictional Discourse." *New Literary History*. 6.2 On Narrative and Narratives (Winter 1975): 319–332. *JSTOR*. Web. 28 Jan. 2013.

Sheehan, Neil. *A Bright Shining Lie: John Paul Vann and America in Vietnam*. London: Pan, 1990.

Weber, Ronald. *The Literature of Fact: Literary Nonfiction in American Writing*. Ohio: Ohio UP, 1985.

Wolfe, Tom & E. W. Johnson. *The New Journalism*. New York: Harper, 1973.

Zavarzadeh, Mas'ud. *The Mythopoeic Reality: The Postwar American Nonfiction Novel*. Urbana: U of Illinois P, 1976.

The Lyric Essay as Non-nonfiction _____

Jay Ellis

If we pretend to respect the artist at all, we must allow him his freedom of choice, in the face, [. . .] of innumerable presumptions that the choice will not fructify.

(Henry James, "Art" 17)

Another Genre

The term "lyric essay" first appears in a Google search confined to the year 2000 online, with only five results: neither the Goodreads synopsis of Anne Marlowe's *How To Stop Time: Heroin A to Z* (1999), nor two essays (by Emily Bass and Laura Sewell Matter) contain the word "lyric" in them. But the Master of Fine Arts in Writing program description from the University of San Francisco turns up as a .PDF file with an interesting inclusion of the term. Goodreads, however, was created in January 2007, and the Bass and Matter essays provide dates in 2014 and 2012, respectively. Checking the "properties" of that .PDF, however, provides the date of creation: "4/5/2007." Thus plies the mysterious good ship Google Search through our recent past, not so good at "time" or "memory" in any senses of those words. We job out our own sense of these words at our peril, even as we inevitably are drawn to playing with them. Both are human, ineluctably. When, and in what ways, should we call our play with them "nonfiction?" This chapter will argue for a more useful reservation of "nonfiction" away from the freedoms of "lyric essay," when writers deliberately stretch their facts.

I begin with Google's misdirection because this type of accident introduces our attention to one form of the lyric essay fittingly—if not exactly lyrically. Such seemingly suggestive correspondences, but ultimately errant claims of fact, are what our main lyric essayist in this chapter specializes in. Also fittingly, the fifth Google result pointed directly to him: a review essay by John D'Agata (of Anne

Carson's *Men in the Off Hours*), in June of 2000. (Good job, Google; blind pigs find truffles.) John D'Agata regularly serves as a champion of the lyric essay, within his work and about the work of others, so it does provide us with a happy correspondence that his is the first mention one finds on the web—at least using America's most popular search engine.[1]

D'Agata, however, also continues to use the term "creative nonfiction" for his work, and that has, at times, been problematic. My point is not at all to act as a judge of any writer or writing, but rather to help readers here understand distinctions between genres that remain arguably important and that do seem to be growing apart: "lyric essay" and "creative nonfiction." Of course these overlap. Of course labels may be uselessly limiting. But it is not uselessly limiting to expect a reasonable amount of truth in advertising, as it were, when writers claim the word "nonfiction." This argument therefore follows some propositions laid out in our introductory chapter; the subject remains problems of creativity and truth, but here follows D'Agata's lyric resistance to facts as most readers expect their relation. D'Agata claims space for aesthetic freedom away from idea, away from logic—an admirable position shared most of the time by this writer (when making things up instead of making arguments), but this space is one that historically has been the provenance of fiction. In any case, D'Agata and others have already solved this problem, when they avow the term "lyric essay." Unfortunately, D'Agata continues to undermine his own championing of that term by continuing also to claim "nonfiction."

In our introduction, I argued for two reasons (among others) why many writers avowing the genre "creative nonfiction" do not simply call their work a form of "fiction:" twin pressures in American literary history; first, the pressure against creativity and imagination; second, the parallel abiding obsession with fact. The genre of the lyric essay (even if some of its practitioners prefer to avoid labels altogether) provides a space for all the creativity and none of the demand for adherence to truth that D'Agata often claims, without the trouble entailed by using the word "nonfiction." We may only recently, however, be seeing writers embrace "lyric essay" and leave "nonfiction" behind. A bit earlier on, we will see, conflating the two led to some interesting trouble.

Essaying Nuclear Facts

In 2005[2], John D'Agata submitted an essay called "What Happens There" to *Harper's* magazine (circulation 149,430)[3]. The essay was rejected because its fact checkers could not verify his details, and he was not calling the piece fiction. D'Agata then found acceptance with *The Believer*, a magazine with much a smaller circulation ("17,000 to 20,000"[4]), but one founded by Dave Eggers, creator of *McSweeney's* magazine and author of *A Heartbreaking Work of Staggering Genius,* a memoir of raising his brother after losing both parents. Eggers has since published much fiction and nonfiction, all of it notably concerned with morally-centered stories and problems of social justice. The masthead's mission statement for *The Believer* reads in part, "We will give people and books the benefit of the doubt." Nonetheless, the magazine did recruit a fact-checker, Jim Fingal, to go over D'Agata's many concrete details. An intern, Fingal contacted D'Agata with queries, beginning a process (claimed at first to be seven years long) that resulted in the essay's appearance in *The Believer*.

D'Agata's style—which seems partly to be the reason for his following—piles detail upon detail, implicitly linking those details to suggest either ironic causality, or a meaningless quality to contemporary life generated by the assault on our perceptions by accumulations of detail. If this seems a tautology, or an aesthetic act of bad faith, readers may want to give the original works a go to be fair. Such associative lists and suggestions draw on lyric poetry; thus one aspect of the "lyric essay" is its piling up of details. Whatever the quality of the work by this now-celebrated author, our test case considers that essay and D'Agata's statements about it in terms of genre because the correspondence, since presented to us, between him and his fact-checker regularly argue over how much "creative" allows one to alter the "non-" and still claim to be something other than fiction inspired by a sadly true event.

"What Happens There" juxtaposes the suicide in Las Vegas of a real person with myriad details suggesting spatial and temporal connection to that city. Here is the opening paragraph as the essay was eventually published in *The Believer*:

> One summer, when sixteen-year-old Levi Presley jumped from the observation deck of the 1,149-foot-high tower of the Stratosphere Hotel in Las Vegas, the local city council was considering a bill that would temporarily ban lap dancing in the city's strip clubs, archaeologists unearthed shards of the world's oldest bottle of Tabasco brand sauce from beneath a parking lot, and a woman from Mississippi beat a chicken named Ginger in a thirty-five-minute-long game of tic-tac-toe. ("What Happens" 3)

The Lifespan of a Fact collates what readers suppose to be D'Agata's and Fingal's correspondence with what readers would suppose to be the text of the original essay into a book. Here is the opening paragraph of the putative original essay, as provided in *Lifespan*:

> On the same day in Las Vegas when sixteen-year-old Levi Presley jumped from the observation deck of the 1,149-foot-high tower of the Stratosphere Hotel and Casino, lap dancing was temporarily banned by the city in thirty-four licensed strip clubs in Vegas, archeologists unearthed parts of the world's oldest bottle of Tabasco-brand sauce from underneath a bar called Buckets of Blood, and a woman from Mississippi beat a chicken named Ginger in a thirty-five-minute-long game of tic-tac-toe. (*Lifespan* 15–16)

Naturally, the essay as provided in *Lifespan* does not match what was actually published in *The Believer* (the version I give above); nowhere in *Lifespan*, however, do we see what D'Agata changed in response to Fingal's queries and arguments. Around its presentation of the essay, the book about its fact-checking process reproduces what readers would naturally assume to be the correspondence (by email? We are not given specifics) between D'Agata and Fingal. *Lifespan*'s back cover claims this took "seven years of arguments, negotiations, and revisions" between them, that "navigate the boundaries of literary nonfiction." The labels "LITERATURE/ ESSAYS" appear in the upper left of that back cover; readers may be forgiven for not seeing this as a warning that this book itself plays with facts.

Lifespan rather presents itself as an arm-wrestling match (indeed, the back photo suggests D'Agata's prominent biceps might overcome the leverage of the taller Fingal's less muscular build). But without the final edited text, readers would have to hunt down a copy of the essay (available in full text only by purchasing the January 2010 issue of *The Believer*, or by Interlibrary Loan through an academic library), in order to see which forearm hit the table on each contested point of fact. To be charitable, this could bolster an assumption—made by a minority of online commentaries from within the publishing business, such as *Overland* editor Jeff Sparrow—that sloppiness resulting from reduced publishing budgets explains more about this controversy than would arch intellectual gamesmanship. Nevertheless, D'Agata and Fingal's apparent contest made the book a hit, and *The New York Times Book Review* editor Jennifer McDonald characterized *Lifespan*'s correspondence as "less a book than a knock-down, drag-out fight between two tenacious combatants, over questions of truth, belief, history, myth, memory and forgetting."

The gist of the book does seem to be arguments over whether D'Agata took too many liberties with facts. Fingal cannot find support for most of the details in the first paragraph of the essay "What Happens There" (nor for much of the rest of the essay). The back and forth on the first paragraph alone fills the first two pages of *The Lifespan of a Fact*. For instance, Fingal finds the original essay reinterred its "world's oldest bottle of Tabasco brand sauce" (in the book, "Tabasco-brand sauce") under "a bar called Buckets of Blood," which readers would presume to be in Las Vegas. Fingal, however, finds the bottle was unearthed "450 miles away from Las Vegas" and under a bar called "Boston Saloon," which is adjacent to one called "Bucket of Blood" (*Lifespan* 16). If that discrepancy doesn't bother readers, the one where D'Agata argues, "I needed him to fall for nine seconds rather than eight in order to help make some of the later themes in the essay work" (*Lifespan* 19) might, as might the one where he "need[ed]" the tic-tac-toe player, a long-time Las Vegas resident, "to be from a place other than Las Vegas in order to underscore the transient nature of the city—that nearly everyone in Vegas is from someplace else" (*Lifespan* 16). Nearly, indeed. In the book's account, Fingal, exasperated by inaccuracies in D'Agata's essay, finally asks him, "what exactly gives you the authority to introduce half-baked legend as fact and sidestep questions of facticity?" D'Agata responds, "It's called art, dickhead" (*Lifespan* 92).

This characteristic attitude toward his seemingly dutiful fact-checker exasperated many readers of *Lifespan* (including this one—for a time). Suicide is inexplicable, an exit from our shared game, so explanations within that shared game make no sense. D'Agata may seem admirably to have tried to express something of our puzzlement, but he also regularly suggested the indifference of most of the world to this suicide, even as his essay—if we assume any detail in it to be factual—implicitly suggests he understands some deeper cause of that suicide. Certainly, he meant to create art. Whether his creative decisions actually succeed aesthetically, or even ethically, is beyond this essay. To any reader (sadly, this could be nearly all readers) having lost someone to that exit, the use of a real suicide to make points about our difficulties perceiving, or remembering, reality, or an entire city's fabled reliance on lies ("What Happens There" stays there, i.e., remains outside the epistemological power outside Las Vegas), might merit D'Agata's apparent struggles with his fact-checker. When he seems rather to be stumping for the power of art over claims of nonfiction, that, too, finds champions among his readers. But why the nastiness ("dickhead"), and why not then avoid the term "nonfiction"?

Ultimately, D'Agata rejects the word "journalism" for what he writes (*Lifespan* 19), rather referring in apparently all his writing about his work, to the "essay" as his genre of choice—one that allows greater artistic license. Unfortunately, however, he also regularly reverts to the term "creative nonfiction," both in *Lifespan*'s arguments, and in his professional writing life. D'Agata's insistence on claiming a special category for his work has all to do with our problems with the "non-" and solves those problems beautifully in particular when he qualifies the word "essay" with "lyric." Why not stick to careful word choice regarding genre, especially as, throughout *Lifespan*, he insists on altering facts when it suits him for purposes of what he argues is an aesthetically superior word choice. Readers of *The Lifespan of a Fact*, however, will find him most consistent in his inconsistency, on all matters, such as calling the difference between "thirty-four" and "thirty-one" strip clubs one of "rhythm." His word choice even about his word choice often makes no sense at all even on the freer field of the aesthetic. Although he received some form of training in poetry for an MFA in poetry (*John D'Agata*), he does not seem to use any reliable means even of counting syllables.

We will proceed first by granting that at least *The Lifespan of a Fact*, if not the original essay that occasioned it, amounts to more than fiction. It has mostly been presented by both D'Agata and Fingal, who often appeared together for interviews on tour to promote that book, as a true account of their struggle over truth and art. Why, however, even on those grounds, does D'Agata not refuse the term "creative nonfiction," which he regularly dismisses, and clarify his championing of the essay—particularly the lyric essay?

D'Agata's faculty profile page at the University of Iowa lists a single research interest, "Nonfiction Writing," but then shifts to the other word: "He teaches courses on the history of the essay, experiments in essaying, and a variety of workshops." The word "essay" is verbed (unusual in American English, but there in my *American Heritage Dictionary*). D'Agata's curriculum vitae, however, is readily available as a Word document linked to that faculty profile, and where he can most freely choose the word for his writing and teaching, the word "essay" appears sixty-nine times, the word "nonfiction" seventy-seven. As an associate professor (tenured) and the director of the Nonfiction Writing Program in the Iowa English Department, he could surely choose his course titles as he wishes, and yet the fact remains that the two terms swap places and seem to bear an interchangeable relation to one another. "Readings in Nonfiction: History of the Essay" places the essay firmly within the claim of the "non-." "Independent Study in Nonfiction: Reading the Essay Canon" suggests that all (or at least important aspects of) "Nonfiction" are to be found under the rubric of "Essay." Here, but also in numerous interviews, as well as regularly in *The Lifespan of a Fact*, D'Agata clearly wants to have it both ways: the status of "nonfiction" as something wholly other than "fiction" makes a truth claim in one direction, while his use of the word "essay" usually runs in the opposite direction of artistic freedom from facticity. Question the hold on the public's attention by mere "art" (the word preceding his epithet for his hard-working fact-checker), and he returns—especially within the walls of academia—to "nonfiction."

Championing the Lyric Essay

Our uneasiness over making things up, over where the truth lies, especially in the culture that D'Agata successfully does convey— of a bombardment of communication and distraction, of competing claims of truth often vetted not by attention to the ethos behind those claims, but instead by their sheer volume—and our awareness of the precarious nature of truth, as well as an abiding uneasiness about pure invention, all haunt us. But when a writer works the seam between "fiction" and "non-" so freely as first to find, but then deliberately alter facts, why not simply stick to the beautiful room of the "lyric essay?" The term draws on its poetic precedent. (Indeed, original definitions of "prose" refer to it as "without metrical structure"— that is, as a form derived from poetry.) The word "lyric" also carries in the *American Heritage Dictionary* its original "category of poetry," but furthermore adds, "that expresses *subjective thoughts and feelings*, often in a songlike style or form" (my emphasis). What better way of describing work that begins in reality and then moves into the freedom of fiction? Because fiction remains as much the enemy of the most combative lyric essayists as does journalism. Recalling our first chapter's argument on the abiding anxieties over both creativity and nonfiction in American culture, we might see how magically some writers are positioning a putatively new genre between the two—and outside the demands of both.

In 2003, D'Agata did nearly this with his anthology, *The Next American Essay*, but again, he could not resist playing with definitions of what might have simply been left behind. Despite its title, the first essay was written the year of D'Agata's birth, in 1975. Living along with the "*Next*," sample essays are given chronologically until a single essay published in the year of the anthology, 2003. The book's first epigraph quotes Cicero, "*These are the facts, my friends, and I have much faith in them*" (original italics, [vii]), only to posture at their delivery in a single paragraph introduction by D'Agata that refutes the value even of the word "fact." Interesting to see how many words the editor devotes to refuting the importance of a straw noun. A hagiographic essay in *The Believer* by Ben Marcus hailed this "new, provocative anthology" by "the form's single-handed shrewd champion." (Again, we see the trope of combat.) Marcus echoed other champions of the lyric essay as nonfiction with their regular logic that beginning with facts, but departing from them, freely allows artists more freedom (somehow) by relieving them of the burden of making up absolutely everything. (As if novelists invent every street, city, food—every detail in their work.)

Three years later, David Shields (who more recently refuses genre distinctions altogether) repeated some of the reasoning by Marcus in a more properly lyric essay championing the form and fully naming it. What to Marcus had been "a new category of writing" was now being championed in a more obvious contest. "Reality Hunter: A Manifesto: Why the Lyric Essay is Better than Fiction" still could not seem to break free from insecurity. Shields chooses writers as if on a basketball court picking players. When he freely includes fiction writers, he pulls them across the new line along with singers (Frank Sinatra), poets, stand-up comedians, and essentially any artist (or philosopher or anyone with work recorded in any way) whom he wants on his team. Because he wants them. The argument is nothing if not a tautological appeal to ethos, in what presumably is a game where one must choose sides—for reasons only hinted at, glanced off, and run from. Somehow, despite its evolution and survival enough that dozens of its writers are recruited to the new Team Lyric Essay, the novel has "squandered its substance, no longer has an object. The character is dying out; the plot, too" (Shields 28). As if the novel had not been pronounced dead before, Shields moves onward, still recruiting—and including novelist Barry Hannah (who was alive and publishing until four years after the Shields "Manifesto").[5]

Poet Christine Hume's review of *The Next American Essay* noted the combative aspect of these arguments, as well as the market necessities framing them.

> The oxymoronic lyric essay is also nom de guerre against the Industry's refusal to consider Essay as Art and its habitual (mindless) need to pigeonhole every literary thing into the same stodgy standby genres, poetry and fiction [. . .]. Wedged awkwardly between hard journalism and the mushy personal essay, it's been forgotten or neglected—by publishers, funding agencies, and readers—and therefore wears the Romantic patina of the alienated form, a solitary displaced thing.

Hume goes on to provide a more persuasive description of the flow of essays as D'Agata has ordered them.

> Because of their unostentatious fascination with language (repetition, elision, materiality), one that interferes with linearity of story or idea while claiming the domain of truth for poetry and imagination for prose, the essays seem to (though this is clearly an illusion) learn from each other *and* teach us how best to read them. (original emphasis)

This works by chance as an excellent description of the way successful lyric essay sentences work. Hume need not have referred readers to the *Seneca Review*'s 1997 description of the "new" genre, but there D'Agata shares credit as associate editor with Deborah Tall behind a description that continues to stand as an early manifesto—with less aggression or defensiveness than Shields, or D'Agata on his own (Tall & D'Agata).

Shields went on to publish *Reality Hunger: A Manifesto* in book form in 2011, and the "new" should be wearing off the "lyric essay" as this separate genre from creative nonfiction perhaps outgrows its defensive relation to fiction and its problematic one to creative nonfiction. By this book's publication date, reactions for and against the claims of Shields and D'Agata and others for the genre have grown. In "The Beautiful, Untrue Things of the Lyric Essay," Joey Franklin opens with Oscar Wilde's famous claim that art has nothing to do with truth, but rather resides in lies. Wilde's 1889 essay was called "The Decay of Lying," and it preceded the lyric essay revolution by over a hundred years. After covering the art for art's sake argument from Wilde, Franklin helps us see the lyric essay's position relative to this book's attention to all forms of creative nonfiction. "[B]efore you divide yourself off in either the D'Agata/Shields/Dominick camp on the left or the Gutkind/Lopate/Levy camp on the right [. . .] let me just say that if Oscar Wilde were here to witness such a debate, I like to think he'd rub his hands with delight, and say we're all missing the point." Franklin then quotes Judith Kitchen, that the work "of the lyric essayist is to find the prosody of fact, finger the emotional instrument, play the intuitive and intrinsic, but all in service to the music of the real. Even if it's an imagined actuality. The aim is to make *of* not *up*. The lyre, not the liar" (original emphasis, Kitchen 47). Franklin ties this in to Wilde's focus on the mind of the essayist (where, in our first chapter, we saw Lee Gutkind find the test of truth). "[T]he heart of the lyric essay is not reality, not nature, but the music of reality, the music of nature as conceived in the mind of the essayist—the music of beautiful untrue things, which, as Wilde says, is the proper aim of art" (Franklin).

Essaying Nuclear Fictions

At times, D'Agata has seemed busier blurring the line of "nonfiction" outside the work than in it, however. Although *Lifespan of a Fact* was widely reviewed, and is still most-often referred to as itself a work of nonfiction, one of its key claims proves to be totally fabricated—by not only D'Agata, but by his fact-checker as well. The book's back cover references "seven years of arguments, negotiations, and revisions," which readers understandably assume are represented by the pages inside that cover: seven years of a back-and-forth correspondence. Given our time, we also naturally expect these to be emails. But nothing in the scant apparatus of the book—published by no less than W. W. Norton, which, although still a reputable house for fiction, still publishes scholarly editions relied on by academics and serious critics—warns the reader that what is inside was wholly created (recreated?) by D'Agata and Fingal. In "Doubling Down: an interview with John D'Agata and Jim Fingal," *Kenyon Review*'s Weston Cutter hardly hunts for trickery in their story, and yet the fact-checker comes clean right away.

> I must clarify that you should consider the "Jim" and "John" of the *essay* to be characters enacting a parallel process / discussion from the one John and I actually had during the factchecking process. What we did—taking the relatively dry factchecking document and dramatizing it a bit—might be seen as a parallel gesture to what John does in his original essay [. . .]. (Cutter, my emphasis)

Once again, a publisher plays sloppy with the truth in putative "nonfiction." All that was needed was sufficient editorial apparatus, any explanation at all to keep readers from being misled.

D'Agata, however, regards any such warning as infantilizing readers. "At some point the reader needs to stop demanding that they be spoon-fed like infants [. . .] without throwing a temper tantrum or banning that art from ever appearing again" (*Lifespan* 110). The hyperbole here adds to the unintentional irony: no one (beyond the usual internet wackos) whom I could find in thorough research has suggested banning writing that crosses generic lines of expectation when it claims to be nonfiction; reasoned argument does not amount to a "temper tantrum." Rather, this and other arguments—such as D'Agata's call for "anarchy" and "shit storms" as the purpose of art (*Lifespan* 109)—recall the *enfant terrible* figure of the romantic poet, who needs to be bad, transgressive, etc., in order to claim a meaningful purpose for his art. That position itself is of course historically situated, a pose only allowable in the embarrassing position of the artist depending on a public support of his or her art. Fingal's response (original? again, we cannot know) in *Lifespan* is, "Great, another writer who despises his readers" (110).

The book has sold quite well according to every available source,[6] and D'Agata and Fingal are easy to find in the numerous interviews and appearances necessary to any heavily-financed book tour. Once a (relatively very) few journalists caught on that the supposedly true account of the conflict over lying in nonfiction was itself fictionalized, the authors' hedging overtook any confession. Fingal replied to Craig Silverman in an email:

> "I'm not really comfortable putting a label on what the book is, since part of the point of the book is to challenge these . . . categories and what they mean for reader expectations," he wrote. "The back of the book describes it as 'literature/essay' which seems close enough / in the spirit of what the book is intended to be."

Silverman had cried foul in an earlier blog post ("'The Lifespan of a Fact' blends fiction with nonfiction"), citing Fingal's admission in the *Kenyon Review* interview with Weston Cutter. An award-winning journalist who focuses on issues of ethics and accuracy in news reporting puts Fingal's email response in evidence for his charge that the two willfully manipulate journalism (through interview responses, but also through *Lifespan*'s entire approach). Noting that the book's Library of Congress publication data on the copyright page lists the book as "Creative nonfiction," Silverman ultimately writes down the book and its promotional performances as a "sales pitch" ("Mike Daisey, 'Lifespan of a Fact'").

Generic Postures

By 2012, backlash against D'Agata's use of the word "nonfiction"—and what we now realize amounted perhaps to more posturing toward combat with his fact-checker than real combat—had reached the hostile review by McDonald in *The New York Times*. In a subsequent letter to the editor of the *Sunday Book Review*, a no less gifted and acclaimed author than Rebecca Solnit complained, "The potential for serious damage grows as this approach creeps out from memoir (where maybe you're sort of entitled to lie about yourself, if not anyone else) and into works about strangers [. . .]." Solnit then ventures a daring analogy:

> I tell my students that it's a slippery slope from the nasty thing their stepfather never really did to the weapons of mass destruction that Iraq never really had.
> A good artist is not hindered by her responsibility to both subject and readers, but stimulated to go deeper, look harder, write better. Maybe that's because the stories don't belong to you. You belong to them.

Unmentioned by Solnit, there's a gender angle on these controversies, at least in terms of traditional stances. The regularly combative tropes in arguments by D'Agata and Shields for freedom from any expectations whatsoever of responsibility in their writing—whether that is to nonfiction, or oddly to some thought that they are indeed writing fiction—sound to this writer like the old tough talk of male novelists arguing against domestic fiction, or, ironically enough, Hemingway's disappointed male idealism revealed in his insistence on writing nothing that isn't true (in his fiction). Comparatively, Solnit implies that responsibility—belonging to someone or something else—is not demeaning at all, but rather a challenge to the artist to do "better."

As of this writing, D'Agata may be softening his tone, settling for a generic category that, despite its imperfections, proves preferable to problems around "creative nonfiction"—at least when writers wish to claim freedom from journalistic or other ethical calls to factual dependability. The Fall 2014 issue of *Seneca Review* (partly the birthplace of at least the term "lyric essay") suspended calls for submissions, instead announcing on its home page "a special double issue on the Lyric Essay edited by John D'Agata" extending into the Spring of 2015. Taking a year off from its regular consideration and publication of submissions for a journal this noteworthy amounts to a declaration. And the journal's website provides two brief essays by D'Agata, one of which is called "We Might As Well Call It The Lyric Essay." Though he now thinks, "'lyric essay' is no less an example of lipstick on a pig," he begins this new declaration with notably humble admissions. "We might as well call it the lyric essay because I don't think 'essay' means for most readers what essayists hope it does. Or, we might as well call it the lyric essay because 'creative nonfiction'—let's face it—is desperate" (D'Agata, "We Might").

Perhaps in a country particularly hostile to art, especially any art that challenges its consumerist demand for distracting comfort, artists remain doomed to jump up and down about their status, to play with personas and call attention to problems of definition, and ultimately, of genre. Witness the growth of alphabetic text as either a necessary accompaniment to or an integral part of so much contemporary visual art, much of which could be missed *as art* without the accompanying placard announcing its intentions. The internet, with its ubiquitous call for commentary and supposedly "meta" discourse, only adds to a situation where successful writers are expected to stump about what they do and who they are, apart from any truly insightful discourse about the nature of their art itself. But this is no new situation. Artists have been in the position of sales for a long time.

Nina Baym speaks gently to this when attempting to understand Nathaniel Hawthorne's claims about his work. The "definitional chaos" she refers to describes the uncertainty around the older generic terms "romance" and "novel."

> It is interesting to speculate, although certainty must elude us, why, in this atmosphere of definitional chaos, and in the evidence of a lack of fit between Hawthorne's label and the public understanding of the meaning of that label, Hawthorne made the distinction that he did, why he claimed that [the term "romance"] was common parlance, and why he so firmly insisted on the membership of his works in this genre. A few possible explanations come to mind, although I confess that they do not satisfy me. First, given his well-known desire for popularity, and his penchant for artistic subterfuge, it is certainly possible that he was intentionally misleading potential readers, taking advantage of definitional confusion to make claims for his work which would not stand up in the reading but would entice a reader into purchasing his book. Literary history is full of examples

of authors misrepresenting their works as a means of insinuating them into the public arena.

If D'Agata has fought for so long for essentially the reasons of a salesman, he has good company in Hawthorne. Creative nonfiction may have some problems (as our writers will find in some of our subsequent chapters) without being, as D'Agata claims, "desperate." But his new Declaration signals another growth spurt for the lyric essay. The term seems persistent, and to writers and readers happy to acknowledge all the freedom lyric essayists might want as long as they don't claim it to be creative nonfiction, that is a good thing.

Let creative nonfiction and lyric essay do their great works of speaking from the selves, from real experience, even if they head in different directions. If they can do so with true confidence, neither will need to keep playing at posturing personas, and they won't need to keep going on about their superiority to fiction and invention. Henry James wrote, "The house of fiction has in short not one window, but a million [. . .]" ("Preface" 7). So much bigger the house of literature. Let us have a wonderfully large space in which we can all live, including all genres, all styles, all voices. If everyone's included, no one will have to be hammering at the door, nor barring it.

Notes

1. Search conducted 12 Nov. 2014, 14:57, using Advanced Search with "Custom date range" limited between 1/1/2000 and 1/1/2001. Google returned no results from previous years back to 1983. Limiting for 2001 returned twenty-seven results, twenty-three in 2002, sixteen in 2003, twenty-seven again in 2004, twenty-four in 2005, thirty-two in 2006 (the year David Shields published "Reality Hunger: A Manifesto, Why the Lyric Essay is Better than Fiction" in *The Believer*), fifty-four in 2007, eighty-one in 2008, 101 in 2009, 216 in 2010, 237 in 2011, 234 in 2012, 276 in 2013, and as of November 12 (16:50) 257 results.

2. The back cover of *Lifespan* gives 2003 as the date, but in an excerpt of that book, published by *Harper's* as "What Happened in Vegas"— to whom D'Agata first offered the essay—the date given is 2005. As

so much of *Lifespan* itself raises questions of fact, I chose the date given by the publisher who refused the original essay on grounds of inaccuracy.

3. Circulation figures from Alliance for Audited Media, "Circulation averages for the six months ended: 6/30/2014."

4. Circulation given in "Dave Eggers," an interview in *The Progressive*, Nov. 2007.

5. Hannah died on March 8, 2010 (Grimes).

6. Accurate data on book sales remain a guarded secret. Not only does my university library not carry the expensive subscription to Nielsen BookScan, the one database tracking approximately 70 percent of US book sales, neither does Harvard's. Memoirist Shirley Showalter provides a Nielsen BookScan figure that "total sales in the categories of Personal Memoirs, Childhood Memoirs, and Parental Memoirs increased more than 400 percent between 2004 and 2008." Readers must find it hard to imagine that trend has abated much in the six years since.

Works Cited

"About the Believer." *The Believer*. Eds. Heidi Julavits, Andrew Leland, & Vendela Vida. Sept. 2014. Web. 15 Oct. 2014.

Alliance for Audited Media. "Consumer Magazines—Search Results: *Harper's*." Alliance for Audited Media, n.d. Web. 24 Oct. 2014.

Bass, Emily. "The Limits of Compassion." *Vela Magazine: Travel-Inspired Creative Nonfiction, Written by Women*. 28 Jul. 2014. Web. 12 Nov. 2014.

Baym, Nina. "Concepts of the Romance in Hawthorne's America." *Nineteenth-Century Fiction*, Special Issue Dedicated to Blake Nevius 38.4 (Mar. 1984): 426–443. JSTOR. 2 Nov. 2014.

Chandler, Otis. "About Goodreads." *Goodreads*. n.d. Web. 12 Nov. 2014.

Cutter, Weston. "Doubling Down: An Interview with John D'Agata and Jim Fingal." *The Kenyon Review*. KR Online, 23 Feb. 2012. Web. 12 Nov. 2014.

"Dave Eggers." Interview with Nina Siegal. *The Progressive*. 71.11 (Nov. 2007), Progressive, Inc. 33–37. EBSCO. 15 Nov. 2014.

D'Agata, John, ed. *The Next American Essay*. Minneapolis: Graywolf P, 2003.

_____. "What Happens There." *The Believer*. 8.1 (Jan. 2010). Web. 9 Aug. 2014.

_____. *John D'Agata* [Curriculum Vitae]. *The University of Iowa: People*. The University of Iowa. 2013. Web. 14 Sept. 2012.

_____. "We Might As Well Call It The Lyric Essay." *Seneca Review*. Fall 2014. Hobart & William Smith Colleges. Web. 2 Dec. 2014.

_____ & Jim Fingal. *The Lifespan of a Fact*. New York: Norton, 2012.

Eggers, Dave. *A Heartbreaking Work of Staggering Genius*. New York: Vintage, 2001.

"Essay." *The American Heritage Dictionary*. 3rd ed. 1992.

Franklin, Joey. "The Beautiful, Untrue Things of the Lyric Essay." *TriQuarterly*. Northwestern UP, 17 Sept. 2014. Web. 2 Dec. 2014.

Goodreads. Synopsis of "*How To Stop Time: Heroin from A to Z* by Ann Marlowe, NY: Basic Books, 1999." *Goodreads*. n.d. Web. 22 Oct. 2014.

Grimes, William. "Barry Hannah, Darkly Comic Writer, Dies at 67." *The New York Times*. 3 Mar. 2010. Web. 1 Dec. 2014.

Hume, Christine. Rev. of *The Next American Essay*. Ed. John D'Agata. *The Constant Critic*. 12 May 2003. Web. 2 Dec. 2014.

James, Henry. "Preface to Volume 3 of the New York edition." *Portrait of a Lady*. By Henry James. New York: Norton, 1995. 7.

_____. "The Art of Fiction." *Essentials of the Theory of Fiction*. 3rd Ed. Michael J. Hoffman & Patrick D. Murphy. Durham, NC: Duke UP, 2005. 13–19.

Kitchen, Judith. "Mending Wall." *Seneca Review*. 37. 2 (2007): 47.

"Lyric." *The American Heritage Dictionary*. 3rd ed. 1992.

Marcus, Ben. "The Genre Artist." *The Believer*. 1.4 (July 2003). Web. 27 Nov. 2014.

Matter, Laura Sewell. "The Long Run." *Vela Magazine: Travel-Inspired Creative Nonfiction, Written by Women*. 22 Oct. 2012. Web. 12 Nov. 2014.

McDonald, Jennifer B. "In the Details: 'The Lifespan of a Fact,' by John D'Agata and Jim Fingal." Rev. of *The Lifespan of a Fact*, by John D'Agata and Jim Fingal. *New York Times Sunday Book Review*. 21 Feb. 2012. Web. 15 Nov. 2014.

"Prose." *The American Heritage Dictionary*. 3rd ed. 1992.

"Seneca Review." *Seneca Review*. Hobart and William Smith Colleges, Fall 2014. Web. 2 Dec. 2014.

Shields, David. "Reality Hunter: A Manifesto: Why the Lyric Essay Is Better Than Fiction." *The Believer*. 4.2 (Mar. 2006).

_____. *Reality Hunger: A Manifesto*. NY: Vintage, 2011.

Showalter, Shirley. "Why Is There a Surge in Memoir? Is It a Good Thing?" *JaneFriedman.com*, 11 Sept. 2012. Web. 12 Nov. 2014.

Silverman, Craig. "'The Lifespan of a Fact' blends fiction with nonfiction to explore nature of truth." *Poynter*. Poynter Institute, 5 Mar. 2012 11:40. Updated 25 Nov. 2014 08:25. Web. 26 Nov. 2014.

_____. "Mike Daisey, 'Lifespan of a Fact' use journalism as a sales strategy." *Poynter*. Poynter Institute, 21 Mar. 2012 11:48. Updated 25 Nov. 2014 08:25. Web. 26 Nov. 2014.

Solnit, Rebecca. Letter. *New York Times Sunday Book Review*. 9 Mar. 2012. Web. 13 Nov. 2014.

Sparrow, Jeff. "'Cats are out, sloths are in'." *Overland*. 60. 214 (Autumn 2014). Web. 20 Oct. 2014.

Tall, Deborah, ed, & John D'Agata, assoc. ed. "The Lyric Essay." *Seneca Review*. 27.2 (Fall 1997).

"What Happened in Vegas." *Harper's Magazine*. February 2012. Web. 14 Nov. 2014.

"Loops and Spins": Autobiography, Autofiction, and Tim O'Brien's Serial Selves_____

David Bahr

In 2002, I interviewed the author Tim O'Brien for a magazine profile. He had just published his eighth and, to date, last book, *July, July*, a novel about the thirtieth college reunion of the class of '69. Unfamiliar with his writing, I prepared by reading *July, July* and O'Brien's major works: his first book and only memoir, *If I Die in a Combat Zone*; his National Book Award–winning novel, *Going After Cacciato*; and the Pulitzer Prize finalist, *The Things They Carried*, a work of metafiction. All are informed by O'Brien's experience in the Vietnam War. During the interview, I was interested in his merging of fact and fiction. He explained how his memoir might have been his most factually accurate book, but that did not make it the "most true" (Bahr). "After writing *If I Die*, I had pretty much come to terms with things," he said. "For me, *Going After Cacciato*, and even more *The Things They Carried*, were about storytelling, how stories can come from lies. Do stories, even from our own life, have to be literally true to be emotionally true?"

I understood what O'Brien meant by the truth of fiction. It was not until a year later, when I tried to write about my own history as a foster child, that I began to appreciate O'Brien's point about the limits of factual truth. Attempting to narrate the events of my troubled past, I found facts wanting, my memories suspect, shifting, and colored by emotions, which often seemed most "true." An academic and journalist, I realized that autobiography is not like fact-based research and reporting. As Micaela Maftei contends in *The Fiction of Autobiography*, autobiographical writing can represent "an honest version of events without understanding this honesty to imply a belief in a single true version, either the author's or anyone else's" (9).

O'Brien has written about his experience as a Vietnam veteran in the form of a memoir, a work of metafiction, and a journalistic essay.

His memoir and essay are evidently works of creative nonfiction. Yet *The Things They Carried* demonstrates that the distinction between fiction and creative nonfiction is not decisive and that the two forms influence and borrow from each other, especially in life writing. The intersection between creative nonfiction and fiction is salient in autobiographical fiction, or autofiction, as it has been classified by French critics. And while *The Things They Carried*, a unique work of American literature, has been categorized as postmodern metafiction, it has not been examined in the context of autofiction. Yet it is the text's autobiographical aspects, both in form and content, that connect it to creative nonfiction. Further, viewing *The Things They Carried* through an autofictional lens reveals why an author might choose to write autofiction instead of a conventional memoir or autobiographical essay.

Patricia Waugh defines metafiction as "a term given to fictional writing which self-consciously and systematically draws attention to its status as an artifact in order to pose questions about the relationship between fiction and reality" (2). *The Things They Carried* raises those questions and, in that sense, can be categorized as metafiction. Waugh also writes that metafiction examines "the fundamental structures of narrative fiction" and explores "the possible fictionality of the world outside the literary fictional text" (2). Yet for someone struggling to provide a written account of an experience, particularly if it is painful, exposing the "fictionality" of the world is not the goal. As O'Brien states, "For me, Vietnam wasn't an unreal experience" (Schroeder 146) and *If I Die* was "published and intended to be a straight autobiography" (136). He acknowledges using fictional devices, such as dialogue, in his memoir, but he does so to get at the "truth."

O'Brien says that he started writing what would become *If I Die* while a soldier in Vietnam. The process began as a form of note-taking. "Partly I began writing little anecdotes," he explains. "But I didn't think of them as a book. [. . .] I wasn't sure what they were or why I was doing it" (O'Brien, *If I Die* 148). Comprised of twenty-three chapters, each titled and some a few pages long, *If I Die* bears its anecdotal origins. The first chapter, "Days," opens *in medias res*, with O'Brien in combat and conversation with a fellow soldier. As with the other stories, "Days" is, as O'Brien says, "just a straightforward telling: 'here's what happened to me'" (148). He describes the memoir as "just there as a document," but "not art" because "I didn't know what literature was" (148).

The conventional, almost photographic realism of *If I Die* provides a structure for the chaos of war. Following "Days," the narrative framework implies a beginning, middle, and end. In the second chapter, "Pro Patria," O'Brien informs the reader, "I grew out of one war and into another" (*If I Die* 11); he connects his father's proud service in World War II with his going off to the Vietnam, suggesting a continuity between generations. But any similarities between father and son are disrupted by the disorder and destruction that follow. The disjunction between the patriotism of his father's generation and O'Brien's fear and loathing of Vietnam is clear in "Beginning," an expository description of O'Brien's struggle and dread after being drafted. "Now, war ended, all I am left with are simple, unprofound scraps of truth," he writes at the chapter's close. "Can the foot soldier teach anything important about war, merely for having been there? I think not. He can tell war stories" (*If I Die* 23). For the next twenty-one chapters, O'Brien tells war stories, ending with "Don't I Know You," about his trip home. Suggesting a conventional denouement in the form of a lesson, O'Brien concludes:

> You add things up. You lost a friend to the war, and you gained a friend. You compromised one principle and fulfilled another. You learned, as old men tell it in front of the courthouse, that war is not all bad; it may not make a man of you, but it teaches you that manhood is not some thing to scoff [.] (*If I Die* 207)

Changing his clothes in the back of an airplane before landing, O'Brien adds, "You smile at yourself in the mirror. You grin, beginning to know you're happy" (*If I Die* 209).

After the chaos, ineptitude, and brutality in the preceding chapters, the ending feels pat. But the conventional narrative structure implied by a beginning, middle, and end requires a conclusion. Considering O'Brien's later writing on the ambiguity and inconclusiveness of his Vietnam experience, the ending of *If I Die* is probably as honest a denouement as O'Brien could have written, given the constraints of conventional mimetic memoir. On *If I Die*, Marilyn Wesley writes "the narrative production of verisimilitude" denies any "genuine differences [that] may exist between a non-combatant reader and the veteran writer" (3). Wesley states how mimesis, as a literary strategy, provides a structure and order that is counter to disruptive forces (such as war). Quoting Leo Bersani, Wesley reiterates that mimesis "constructs 'a secret complicity between the novelist and his society's illusions about its own order . . . by providing [society] with strategies for containing (and repressing) its disorder within significantly structured stories about itself'" (3–4). In this context, *If I Die* reads more like traditional fiction than *The Things They Carried*, which disrupts mimesis with authorial and narrative instability, reflexivity, and unreliability.

After the first two chapters, *If I Die* becomes, as Wesley observes, "an identifiable succession of incidents from his introduction to the military to his exit, generally presented as historical movement from month to month" (3). Although some memoirs are not written in a linear, but recursive chronology, most attempt to be mimetic, an accurate representation of events as recalled by the author. Pioneering autobiography theorist Philippe Lejeune has identified this commitment to accurate self-representation as the "autobiographical pact." Defined by Lejeune, this "pact" is not grounded on empirically verifiable facts:

> The oath rarely takes such an abrupt and total form; it is a supplementary proof of honesty to restrict it to the possibility (the truth such as it appears to me, in as much as I can know it, etc., making allowances for lapses of memory, errors, involuntary distortions, etc.), and to indicate explicitly the field to which this oath applies (the truth about such and such an aspect of my life, not committing myself in any way about some other aspect). (22)

Whether objective or subjective, mimesis has its limits, and O'Brien acknowledges as much. "In writing *If I Die*, I learned distrust of truth," he says ("A Conversation" 100). He notes that even in news journalism, which, ideally, is an account of "absolute truth" (100), the reporter must make choices about what to include, the rest "is thrown away" (100). O'Brien adds that "I'm not saying that historians or newspaper writers lie," but that "to bill something as the truth is suspect, and I learned that in *If I Die*" (100). In writing the memoir, he believes that he "was reasonably faithful to what had occurred," but he "hadn't held a mirror up to what had actually happened" (101). This realization prompted O'Brien's to turn to fiction to communicate those aspects of his experience that were discarded or could not be conveyed in a conventional mimetic form. "It was liberating to think, Well, if you could do that in a memoir [i.e., construct dialogue and scenes], why not write a work of fiction, in which, through fictional strategies, you don't have to worry about being faithful to the truth?" (101). With fiction, he adds, there "are different kind of truths you're after, a feeling, an emotional truth, a spiritual and psychological truth not tethered to the world we live in" (101).

Ironically, it is a nonfiction essay by O'Brien that reveals the emotional truths of his metafiction that could not be conveyed by the memoir. Twenty years after the publication of *If I Die*, O'Brien returned to where he was stationed as a soldier in Vietnam. He wrote about this "homecoming" for the *New York Times Magazine*, an essay entitled "The Vietnam in Me." The piece juxtaposes memories of the past with struggles of the present, including the breakup with his girlfriend, Kate, who accompanied him on the journey. The essay confirms that *If I Die*, and its implied resolution, was inconclusive. O'Brien admits to years of treatment for depression and chronicles his suicidal thoughts while writing the article, provoked by rekindled war memories and his separation from Kate. When O'Brien writes, "Evil has no place, it seems, in our national mythology. We erase it. We use ellipses" ("Vietnam" 52), he echoes what Wesley identified as the constraints of conventional, mimetic autobiography, in which structure contains, and represses, chaos. The essay reveals that there is no "lesson" or happy ending, as suggested by *If I Die*. The struggle is ongoing.

O'Brien addresses the ellipses and erasures of *If I Die* with *The Things They Carried*. Comprised of twenty-two individually titled "chapters," the book alternates between longer "stories" and shorter pieces that comment on and/or connect the lengthier texts. The narrator is introduced in the third anecdotal chapter, "Spin," when the character Norman Bowker addresses "O'Brien" (*Things* 39). In the fourth chapter, "On A Rainy River," the possible parallels between author and protagonist—now explicitly identified as "Tim O'Brien"—emerge for readers of *If I Die*. As with "Beginning," "On A Rainy River" tells of O'Brien's draft and subsequent conflict about dodging military conscription for a war he does not support. In *If I Die*, O'Brien writes of his decision not to evade the draft:

> It was an intellectual and physical standoff, and I did not have the energy to see it to an end. I did not want to be a soldier, not even an observer to war. But neither did I want to upset a peculiar balance between the order I knew [. . .]. It was not just that I valued that order. I also feared its opposite—inevitable chaos, censure, embarrassment [. . .] (22)

The circumstances of O'Brien's choice to go to war were neither atypical nor particularly dramatic. Yet his internal battle, and consequences of his decision, were impactful for O'Brien. To convey the internal drama, O'Brien builds on the situation described in his memoir and constructs a tale in which "O'Brien" runs away and encounters an eighty-one year old man, Elroy Berdahl, "skinny and shrunken and mostly bald" (*Things* 51). O'Brien spends thirteen of the story's twenty pages relaying "O'Brien's" experience on the lam along the Rainy River and at Elroy's Tip Top Lodge. The effect is to immerse the reader in the isolation of the protagonist's conflict. Perhaps representing the older O'Brien, or the absence of adult guidance, Elroy offers no advice, only listens, and quietly lets the protagonist struggle, finally taking him by boat to the shores of Canada. As O'Brien is about to leave the United States, he hesitates.

> Inside me, in my chest, I felt a terrible squeezing pressure. Even now, as I write this, I can still feel that tightness. And I want you to feel

it—the wind coming off the river, the waves, the silence, the wooded frontier. You're at the bow of a boat on the Rainy River. You're twenty-one years old, you're scared, and there's a hard squeezing pressure in your chest. (*Things* 59)

He then asks "What would you do?" (O'Brien, *Things* 59). The protagonist's effort to flee is detailed for several more pages, resulting, as it did in the memoir, with O'Brien going to Vietnam. Less expository than "Beginning," "On The Rainy River" offers an imagined narrative, suggesting a myth with touches of magical realism. It affirms what O'Brien wrote twenty years earlier about fighting in a war he did not support: "the standoff is still there" (*If I Die* 22).

The emotional baggage that O'Brien carries as a Vietnam veteran is given greater metaphoric weight in "Speaking of Courage," a third-person narrative about Norman Bowker, who has trouble re-assimilating to civilian life. Set during July 4, Bowker drives around town, isolated and conversing with the ghosts in his head, reliving the combat death of a friend. Not unlike *If I Die*, the story ends on a note of hope: Bowker gets out of the car, dips his head in the lake, suggesting a baptism, and watches the local fireworks. "For a small town, he decided, it was a pretty good show" (*Things* 172).

Milton Bates calls "Speaking of Courage" "a model of the well-wrought short story," laudable for its "symmetries," although in "Notes," the next chapter, that "symmetry comes undone" (250). Robin Silbergleid states how "Notes" works like a piece of creative nonfiction, "even on the level of tone and diction" (139). "Notes" begins: "'Speaking of Courage' was written in 1975 at the suggestion of Norman Bowker, who three years later hanged himself in the locker room of a YMCA in his hometown in central Iowa" (O'Brien, *Things* 177). Silbergleid explains that "Notes" "isn't actually nonfiction, but adopts the rhetorical devices of essay writing," and "while both naïve and cynical readers might wonder if the story of Norman Bowker is true, in the end, it doesn't matter if Bowker's story actually happened; what matters is that, within the context of *The Things They Carried*, Bowker's story needs to be understood as 'true'" (139). I first read "Notes" in preparation for my interview with O'Brien. I believed his gloss on "Speaking of Courage" as a statement of fact, yet, during our conversation, the issue of what was fact and fiction arose. I recall him saying that the entire book was fiction except for the suicide of an army buddy, which had prompted him to write "Speaking of Courage" and "Notes." Years later, I read an interview with O'Brien from 1991, in which he states that the story was based on "Norman Bowker, a real guy, who committed suicide after I received his letter" ("An Interview" 7). Then, assessing the recently published *The Things They Carried*, O'Brien says:

> It's a new form, I think. I blended my own personality with the stories, and I'm writing about the stories, and yet everything is made up, including the commentary. The story about Norman Bowker is made up. There was no Norman Bowker. The point being, among others, that in fiction we not only transform reality, we sort of invent our own lives, invent our histories, our autobiographies. ("An Interview" 8)

Within the same conversation, O'Brien asserts that "Speaking of Courage" *is* and *is not* based on a man named Norman Bowker. In the construction of personal narratives, O'Brien is more interested in the instability between fact and fiction. "To try to classify different elements of the story as fact or fiction seems to me artificial," he says. "What matters in literature, I think, are pretty simple things—whether it moves me or not, whether it feels true" ("An Interview" 9).

Unlike *If I Die*, *The Things They Carried* destabilizes narrative conventions, preventing any one story from becoming *the* story. This allows for the Tim O'Brien of *If I Die* and the Tim O'Brien of *The Things They Carried* to co-exist and, in fact, be supplementary. The memoir's factual truths and his fiction's emotional truths—often shifting, contradictory, and variable—are not mutually exclusive. Maftei contends that the implied and sometimes explicit "unity (both temporal and in terms of identity)" (10) associated with memoir and autobiography needs to be challenged. "This rejection exemplifies the way our lives can be said to consist of a series of successive selves, often overlapping, rather than a single, constant self" (Maftei 10). The O'Brien of *If I Die* is not the same O'Brien, literally and figuratively, of *The Things They Carried*, but, considered in tandem, O'Brien's serial selves offer a more truthful account of a life lived.

Our changing roles and perspectives are not the only reasons that autobiographical writing may be a life-long project of revisiting and revising. For those, like O'Brien, who experienced a traumatic event, the need to write about it can be a way to manage, shape, and renegotiate memories that are not easily, or ever, exorcised. The expectations of unity attached to conventional autobiography are at odds with a serial self. As a result, fiction has been more amenable to the project of autobiographical revisiting and revising. But, maybe, as Maftei proposes, we need to re-envision autobiography: "Can we divorce autobiographical writing from traditional fiction/nonfiction categorization by understanding it as a totally new creation that relies on the past but is not bound by it?" (10).

Conceived and debated by French theorists, autofiction destabilizes the boundaries between fiction and nonfiction. In her historical overview of autofiction, Karen Ferreira-Meyers cites how scholars date the term's origin to 1977 and the French writer Serge Doubrovsky, although it has only recently been adopted by Anglophone literatures. Doubrovsky defines autofiction as fiction in which the "events and facts" of an author's life are "accurately reported," but the author "assembles them in a radically altered presentation, disorderly or in an order, which deconstructs and reconstructs the narrative according to its own logic with a novelistic design of its own. [. . .] In other words, one could say that all this is a postmodern version of autobiography" (1–2). Meyers notes how, over the years, variations of this definition have emerged, with the accuracy of events given more or less emphasis. The main point of contention seems to be between the terms autofiction and autobiographical novel, with some viewing one or the other as closer to autobiography. But, as Maftei, O'Brien, and others have indicated, "accuracy" and "facts" are problematic when memory and emotions are involved. In the end, the distinction between autofiction and autobiographical fiction seems moot, as least in terms of the possibilities that they offer a writer like O'Brien, struggling to write his autobiographical truth. Nina Schmidt views the tension between fact and fiction in autofiction as "decidedly positively: it enables agency, a creative way of dealing with issues otherwise unspeakable" (Schmidt 56).

O'Brien has said that the "fiction writer combines memory with imaginative skills" (Schroeder 143). The process is "also about how life itself operates" because "our lives are largely, maybe totally, determined by what we remember and by what we imagine" (144). He concludes, "Memory and imagination as devices of survival apply to all of us whether we are in a war situation or not" (144). While he states that "Memory, by itself, is the province of nonfiction—you write what you remember, you remember what you take in notes or on a tape recorder" (143), he adds that few of us document our lives in this way. Of course, personal recordkeeping is selective and often subjective. And the act of remembering always involves a reimagining. "Recollection," as Israel Rosenfield states in *The Invention of Memory*, "is a kind of perception, and [. . .] every context will alter the nature of what is recalled" (89). For those whose pasts weigh on us, in the form of fragmented recollections or sense memories that elude mimetic language, autofiction allows us to manage and navigate these ghosts. For O'Brien, this "sense of embellishment," of "letting one's imagination heighten detail," is "not lying"; rather, it is "trying to produce story detail which will somehow get at a felt experience" (Schroeder 140).

The last chapter of *The Things They Carried*, "Lives of the Dead," an episodic narrative photographic in its effects, shifts between scenes of war, the protagonist Tim O'Brien's childhood, and the present. The piece, about the living process of writing, is also about what Elaine Scarry calls "the objectifying power of the imagination" (164). As O'Brien states in "Notes": "By telling stories, you objectify your own experience. . . . You separate it from yourself" (*Things* 179). Throughout "The Lives of The Dead," O'Brien shifts between these three periods, playing the memories against each other. In "The Vietnam in Me," O'Brien writes, "The hardest part, by far, is to make the bad pictures go away. On war time, the world is one long horror movie, image after image, and if it's anything like Vietnam, I'm in for a lifetime of wee-hour creeps" (56). Similarly, "The Lives of the Dead" is a story about a man struggling, through the process of writing, to manage these "pictures." He concludes:

> I'm skimming across the surface of my own history, moving fast, riding the melt beneath the blades, doing loops and spins, and when I take a high leap into the dark and come down thirty years later, I realize it is as Tim trying to save Timmy's life with a story. (O'Brien, *Things* 273)

Unlike *If I Die*, which concludes with a literal and figurative arrival, *The Things They Carried* suggests there is no denouement. Life writing is an ongoing process. When a well-intentioned woman in "How To tell a True War Story" tells "O'Brien" to leave behind his painful past and "find new stories to tell," the fictional O'Brien could be speaking for the living author, when, exasperated but undaunted, he narrates: "All you can do is tell it one more time, patiently, adding and subtracting, making up a few things to get at the real truth" (*Things* 91).

Works Cited

Bahr, David. "Book of Illusions." *Time Out New York*. 24 Oct. 2002. n.p.

Bates, Milton J. *The Wars We Took to Vietnam: Cultural Conflict and Storytelling*. Berkeley: U of California P, 1996.

Doubrovsky, Serge. "Autofiction." *Autofiction* 1.1 (2013): 1–3.

Ferreira-Meyers, Karen. "Historical Overview of a New Literary Genre: Autofiction." *Autofiction* 1.1 (2013): 15–35.

Lejeune, Philippe. *On Autobiography*. Trans. Katherine Leary. Ed. Paul John Eakin. Minneapolis: U of Minnesota P, 1989.

Maftei, Micaela. *The Fiction of Autobiography: Reading and Writing Identity*. London: Bloomsbury Academic, 2013.

O'Brien, Tim. "The Vietnam in Me." *The New York Times Magazine*. 2 Oct. 1994: 48–57.

_____. *The Things They Carried*. Boston: Houghton Mifflin, 1990.

_____. *Going After Cacciato*. New York: Delacorte Press/Seymour Lawrence, 1978.

_____. *If I Die in a Combat Zone Box Me Up & Ship Me Home*. New York: Delta/Seymour Lawrence, 1975.

O'Brien, Tim & Martin Naparsteck. "An Interview with Tim O'Brien." *Contemporary Literature* 32.1 (Spring 1991): 1–11.

Rosenfield, Israel. *The Invention of Memory: A New View from the Brain*. New York: Basic, 1988.

Scarry, Elaine. *The Body in Pain: The Making and Unmaking of the World*. London: Oxford UP, 1987.

Schroeder, Eric James. "Two Interviews: Talks with Tim O'Brien and Robert Stone." *Modern Fiction Studies* 30.1 (Spring 1984): 136–163.

Silbergleid, Robin. "Making Things Present: Tim O'Brien's Autobiographical Metafiction." *Contemporary Literature* 50.1 (Spring 2009): 129–155.

Waugh, Patricia. *Metafiction: The Theory and Practice of Self-Conscious*. Florence, KY: Routledge, 1984.

Wesley, Marilyn. "Truth and Fiction in Tim O'Brien's *If I Die in a Combat Zone* and *The Things They Carried*." *College Literature* 29.2 (2002): 1–18.

CRITICAL
READINGS

Benjamin Franklin's Middle Way and the Argumentative Nature of Autobiography____

Peter Kratzke

Across the texts constituting how American history is told flickers the genre of *creative nonfiction*, both words operative in meaning and practice: how does literary creativity affect the recording of nonfictional information? Long before there were twentieth-century writers such as Truman Capote, there was John Smith, who amplified details of his experience—including his rescue by Pocahontas—between his 1608 *A True Relation of Virginia* and his 1624 *Generall Historie of Virginia.* About the difference between the first account and the second, Randolph G. Adams parses, "Perhaps the 1608 text is history and the 1624 version is literature" (33). North of Smith's Virginia, William Bradford, who did not begin writing *Of Plymouth Plantation* until a decade after the Pilgrims arrived in the New World, employed a "plain style" that underscored his plea that the colony needed greater social stability. In the ensuing century, Jonathan Edwards described, in his wonderfully-titled 1737 essay *A Faithful Narrative of the Surprising Work of God in the Conversion of Many Hundred Souls in Northampton*, the town and its residents while, more importantly, formulating the process behind their respective epiphanies. Categorizing any of these early American figures as writers of creative nonfiction, though, only anticipates Edwards' contemporary, Benjamin Franklin. Franklin's depiction of eighteenth-century life in his *Autobiography* provides a great deal of interesting nonfictional information, but the quality that has maintained the text's towering position in American culture is how and why it confirms that all writing of history is inevitably creative and that all creativity, in turn, is argumentative.

As the most self-referential genre in the writing of history, autobiography attempts to stop life's clock and account for the barren data of chronology. Franklin did so no fewer than four times in telling his rags-to-riches story: in 1771, when he served in England as Agent for Pennsylvania; in 1784, when he was sent by Congress as its Commissioner to France; in 1788, when he was in Philadelphia; and, finally, just before his death in 1790. The resulting posthumously published account, unfinished given an outline that Franklin etched of the topics he wished to cover, stops short in 1758, but scholarship and popular interest, especially in celebrating the 2006 tercentenary of Franklin's birth, have attempted to fill in the gap between Franklin the narrative hero and Franklin the narrator of what he called his "memoirs"—the term *autobiography* was not coined until 1797 (Chaplin xiii). However, as indicated by the bibliographic difference between using the present tense for discussing authorial voice and currency of ideas ("In his *Autobiography*, Franklin discusses the importance of appearances") and the past tense for historical and biographical reference ("Franklin described in his *Autobiography* how he established a lending library"), the gap can be fraught with questions about theme involving what authors intend and what readers interpret.

Although at times perplexing, autobiography's gap between creative narrative and nonfictional information must not be either too wide or too transparent if an account is to remain classified substantively as nonfiction. The formulaic job cover letter is a familiar counterexample in which never was heard a discouraging word: the applicant is *passionate* about skills, *enthusiastic* about the prospective company, and *sincere* in waiting for the company's response. Order and the exemplary are created from disorder and the average represented in the applicant's resume. Unfortunately, the same letter is also quickly read and discarded for its unrealistic "purple prose," and the writer remains unemployed. Franklin's *Autobiography*, the form of which is ostensibly a letter to his son William, is different for three important reasons. First, Franklin wished to demonstrate to average citizens how they could lead their not-so-exemplary lives. Second, Franklin's creativity almost never calls attention to itself, his prose style spare and clear. The third reason comments on and even undercuts the previous two: Franklin just so happened to be a genius. After describing his lineage to begin Part One, Franklin muses, "By my rambling Digressions I perceive my self to be grown old. I us'd to write more methodically. But one does not dress for private Company as for a publick Ball. 'Tis perhaps only Negligence" (1316).[1] Negligence in personal action is one matter. For an author to plead negligence about the act of writing autobiography is another. When the author is a genius, it is another altogether.

Polemical Argumentation and the Middle Way

Almost all literary and historical assessments about Franklin comment on his elusiveness. Simon P. Newman remarks, "A true master of spin, Franklin enjoyed an enviable ability to construct and popularize certain public faces and images for himself while yet contriving to obscure others" (161). Not only did Franklin "spin," he revised. As anyone who has touched a dot of ink to paper knows, revision is a recursive process, continually doubling back on itself. The result is that, throughout his *Autobiography*, Franklin is acutely self-aware about the difference between narrative and narrator, and the whole emerges as less a record of his life than an account of his writing that record through what he otherwise disclaims as his ability to "scribble" (1365). Not surprisingly, critical assessments get tangled in Franklin's "spin[ning]," the effect at once delightful and maddening. Franklin, as Walter Isaacson envisions in his biography, is "the founding father who winks at us" (2), but at what is Franklin winking? Is it that he invites his readers to share his insight, or is it that he knows that completely accurate human communication is hopeless?

Across his long career, Franklin argued in an astonishing variety of genres and about all sorts of difficult questions, but consistent from early to late was his use of polemical argumentation in turning on its head the illogic of his opponents. Polemical argumentation, to define the term, is driven by categorical one-side-or-the-other seeming certainties that then can (but not always) give perspective for understanding what may be termed the *middle way*. In an early example, Franklin praised in a 1722 poem a style of writing that shunned the extremes of both poetic diction and purpose prose. Rather, Franklin advocates "The middle Way between good Verse and Prose" (23). Rarely is Franklin as explicit; more typically in his writings, he explores categories and thereby shows to tell the middle way. "He that changes his [political] Party," Franklin argued in a 1732 agenda for the Junto (an intellectual club he helped to form), "is either sincere, or not sincere [. . .]" (209), and his career as a diplomat would testify to the contentious ambiguities between these two poles. Nearly fifty years later, Franklin observed in his 1780 essay titled "The Handsome and the Deformed Leg," "There are two sorts of People in the World, who with equal Degrees of Health & Wealth and the other Comforts of Life, become, the one happy, the other unhappy" (950). Emotional happiness, Franklin knew by that time in his life, is as unstable as life's physical circumstances. Most significantly to his role as a Founding Father, Franklin adapted polemical argumentation throughout the turmoil of the American Revolution: "Join, or Die," Franklin famously enjoined in his 1754 cartoon about the French and Indian War (377), and, in a 1783 letter, he observed even in the wake of victory that "*there never was a good War, or a bad Peace*" (1073). Compromise in cementing national and international alliances alike was never far from Franklin's mind. To turn this mode on itself, polemical argumentation can be either constructive or destructive: black-or-white categorical boundaries must be drawn, but doing so risks overlooking the vast gray of human existence. At every step in life's journey told in his *Autobiography*, Franklin was aware—or became aware—of this problem.

Behind Franklin's flexible use of polemical argumentation were his equally flexible views about human nature. As an optimist, Franklin embraced freedom for citizens to choose their own destinies; as a pessimist, he knew that human corruptions signaled, at best, compromise and, at worst, distortion. Esmond Wright offers good advice for any reader or critic: "Efforts to give consistency to his [Franklin's] ideas or to his views [. . .] are imperiled by the many experiences and challenges he encountered. He was, first and last, versatile, adaptable, adept at swimming with tides" (vii). Compounding these "experiences and challenges" was that, despite what he saw as the marvelous potential of science, Franklin found human nature—and a large part of human experience—as vexing.

Franklin addressed this problem in reference to the Locke-Hobbes polemical argument as early as in a 1737 letter: "Hobbes [. . .] is somewhat nearer the Truth than that which makes the State of Nature a State of Love: But the Truth perhaps lies between both Extreams" (425). Franklin's hedging "somewhat" is crucial. Ronald A. Bosco has considered what might at first seem strange to the popular conception of Franklin:

> one invariably comes up against what I would call his [Franklin's] "dark side," a side from which expressions such as "Franklin's pessimism," "Franklin's concept for mankind and human pride," and "Franklin's disdain for human nature" provide just as apt indices to his life and opinion as to those well-worn reminders of his optimism typically found in the indices of Franklin biographies. (526)

From theory to action, Franklin looked to a resolving moderation in all things. Isaacson is not alone among Franklin's readers in asserting, "Franklin's most important vision: an American national identity based on the virtues and values of its middle class" (3). Although the middle class was Franklin's socio-economic focus, its "virtues and values" were anything but, in one of Franklin's favorite words, "middling." With his *Autobiography*, Franklin had the perfect genre to show exactly what he meant by this difference.

The Middle Way in and beyond the *Autobiography*

The most obvious prefatory reading for the *Autobiography*'s line between creative narrative and nonfictional information is *Poor Richard's Almanack*, which Franklin published between 1732 and 1758. Full of homespun proverbs, miscellaneous information, and occasional illustrations, *Poor Richard's* is driven by the push-pull between polemical certainties given voice by the character "Poor" Richard Saunders, who, as the narrative hero, differs from Franklin the narrator, whom Poor Richard calls his "Printer." On the one hand, Poor Richard exhorts his readers to seize the day: "Since thou art not sure of a minute, throw not away an hour" (1209) and "You may delay, but *Time* will not" (1303) are among his many proverbs. On the other hand, he advises deliberate application: "Snowy winter, a plentiful harvest" (1188) and "Make haste slowly" (1232). Every categorical proverb seems to have a counter-proverb, but, once in a while, Franklin the narrator's advocacy for the middle way peeks through the exceptions that prove the rule to Poor Richard's certainties: "Half the Truth is often a great Lie," Poor Richard allows, and "In a corrupt Age, the putting the World in order would breed Confusion; then e'en mind your own Business" (1304). For his final, twenty-fifth-anniversary edition of *Poor Richard's*, Franklin included a preface titled "Father's Abraham's Speech, or, The Way to Wealth" that is a veritable *tour de force* of the tension between Poor Richard and his Printer. In his speech, Father Abraham, one of the most memorable among Franklin's many literary creations and whose views might be assumed to align with the author's, offers amid his flurry of advice about thrift and moderation, "*a Ploughman on his Legs is higher than a Gentleman on his Knees* [. . .]" (1300). Whether rising rusticity is truly better than falling nobility, though, is not so clear. Following Father Abraham's droning advice (Father Abraham acknowledges "Poor Dick" or "Poor Richard" some forty-nine times in referring to previous almanacs), Franklin the narrator has a merry, slightly sardonic laugh after Father Abraham has finished: "Thus the old Gentleman ended his Harangue. The People heard it, and approved the Doctrine, and immediately practiced the contrary, just as if it had been a common Sermon [. . .]" (1302). Undaunted by the stubborn human nature of both Father Abraham and his audience, Franklin again attempted to preach his doctrine of the middle way in writing his *Autobiography*.

Without question, the creative achievement of Franklin's *Autobiography* lies in those moments centered on *Almanack*-like lessons. Douglas Anderson, whose *The Unfinished Life of Benjamin Franklin* analyzes Franklin's literary technique, calls these moments "little anecdotes" in connecting Franklin to writers such as John Bunyan, a favorite of Franklin. "Little anecdotes," Anderson explains, "can unexpectedly acquire an expansive potential in Franklin's pages. Such evocative reserves call for a carefully-schooled audience to register their impact. [. . .] Franklin's little anecdotes draw his reader gradually, almost imperceptibly, back into an atmosphere of a tumultuous past, from the threshold of a tumultuous future" (15). Anderson's description complements Franklin's polemical sensibilities, for, in these anecdotes, Franklin the hero explores the edges of categories in negotiating his middle way. At the same time, how Franklin the narrator describes and evaluates these anecdotes, especially those found in Parts One and Two, is what makes the *Autobiography* so unnerving as well as delightful. Instead of easy and wide, the middle way turns out to be straight and narrow, especially when envisioning Franklin over the reader's shoulder, peering through his near-and-far bifocals and effectively advising, "Do as I say, not as I do."

The anecdotes of Franklin's *Autobiography* may be categorized in terms of his approach to rhetoric, social relationships, public practice, and sense of selfhood. Across the blurred overlaps of these categories, Franklin the hero is sometimes better, sometimes worse than the characters he encounters. One way or the other, he is ultimately integrated into the world through the middle way. Franklin the narrator, meanwhile, clearly has a larger creative objective, one that may be interpreted variously. For instance, Malcolm Bradbury and Richard Ruland argue, *"The Autobiography* is also the tale of Franklin's life seen *as* a book. To that end, he liked to call himself 'B. Franklin, Printer,' to regard his mistakes as 'errata,' his task as the making of a 'character,' his business the finding of a 'style' of writing and of life" (44). This kind of view quickly deconstructs any notion that autobiography is not, at its core, argumentative, for creating autobiography entails a critical eye through which inclusion implies exclusion and appreciation implies depreciation. Within the generic confines of autobiography, in other words, disclosure is always *controlled* disclosure.

Weaving its way through his *Autobiography* is Franklin's emphasis on a middle way of rhetoric. Early in his life, Franklin reads from his father's library books that "consisted chiefly of Books in polemic Divinity, most of which I read, and have since often regretted, that at a time when I had such a Thirst for Knowledge, more proper Books had not fallen in my Way [. . .]" (1317). Although the young hero misses the opportunity to read the "proper Books," his using the Socratic method with his friend John Collins helps to correct the problem. Indeed, Franklin retains throughout his life

> the Habit of expressing my self in Terms of modest Diffidence, never using when I advance any thing that may possibly be disputed, the Words, *Certainly*, *undoubtedly*, or any others that give the Air of Positiveness to an Opinion; but rather say, *I conceive*, or *I apprehend* a Thing to be so or so, *It appears to me*, or *I should think it so or so for such & such Reasons*, or *I imagine* it to be so, or *it is so if I am not mistaken*. *(*1321–22*)*

As with style, so with genre: Franklin's middle way of rhetoric surfaces in his thoroughly eighteenth-century aesthetic that "the chief Ends of Conversation are to *inform*, or to be *informed*, to *please* or to *persuade* [. . .]" (1322). Exemplary of these three purposes to literature, in Franklin's estimation, is Bunyan's *Pilgrim's Progress*. "Honest John," Franklin notes, "was the first that I know of who mix'd Narration & Dialogue, a Method of Writing very engaging to the Reader [. . .]" (1326). Franklin followed suit, of course, with his *Poor Richard's*, an endeavor he describes in his *Autobiography* as "both entertaining and useful [. . .]" (1397). The proof that the *Poor Richard's* persuaded its readers Franklin leaves to its robust annual profits.

From style to genre to real-world negotiations, Franklin's approach to rhetoric is that persuasion means getting a job done. Most notably, Franklin asserts in Part Two "the Impropriety of presenting one's self as the Proposer of any useful Project that may be suppos'd to raise one's Reputation in the smallest degree above that of one's Neighbours, when one has need of their Assistance to accomplish that Project" (1380–81). In Part Three, Franklin applies this principle in negotiating all sorts of Philadelphia community projects, from organizing city watches to building a hospital for the poor. On a national scale, his Albany Plan, which looked to unite the colonies for defense on the occasion of the French and Indian War, is not adopted, but Franklin's defense of his ideas typifies his middle way: "The different & contrary Reasons of dislike to my Plan," he argues, "makes me suspect that it was really the true

Medium [. . .]" (1431). Franklin follows this episode with a portrait of the intractable Governor of Pennsylvania, Robert Morris: "these disputing, contradicting & confuting People," Franklin observes, "are generally unfortunate in their Affairs. They get Victory sometimes, but they never get Good Will, which would be of more use to them" (1432). As Franklin's later career would show, to bite one's tongue is often what truly persuades.

How Franklin explores his social relationships builds on his middle way of rhetoric. No anecdote is more polemical (and iconic) in these terms than when, in 1723, the young hero initially enters Philadelphia and buys "three great Puffy Rolls," one of which he eats while he holds the others under his arms, eventually giving them away. "Thus I went up Market Street as far as Fourth Street," Franklin recalls, "passing by the Door of Mr. Read, my future Wife's Father, when she [Deborah] standing at the Door saw me, & thought I made as I certainly did a most awkward ridiculous Appearance" (1329). Franklin would not remain the bumpkin for long, and, when he returns to Boston, he is quite the opposite, showing off with James' workmen and even buys them a drink. To his brother's "Raree-Show," James' response is "grum & sullen [. . .]" (1334), but Franklin argues that his intentions were not polemical. Whether he is convincing is debatable; regardless, the point for Franklin's middle way—one that he demonstrates time and again—is, simply but elusively, to learn to get along with others.

Distinguishing Franklin's negotiation of the social middle way from a creative as well as historical perspective are his "errata." Begun by his composing the text as marginal notes (Chaplin xv), these moments when he admits fault show Franklin's tendency toward rash action. He calls breaking his indentures with James his first such erratum—"Perhaps I was too saucy and provoking" (1325), Franklin coyly says—and he again errs when he lends money of Vernon, a friend of his brother John, to the untrustworthy Collins. Franklin's neglect in writing Deborah after he arrives in London is another notable erratum, and, in each case, he looks to counterbalance the scales: he later cares for the diseased James' son, eventually pays Vernon with interest, and enters into a common-law marriage with Deborah. To the prospect of marriage, though, Franklin's middle-way motivations are a bit discordant, for, rather than the immoderation of love that normatively leads to the altar, Franklin reasons that he can answer

> that hard-to-be-govern'd Passion of Youth, [which] had hurried me frequently into Intrigues with low Women that fell in my Way, which were attended with some Expense & great Inconvenience, besides a continual Risque to my Health by a Distemper which of all Things I dreaded, tho' by great good Luck I escaped it. (1371)

Deborah might have subsequently well served Franklin's social middle way, but whether she would have approved her husband's sentiment is far less certain.

Although Franklin's social relationships are interesting—if not interestingly problematic—they are secondary to his public practice. As ever, he widely explores the category. After first arriving in Philadelphia, Franklin meets two printers, Andrew Bradford and Samuel Keimer, who polemically embody the printing trade: the one "was a crafty old Sophister, and the other a mere Novice" (1331). "These two Printers," Franklin continues, "I found poorly qualified for their Business. Bradford had not been bred to it, & was very illiterate; and Keimer tho' something of a Scholar, was a mere Compositor, knowing nothing of Presswork" (1331). In Franklin's view, personal interest, technical competency, and responsible action must all be fused in whatever public practice, a principle he emphasizes in developing his day-to-day business. "I took care not only to be in *Reality* Industrious & frugal," Franklin comments about his opening a stationer's store, "but to avoid all *Appearances* of the Contrary" (1369), and, in the second most-famous polemical anecdote of the *Autobiography*, he recounts that "I sometimes brought home the Paper I purchas'd at the Stores, thro' the Streets on a Wheelbarrow" (1369). For his part, the impulsive and hot-headed Keimer takes his failing business to Barbados, where, in a note that Franklin perhaps relishes too much, Keimer "lived some Years, in very poor Circumstances" (1369). Immoderate character leads to immoderate destiny, and, in contrast to his former employer's dismal fate, Franklin retires at the age of forty-two with a "sufficient tho' moderate Fortune [. . .]" (1420).

Integrated into how Franklin negotiates a middle way of public practice is his arch principle of usefulness. When just a boy, Franklin leads others to construct a wharf, but, because he and the others had stolen the stones to build it, he concludes "that nothing was useful which was not honest" (1314). The lesson sticks. Later, in a kind of "pay it forward" public gesture, Franklin foregoes patenting his famous stove because "*That as we enjoy great Advances from the Inventions of others, we should be glad of an Opportunity to serve others by any Inventions of ours, and this we should do freely and generously*" (1417–18). However, what constitutes usefulness for Franklin is not always so clear as in the case of his stove. For example, when he is rising in the world while in England, Franklin finds himself lodging in a home in which a seventy-year-old Catholic woman dwells in the garret. Subsisting on only "water-gruel," the elderly woman constantly studies her Bible and donates to charity almost all her income. In remembering this saintly figure, Franklin shrugs, "I give it as another Instance on how small an Income Life & Health may be supported" (1351). Is Franklin being serious, adding just another example about how foregoing expenditures helps to sustain a living? Or is he being facetious, going for the quick joke that the woman could be doing something more useful for the public? Neither polemical implication is very appealing; happily for the reader, the anecdote passes quickly, the *Autobiography* rolling along at its brisk pace.

Underlying the overall middle way of Franklin's *Autobiography* is the question of selfhood that propelled Western culture from the Renaissance to the Enlightenment: can human beings willfully modify their moral character and, consequently, their destinies? The question still haunts. For Franklin, any definition of morality derives from usefulness, not usefulness from morality. "This is the Age of Experiments [. . .]" (1463), Franklin declares in Part Three, and the most famous experiment in the *Autobiography* about morality is when, in Part Two, Franklin attempts the "the bold and arduous Project of arriving at moral Perfection" (1383) by mastering twelve within-human-reach virtues: temperance, silence, order, resolution, frugality, industry, sincerity, justice, moderation, cleanliness, tranquility, and chastity. Importantly, the word *perfection* did not have during the eighteenth century today's meaning of absolute completion (Lemay and Zall 226). Instead, underlying perfection was the sense of process, so comparison—as in the *Constitution*'s "more perfect Union"—was possible. With Franklin's project, the middle way of perfection lies between achievement and method, a condition reflected in the name of a secret sect Franklin only half-jokingly proposes to circulate among the country's youth: the "Society of the *Free* and *Easy* [. . .]" (1396). In Franklin's own project, though, pride casts its spell, and Franklin must add the humility to his list: "I cannot boast of much Success in acquiring the *Reality* of this Virtue," he explains about his battle against pride, "but I had a good deal with regard to the *Appearance* of it" (1393). Franklin knows that he cannot fool himself, and he concludes Part Two, "For even if I could conceive that I had completely overcome it, I should probably be proud of my Humility" (1394). If nothing else, Franklin shows in the middle way of his self-deprecation why scholars have labeled him the Father of American Humor.

Beyond exploring selfhood and negotiating his middle way toward perfection, Franklin died before writing about what he noted in his outline and may be taken as the most important of his career's anecdotes about the category: under an hour-long, withering attack of Solicitor General Alexander Wedderburn, Franklin all but personified the virtue of silence by uttering not a word when standing before Britain's Privy Council on January 29, 1774. The reason Franklin found himself in the "Cockpit" in the first place is a complicated story about purloined letters and political miscalculation, but the upshot is that Franklin's Anglophilism all but evaporated. H. W. Brands even uses the scene to preface his biography of Franklin: "A lesser man would have been humiliated" (1) is Brands' opening sentence. The incident was so important, in fact, that a six-city exhibition to celebrate Franklin's tercentenary featured an *in situ* display in which visitors could look over the Franklin figure's shoulder, push a button, and hear a recording of

Wedderburn's invective. The display's effect is visceral enough, but how Franklin himself would have told the story remains one of the great "What if?" questions in American autobiography, if not all creative nonfiction. What history does tell is that Franklin would subsequently be the only Founding Father to sign (as well as play a part in composing) the four principal documents of the American Revolution: the *Declaration of Independence* (1776), the *Treaty of Paris* (1783), and the *Constitution* (1787). For the occasion of the other document, the *Treaty of Alliance with France* (1778), Franklin wore the same distinctive suit that he had worn four years earlier when standing in the Cockpit (Isaacson 347). Sartorial style, in this case, made the man's argument about the middle way, for Franklin was not one to suffer polemical fools gladly.

A Real Renaissance Man

That Franklin would respond to various occasions through polemical argumentation is of a piece with eighteenth-century literary history. Bradbury and Ruland ask, in light of "the contentious literary debates of new America," "Do true artists innovate, or do they imitate? Would they merge from the spirit of nationality, or cosmopolitanism? Should they serve public purpose, or aesthetic and possibly therefore decadent pleasure? Had they a legacy from the past, or must they be born anew in the radical energy of the present?" (64). Franklin's responses shifted with occasion, but the middle way was his consistent principle. Tom Bailey comments in a position typical of the *Autobiography*'s readers,

> The book's central message, in its content, language, and shape, is that personal energies must be devoted to, subsumed into, the creation of an orderly state[. . .]. Franklin, that is to say, does not preach mindless self-reliance and self-aggrandizement, but a radical, generous displacing of selfishness for cultural goals. (94)

In this middle way of the greater good, Franklin saw America's best hope for a bright future.

As much as any label, Franklin's admirers have labeled him Revolutionary America's "Renaissance Man." Given the scope of

Franklin's life, the term fits—but how? As the ups and downs told by Franklin in his *Autobiography* demonstrate, the middle way is inevitably prone to ambiguity. Moreover, what lies, in etching the line between the text's narrative and narrator, at a human being's core? The *Autobiography* teaches that no autobiography will or can answer the question. After collaborating with Eugenia W. Herbert to write *The Private Franklin*, Claude-Anne Lopez contemplates that Franklin "still perplexes me after more than fifty years of deciphering and transcribing his correspondence. [. . .] Neither demigod nor unfeeling egotist [. . . he had] some warts, some laurels, some sins, some virtues" (xiii). Not all readers are so open-minded as Lopez, and attempts to simplify Franklin have led to some decidedly polemical arguments of their own. By 1868, an anonymous review in *The Nation* would observe, "From the beginning of the world till now, mankind divides into two classes, of which you may say that one are natural-born lovers and believers, and the other are natural-born haters and despisers of this 'Autobiography'" (270). To pick only the most famous (or notorious, to Franklin defenders) example of the "haters," D. H. Lawrence teeters on the brink of polemical absurdity: "Oh, Franklin was the first down-right American. He knew what he was about," Lawrence wrote in his 1923 *Studies in Classic American Literature*, "the sharp little man. He set up the first dummy American" (20). Lawrence's words have an ounce of truth, but, in trying to compete with Franklin's creative wit, Lawrence ignores that the middle way carries no guarantees, a complex implication best captured in Carl Van Doren's label of Franklin as "a harmonious human multitude" (782). Between Lawrence's stridency and Van Doren's exuberance, the matter may be best settled with Walter Blair's assessment that Franklin was a "Muddied Giant" (53), and that label is probably just as Franklin would have had it.

Perhaps what most solidifies Franklin's *Autobiography* in the canon of creative nonfiction has little to do with either the creativity that makes it literary or the biographical that makes it nonfictional. Rather, Franklin legacy resides in the daily intellectual lives of almost all Americans. *Everything's an Argument* is the title to a well-circulated textbook for college composition, and that Franklin should be pictured front and off-center on today's $100 bill represents a kind of argument about socio-economic power beyond Franklin's advocacy for printed currency. "It's all about the Benjamins," Sean Combs advises in his 1997 hip-hop song about why the appearance of wealth is as important as the reality of it. At least when holding the actual paper currency, Combs should take a closer look. Frozen in the famous 1778 portrait by Joseph-Siffred Duplessis, an elderly Franklin seems to warn holders of a "C-note" that they pause even while contemplating their range of immediate options. The amount will buy a good night on the town, readers of the *Autobiography* know, but it cannot sustain the good times. As legacies go, Franklin could have done worse.

Note

1.   All references for Franklin's writings are to the Library of America edition.

Works Cited

Adams, Randolph G. "Reports and Chronicles." *Literary History of the United States*. Ed. Robert E. Spiller, et al. 3rd ed. New York: Macmillan, 1963. 24–39.

Anderson, Douglas. *The Unfinished Life of Benjamin Franklin*. Baltimore: Johns Hopkins UP, 2012.

Bailey, Tom. "Benjamin Franklin's *Autobiography*: The Self and Society in a New World." *Midwest Quarterly* 22 (Winter 1981): 93–104.

Blair, Walter & Hamlin Hill. *America's Humor: From Poor Richard to Doonesbury*. New York: Oxford UP, 1978.

Bosco, Ronald A. "'He that best understands the World, least likes it': The Dark Side of Benjamin Franklin." *The Pennsylvania Magazine of History and Biography* 111 (1987): 525–54.

Brands, H. W. *The First American: The Life and Times of Benjamin Franklin*. New York: Doubleday, 2000.

Bradbury, Malcolm & Richard Ruland. *From Puritanism to Postmodernism: A History of American Literature*. New York: Viking, 1991.

Chaplin, Joyce E. Introduction. *Benjamin Franklin's Autobiography: An Authoritative Text, Contents, Criticism*. Ed. Joyce E. Chalpin. New York: Norton, 2012. xiii–xxvi.

Combs, Sean [Puff Daddy]. "It's All about the Benjamins." *Lyricsfreak. com*, 2014. Web. 13 April 2014.

Franklin, Benjamin. *Benjamin Franklin: Writings*. Ed. J. A. Leo Lemay. New York: Library of America, 1987.

"From *The Nation*, 1868." *Benjamin Franklin's Autobiography: An Authoritative Text, Backgrounds, Criticism*. Ed. J. A. Leo Lemay & P. M. Zall. New York: Norton, 1986. 270–71.

Isaacson, Walter. *Benjamin Franklin: An American Life*. New York: Simon & Schuster, 2003.

Lawrence, D. H. *Studies in Classic American Literature*. 1923. Garden City, NY: Doubleday, 1953.

Lemay, J. A. Leo & P. M. Zall. "Perfection." *Benjamin Franklin's Autobiography: An Authoritative Text, Backgrounds, Criticism*. Eds. J. A. Leo Lemay & P. M. Zall. New York: Norton, 1986. 226–28.

Lopez, Claude-Anne. "A Subjective Preface." *The Private Franklin: The Man and His Family*. Claude-Anne Lopez & Eugenia W. Herbert. New York: Norton, 1975. xiii–xiv.

Lunsford, Andrea A., John J. Ruszkiewicz, & Keith Walters. *Everything's an Argument*. 6th ed. Boston: Bedford/St. Martin's, 2012.

Newman, Simon P. "Benjamin Franklin and the Leather-Apron Men: The Politics of Class in Eighteenth-Century Philadelphia." *Journal of American Studies* 43 (2009): 161–75.

Van Doren, Carl. *Benjamin Franklin*. New York: Viking, 1938.

Wright, Esmond. *Franklin of Philadelphia*. Cambridge, MA: Belknap P of Harvard UP, 1986.

Gender and Genre in Susan Fenimore Cooper's Nature Writing_____

Kelly Clasen

In the preface to *Rural Hours* (1850), Susan Fenimore Cooper downplays the importance of her reportage on the season-to-season changes in the landscape surrounding her home in Cooperstown, New York. She describes her "trifling observations" of these "trifling incidents" as the type of material that might be "afterward remembered with pleasure by the fireside, and gladly shared, perhaps, with one's friends."[1] Cooper's preface suggests humility and uncertainty, as she goes on to express her hope that any pleasure gleaned by the book's readers might be worth the "reluctance with which it was printed" (3). These rhetorical gestures indicate her awareness of the limited expectations for women writers at the time and also alert readers to the novelty of the project, as *Rural Hours* would make Cooper, the daughter of James Fenimore Cooper, the first published American woman nature writer. The book, which was well-received by the nineteenth-century public, continues to gain scholarly recognition, in particular because of its similarities to and publication four years before *Walden*, the most celebrated piece of nature writing from that era. Its reputation lags well behind that of *Walden* (which includes information from *Rural Hours* in a passage on loons), yet *Rural Hours* should be as prominent as *Walden* in scholarship on nature writing and environmental rhetoric because of Cooper's more direct call for increased sustainability. Cooper, who is primarily externally focused on her surroundings in *Rural Hours*, advances a conservationist message that is rooted in scientific understanding, while Henry David Thoreau, who is more attuned to personal reflection, records a mostly private, hypermetaphorical celebration of nature in *Walden*.

Among examples of American creative nonfiction from the era, *Rural Hours* stands out because of its adherence to traditional nature writing techniques, such as its incorporation of scientific facts and debt to natural history, alongside the female author/narrator's inclusion and refinement of strategies frequently employed by the sentimental or domestic novelist. *Rural Hours* is historically important not only as an early example of American nature writing, but also as a starting point in identifying the noticeable differences in environmental thinking between men and women—the sort of analysis ecofeminist critic Patrick Murphy calls for in response to feminists' efforts to expose Dorothy Wordsworth's influence on her brother William's poetry by studying her writing. "What is needed now," Murphy suggests, "is criticism that can evaluate the differences between their writings in terms of ecological criteria, analyzing the implications of Dorothy's willingness to record rather than order nature and to efface the speaker of the text as a domineering, central observer" (25). Such a model can be productively applied to *Rural Hours*, which Lawrence Buell has described as "the nineteenth-century American literary season book that comes closest to rivaling Thoreau, [...] a calendar of natural and cultural history observations that reveals a Dorothy Wordsworth-like keenness of environmental perception" (47). The "keenness" of observation and unassuming mode of expression that are central to *Rural Hours* illustrate gender's influence on the authors' appraisals of nature. By studying Cooper's and Thoreau's different approaches to addressing similar issues that are inherent to the development of broader arguments about humans' responsibility to nature, we gain a better sense of the perceptual framework within which these authors were writing, and can acknowledge, as Karen J. Warren urges, that the "socially constructed *lens* through which one perceives reality" differs according to gender, among other factors (46; emphasis in original). Cooper's constant subjugation of herself to the natural world in her writing surfaces as symptomatic of the effects of patriarchal influence; nevertheless, this traditionally oppressive sociological framework contributes to her move toward ecological understanding in *Rural Hours*.

The book chronicles its author's detailed observations about her rural surroundings—weather conditions, animal behaviors, agricultural practices, plant cycles, and human activity—in near-daily entries beginning in March and ending in February and is often categorized as a nature diary. Yet other literary forms exert their influence upon the text, nudging it into the category of creative nonfiction because of the author's clear consideration of literary style. Cooper had tried her hand at the popular genre of domestic fiction with the 1846 publication of *Elinor Wyllys; or, The Young Folks of Longbridge, a Tale* under the pseudonym Amabel Penfeather, a work that never achieved the success of *Rural Hours*. The influence of domestic fiction likely discouraged Cooper, in her later creative nonfiction, from focusing primarily on the individual's experience in nature and encouraged her to concentrate instead, as Vera Norwood has noted, on "the American landscape's new image as home," an artistic trend that is traceable to the growing nationalistic pride of the early nineteenth century (*Made From this Earth* 27–28). As most critics of Cooper's work have observed, *Rural Hours* stresses the need for its readers to become educated, as she had, about the flora and fauna surrounding their homes, thereby extending expectations of domestic knowledge beyond the walls of the home to include the outdoors. Norwood sees in Cooper's work a reconciliation of the reading public's appetite for domestic novels with American writers' development of "a narrative about the native American landscape as, uniquely, 'their' home" ("Women's Roles" 13). Richard M. Magee has noted an "overlap" in genres in *Rural Hours*—"the domestic/sentimental" and the "natural history/environmental"—and characterizes this convergence as "sentimental ecology" (27–28). And Nina Baym identifies the purpose of *Rural Hours* as an attempt to "model country life as a constant intellectual, civilized, rational pleasure and therefore to show ladies a rational, civilized way of being ladylike" (75). Ultimately, Cooper's fusion of genres suggests a conscious attempt to stretch the expectations of women's writing beyond the boundaries imposed by the domestic novel and its characteristic focus on the struggles of its heroine and into the realm of nature writing.

As its narrator, Cooper eschews the role of heroine in *Rural Hours*, which is therefore unlike *Walden* in that its primary concern is the natural world and its ecological and historical relationships, rather than the experience of the individual therein. In subjugating herself to the outside world and examining her expanded household from the perspective of female overseer, Cooper recognizes the fragile interconnectivity of living things and the necessity for Americans to adopt an ethic of stewardship. Cooper privileges literal description, and her text urges a move toward more realistic representations, as in the following passage, in which she traces the growth of realism in English painting:

> And so, writers began to look out of the window more frequently; when writing a pastoral they turned away from the little porcelain shepherds and shepherdesses, standing in high-heeled shoes and powdered wigs upon every mantel-piece, and they fixed their eyes upon the real living Roger and Dolly in the hay-field. Then they came to see that it would do just as well, nay, far better, to seat Roger and Dolly under a hawthorn, or an oak of merry England, than to paint them beneath a laurel, or an ilex of Greece or Rome; in short, they learned at length to look at nature by the light of the sun, and not by the glimmerings of the poet's lamp. And a great step this was, not only in art, but in moral and intellectual progress. (208)

Cooper's method of studying her surroundings objectively— or "by the light of the sun"—exemplifies important rhetorical distinctions between *Rural Hours* and *Walden*. Although each author writes with the overarching goal of inspiring respect for one's natural surroundings, Thoreau's imaginative wanderings often lead him back to self-reflection, whereas Cooper's are more likely to span different continents and centuries, without beginning with or returning to first-person narration. The humility of Cooper's prose contributes to her more consistent focus on the world around her and highlights the intricacies of global plant, animal, and human interconnections. Rochelle Johnson has demonstrated Cooper's superior ability to elevate "the prominence of the objects of her literary attention—most often natural objects and phenomena—over both her persona and her necessarily human orientation toward place" ("*Walden, Rural Hours*" 182), but Cooper's rhetorical divergence from Thoreau has implications that extend beyond our understanding of American nature writing, as it signals the emergence of a distinctly feminine environmental ethos that is rooted in historically limited expectations for women. Indeed, although Josh Weinstein has recently explored the importance of Cooper's Episcopalian faith on the development of her "humble Christian ecological vision" (67), the influence of gender roles in the development of such a philosophy warrants greater attention.

The authors' accounts of the health of their respective surroundings provide a starting point for such an inquiry, as they illustrate the ways in which gender expectations shaped mid-century writers' perceptions of and relationships to nature. Tina Gianquitto has observed that Cooper is "capable not only of seeing specific objects in nature but also of seeing them in the context of larger social, moral, and scientific debates and discussions" (104–05). This tendency for Cooper's observations to inspire reflections on "larger" issues, rather than the self, contributes significantly to the differences between her and Thoreau's environmental appraisals. The authors demonstrate great variations in their perceptions of the resiliency of nature, and comparing passages from each text in which environmental health is a prominent theme—Cooper's critique of timber consumption and Thoreau's appraisal of Walden Pond's purity—exemplifies the directness of Cooper's argument and the often abstract, though more lyrical, qualities of Thoreau's.

One of the most groundbreaking aspects of Cooper's book is her warning about the dangers of deforestation well before any knowledge of its harmful effects upon global ecological stability and her corresponding appeal for conservation. Cooper writes, "One would think that by this time, when the forest has fallen in all the valleys—when the hills are becoming more bare every day—when timber and fuel are rising in prices, and new uses are found for even indifferent woods—some forethought and care in this respect would be natural in people laying claim to common sense" (132). Cooper's concerns are multifaceted, originating from economic, aesthetic, and moral standpoints. She criticizes this "rapid consumption of the large pine timber" (132) and suggests that the value of trees extends well beyond "market price in dollars and cents" to include "importance in an intellectual and in a moral sense" to the civilization in which they exist (133). For Cooper, "[t]here is also something in the care of trees which rises above the common labors of husbandry, and speaks of a generous mind" (134). Although Cooper could not have foreseen the environmental impact of deforestation evident to the modern reader, her recognition of the moral implications of land misuse, her critique of the "spirit of destructiveness" (134), is innovative, considering the historical tendency for Americans to view uncultivated land as a site of conquest.

Thoreau laments the vigorous activities of the "woodchoppers" along Walden's shores (132) and expresses a similar need for people to expand their valuation of forests beyond the pecuniary to include the spiritual: "I would that our farmers when they cut down a forest felt some of that awe which the old Romans did when they came to thin, or let the light to, a consecrated grove [...] that is, would believe it is sacred to some god" (169). However, his writing style here clashes with Cooper's vision of ideal art, a more realistic art that situates its subjects among local natural features rather than "a laurel, or an ilex of Greece or Rome" (208). Thoreau's wish that American farmers toiling in their fields might suddenly experience the awe of the ancients, though it indicates his disapproval of deforestation, signals his tendency "to look at nature by [...] the glimmerings of the poet's lamp" (as Cooper might describe such a tactic). He does not express the same level of awareness as Cooper does about the long-term financial, aesthetic, and moral repercussions of deforestation, although the practice would have been ongoing and apparent to the author during his tenure at Walden.

According to Robert Sattelmeyer, because of the "pressures of settlement and cultivation and environmental change" in the Concord area for more than two hundred years before Thoreau's time at Walden, forest coverage was actually at its lowest in Concord in 1850, and the area around Walden Pond had seen a similar, though less drastic, decline in trees (241). Carolyn Merchant records the total forest coverage in 1850 Massachusetts as 40 percent, down from 95 percent in 1620 (225). Thoreau may have chosen to downplay the deforestation around Walden in his book because, as

Sattelmeyer has suggested, it contradicts the romanticized picture of his environs he wanted to establish for his literary experiment (242). Buell also attributes Thoreau's reluctance to "sound the preservationist note loudly" to this "pastoralizing impulse": "One cannot argue simultaneously that sylvan utopia can be found within the town limits and that the locale is being devastated at an appalling rate; and the vision of a pristine nature close by appealed irresistibly to Thoreau for personal as well as rhetorical reasons" (120). These romantic tendencies obfuscate his representations of the natural world around him.

Even if Thoreau's motivations for attaching little importance to the ongoing deforestation at Walden were rhetorically driven, traceable to the no-less-admirable goal of inspiring reverence for nature by exaggerating its vigor at Walden and exacerbated by the pastoral literary tradition, he does not call for reform and thus seems, in *Walden*, to accept deforestation as inevitable—quite unlike Cooper, who considers in detail the ways farms near Cooperstown might be improved through "a little attention to the woods and trees" (134). Cooper, in this passage, moves beyond an expression of regret over the changing rural New York landscape to recommend deliberate conservation. Her plan, though aesthetics-focused and overly optimistic, is also pragmatic. She suggests:

> Thinning woods and not blasting them; clearing only such ground as is marked for immediate tillage; preserving the wood on the hill-tops and rough side-hills; encouraging a coppice on this or that knoll; permitting bushes and young trees to grow at will along the brooks and water-courses; sowing, if need be, a grove on the bank of the pool, such as are now found on many of our farms; sparing and elm or two about the spring, with a willow also to overhang the well; planting one or two chestnuts, or oaks, or beeches, near the gates or bars; leaving a few others scattered about every field to shade the cattle in summer […] how little would be the labor or expense required to accomplish all this, and how desirable would be the result! (Cooper 134)

What is perhaps most important about Cooper's consideration for trees is her call for reform, her direct attention to "preserving the wood." As Roderick Frazier Nash has explained, many American writers in the early- to mid-nineteenth century expressed anxiety about the destruction of nature, John James Audubon, James Fenimore Cooper, and Washington Irving among them, and "[c]oncern over the loss of wilderness necessarily preceded the first call for its protection" (95–98). Although Nash overlooks Cooper's book in his study of the historical progression of preservationist ideals, the 1850 publication of *Rural Hours* places it at the forefront of such thinking. Cooper's suggestions are not radical—she does not call for the immediate halt of timber harvesting or for government protection of forests—but they urge both an alteration in attitude toward deforestation and methods of conservation. Typical of her practicality, Cooper, in this vision, carefully eliminates clear-cutting, while still considering the economic welfare of rural New Yorkers. The passage suggests that conservation need not presage financial degradation, and the euphoric tone of its final sentence indicates that residents would also benefit spiritually from the aesthetic benefits of such attention to trees.

In contrast to Cooper's anxiety about the multifaceted potential harmful effects of deforestation on her rural New York environment is Thoreau's confidence in the inalterability of Walden—a viable comparison because of each author's repeated focus, within a broader conversation about the natural world, on a more specific natural realm: the forest and Walden Pond. In exultant prose, he employs the extended metaphor of Walden as an unbreakable mirror as a tribute to nature's regenerative powers. He writes:

> Nothing so fair, so pure, and at the same time so large, as a lake, perchance, lies on the surface of the earth. Sky water. It needs no fence. Nations come and go without defiling it. It is a mirror which no stone can crack, whose quicksilver will never wear off, whose gilding Nature continually repairs; no storms, no dust, can dim its surface ever fresh—a mirror in which all impurity presented to it sinks, swept and dusted by the sun's hazy brush,—this the light dust-cloth,—which retains no breath that is breathed on it, but sends its own to float as clouds high above its surface, and be reflected in its bosom still. (Thoreau 129)

While Cooper recognizes the potentially devastating dynamism of her rural landscape, Thoreau offers a static vision of Walden that is lovely, but deceiving. Despite the metaphorical novelty of the passage, Thoreau's image of Walden as inalterable is imprudent, considering the effects of human activities on the pond. A few pages later, he chastises the villagers of Concord for considering piping in Walden's water for use in domestic chores, but he reassures himself that despite the woodchoppers' and ice-cutters' work and the encroachment of the railroad, Walden "is itself unchanged, the same water which my youthful eyes fell on," and concludes that "the change is in [him]," who has aged while Walden has remained "perennially young" (Thoreau 132).

This tendency for Thoreau to move from metaphor-laden environmental commentary to self-exploration contributes to the differences between his and Cooper's nature diaries. Although both authors exalt nature—with Thoreau's text bearing an eloquence rarely equaled by Cooper—only Cooper's text might be viewed in aggregate as a direct entreaty for conservation. Thoreau's figurative language establishes a mood of reverence that inspires readers' admiration for Walden and, by extension, nature. As Karl Kroeber points out, "Thoreau's most remarkable accomplishments are in his representations; his greatest skill is as a rhetorician. This is why even writers who regard nature in an un-Thoreauvian fashion may still sincerely admire his achievement" (Kroeber 313). Nevertheless, *Walden* fails to address the need for residents nearby to protect the pond and ultimately sends a misguided message about nature's immutability. According to Marti Kheel, "While the deliberate attempt to cultivate images that positively influence ethical conduct toward nature is a welcome development, metaphors should not be considered a conceptual *foundation* for a nature ethic" (214; emphasis in original). The naïveté of Thoreau's metaphor becomes especially clear when one takes into account the now-apparent anthropogenic effects on the area, for a study performed in 2005 documents humans' contributions to changes in the nutrient status of Walden from about 1750 (Köster, et al. 129), and in more recent years, Thoreau's book has been an asset to scientists tracking the effects of global warming on plants around Walden.[2]

Thoreau recognizes the spiritual benefits available to the individual who spends time observing natural phenomena, like Walden and its surroundings, but he does not acknowledge the possible threats to the pond posed by humans. He emerges as more concerned with the abstract possibilities of thinking about nature—with using the idea of Walden, the "earth's eye" (Thoreau 128)—as a catalyst for philosophy and self-exploration than with the pond itself. This strategy suggests Thoreau's lack of ecological awareness, for, as Dana Phillips reminds us, "emotion and personal uplift are not the central concerns of ecology" (204). Thoreau's anti-materialist and subjective outlook facilitates his production of moving, nature-themed rhetoric, but it also clouds his ability to objectively record the ongoing changes in the landscape.

Cooper, in contrast to Thoreau and his focus on the self, exhibits greater attention to detail and deftness in recording the goings-on around her, including, as Gianquitto has noted, "the minutiae of the plants, animals, and especially birds that inhabited her landscape" (103). As a result, in addition to her exhortations against deforestation, Cooper exhibits a keen awareness of the damaging effects of civilization upon New York plants and animals. Her records help chronicle a process of species decline that had started to become evident as early as the end of the seventeenth century in the United States. Michael Branch has helpfully summarized the species that Cooper identifies as having declined in population or disappeared as:

> quail, pine, passenger pigeon, martin, pitcher plant, moccasin flower, fragrant azalea, hemlock, rattlesnake, mountain lion, ladyslipper, whip-poor-will, old-growth trees (all species), killdeer, crested woodpecker, blue gentian, deer, oak, moose, beaver, red-headed woodpecker, ruffed grouse, ducks, bass, large fish (all species), herring, panther, bear, pinnate grouse, white pelican, wolf, bison, fox, otter, fisher, wolverine, rabbit, hare, and squirrel. (69)

Such observations, taken in aggregate, contribute to Cooper's ability raise environmental awareness.

Thoreau in *Walden* also acknowledges the disappearance of animal species in his rural environment; in his discussion of the decline of hunting among New England youths, he observes that "a change is taking place, owing, not to an increased humanity, but to an increased scarcity of game" (144). However, whereas Cooper primarily considers the alterability of her rural environment in her recognition of species decline, Thoreau expresses concern over the potential moral ramifications of hunting, fishing, and consuming flesh for the individual and suggests the need for "increased humanity." He advocates abstaining from "animal food" not for the benefit of the creatures, but for the man. Substituting "a little bread or a few potatoes" for meat and fish is, according to Thoreau, both easier and cleaner, and it contributes to the development of the imagination (146). He argues that to obtain sustenance by "preying on other animals [...] is a miserable way" to live and prophesies that "it is a part of the destiny of the human race, in its gradual improvement, to leave off eating animals, as surely as the savage tribes have left off eating each other when they came in contact with the more civilized" (147). A widespread shift in eating habits toward vegetarianism would presumably contribute to the protection of hunted species, but Thoreau approaches the subject from an anthropocentric angle. Cooper repeatedly references species decline to suggest the changes being wrought on her farming community by the trend toward large-scale production and the corresponding deforestation; Thoreau employs recognition of species decline as an entrée into a discussion of the moral benefits of appetite temperance upon the individual.

In her diligent reportage, Cooper promotes, through repeated instances of straightforward observation, a conservationist message that diverges from, but is no less remarkable than, what Thoreau accomplishes through careful employment of figurative language. Although Cooper tends to avoid sentimentalizing the emotional effects of the ongoing ecological transformation she observes, she occasionally incorporates the sort of euphoric prose mastered by Thoreau and frames her rural experiences in terms of aesthetics, further aligning the work with creative nonfiction. Her impetus for doing so contradicts Thoreau's, however, and also can be linked to her female domestic vision. According to Buell, although both authors would deem a large tree a finer embellishment to a home than new paint or grand furniture, "Cooper praises nature over artifice not because nature is wild rather than tame, but because it 'marks a farther progress' in civility than the axe-wielding phase of frontier living" (407). Despite what she considers her rural environment's physical blights, namely felled trees, Cooper views the landscape as ripe with beauty. In an entry from May, she declares: "How rapid is the advance of spring at this moment of her joyous approach! And how beautiful are all the plants in their graceful growth, the humblest herb unfolding its every leaf in beauty, full of purpose and power!" (Cooper 37). Her tone here is not unlike Thoreau's in his welcoming of spring to Walden, particularly his delighted recognition of the sudden return of "sand foliage" along the railroad, which causes him to feel as though he "stood in the laboratory of the Artist who made the world and [him]" (Thoreau 205). Hence, Cooper inspires environmental awareness not only by identifying trends in species decline and calling for reform, but, like Thoreau, by sometimes aestheticizing her environment—with different motivations. By assuming the socially-prescribed position of the educated woman promoting proper stewardship of the home (and, by extension, the homeland), Cooper promotes interest in natural history and in the relationships between the living things she aestheticizes, which prevents her from offering simply a picturesque interpretation of her surroundings.

Cooper's book does not suggest a return to a wilderness state, as to do so would imply the necessary removal of humans, an idea that would counter her general conservatism; rather, *Rural Hours* promotes the adoption of an environmental ethos based on practical sustainability and conservation and rooted in her awareness of the interconnectedness of species. When describing the "mandrakes, or May-apples" near her rural home, Cooper reminds us that they are also "found under a different variety in the hilly countries of Central Asia" and declares: "One likes to trace these links, connecting lands and races, so far apart, reminding us, as they do, that the earth is the common home of all" (56). Another example of this sort of ecological awareness (expressed more than a decade before the initial development of the scientific field of ecology) arises in Cooper's explanation of the European red poppy's relationship to a small insect known as the "upholster bee." According to Cooper, after the bee makes a nest in a grain field, it uses tiny pieces of poppy petals to pad the nest, only laying a single egg when the "brilliant cradle" is complete (123). Because of the poppy's "connection with the precious grain," it appears in many ancient myths and was "considered as sacred" by Ceres, Roman goddess of agriculture (123). Cooper's desire to establish connectivity between insect, plant, man, and mythology is especially evident in this account of natural history. Because of her understanding of the world as a "web," her work, as Johnson and Patterson have observed, "contributes to the move that the genre of nature writing was making toward an emphasis on process and on the interconnectedness of things (that is, toward ecology)"; ultimately, "[t]he vision she expresses in *Rural Hours* brings an ecological awareness to what might have been a much shallower anthropocentric aesthetic presentation" (xxi). Her devout faith contributes to this progressive vision, as she considers the presence of similar plants on other continents to be divine evidence of the interrelatedness of all life forms.

Ultimately, the important rhetorical differences between *Rural Hours* and *Walden* are largely attributable to the authors' different lives, as they were shaped by gender expectations and, more specifically, the way these expectations applied to writers of this era. Resisting the urge to align and, thereby, simplify Cooper and Thoreau as contemporary nature writers with similar environmentalist objectives and acknowledging instead their different rhetorical paths provides a framework for analyzing the continued prominence of environmental themes in literature produced by men *and* women as the country entered the increasingly industrialized postwar era. In *Rural Hours*, Cooper created a literary model for Thoreau, the most influential nature writer in American history; urged women to challenge literary expectations; advocated an ecological awareness of plant and animal species; and, most importantly, issued the warning that rural Americans needed to begin conservation efforts. Because of her ability to "look at nature by the light of the sun" and record, with minutest detail, her observations of its beauty and scars, Cooper's work continues to help readers understand more clearly mid-nineteenth-century rural America and the environmental threats it faced.

Notes

1. Susan Fenimore Cooper, *Rural Hours*, ed. Rochelle Johnson and Daniel Patterson (Athens: U of Georgia P, 1998) 3. Subsequent references are cited parenthetically by page number. This edition reproduces the full text of Putnam's 1850 edition of *Rural Hours*, the edition Henry David Thoreau would have accessed, rather than the abridged version first issued in 1968.

2. See Edward Nickens, who discusses Boston University researchers' use of Thoreau's observations of seasonal events at Walden Pond to help create a record of springtime events in Concord as a means of tracking global climate change in the area, as well as Elizabeth Pennisi, who uses Thoreau's data on the plants around Walden to suggest the effects of climate change on these species.

Works Cited

Baym, Nina. *American Women of Letters and the Nineteenth-Century Sciences.* New Brunswick: Rutgers UP, 2002.

Branch, Michael. "Five Generations of Literary Coopers: Intergenerational Valuations of the American Frontier." *Susan Fenimore Cooper: New Essays on Rural Hours and Other Works.* Ed. Rochelle Johnson & Daniel Patterson. Athens: U of Georgia P, 2001. 61–82.

Buell, Lawrence. *The Environmental Imagination: Thoreau, Nature Writing, and the Formation of American Culture.* Cambridge, MA: Harvard UP, 1995.

Cooper, Susan Fenimore. *Rural Hours.* Ed. Rochelle Johnson & Daniel Patterson. Athens: U of Georgia P, 1998.

Gianquitto, Tina. *"Good Observers of Nature": American Women and the Scientific Study of the Natural World, 1820–1885.* Athens: U of Georgia P, 2007.

Johnson, Rochelle & Daniel Patterson. Introduction. *Susan Fenimore Cooper: New Essays on Rural Hours.* Ed. Rochelle Johnson & Daniel Patterson. Athens: U of Georgia P, 2001. xi–xxxii.

Johnson, Rochelle. "Placing *Rural Hours.*" *Reading Under the Sign of Nature: New Essays in Ecocriticism.* Ed. John Tallmadge & Henry Harrington. Salt Lake City: U of Utah P, 2000. 64–84.

_____. "*Walden, Rural Hours,* and the Dilemma of Representation." *Thoreau's Sense of Place: Essays in American Environmental Writing.* Ed. Richard J. Schneider. Iowa City: U of Iowa P: 2000. 179–206.

Kheel, Marti. *Nature Ethics: An Ecofeminist Perspective.* Lanham: Rowman & Littlefield, 2008.

Köster, Dörte, et al. "Paleolimnological assessment of human-induced impacts on Walden Pond (Massachusetts, USA) using diatoms and stable isotopes." *Aquatic Ecosystem Health & Management* 8.2 (Apr. 2005): 117–31.

Kroeber, Karl. "Ecology and American Literature: Thoreau and Un-Thoreau." *American Literary History* 9.2 (Summer 1997): 309–28.

Magee, Richard M. "Sentimental Ecology: Susan Fenimore Cooper's *Rural Hours.*" *Such News of the Land: U.S. Women Nature Writers.* Ed. Thomas S. Edwards & Elizabeth A. De Wolfe. Hanover: UP of New England, 2001. 27–36.

Merchant, Carolyn. *Ecological Revolutions: Nature, Gender, and Science in New England.* Chapel Hill: U of North Carolina P, 1989.

Murphy, Patrick D. *Literature, Nature, and Other: Ecofeminist Critiques.* Albany: State U of New York P, 1995.

Nash, Roderick Frazier. *Wilderness and the American Mind.* 4th ed. New Haven: Yale UP, 2001.

Nickens, T. Edward. "Walden Warming." *National Wildlife* 45.6 (Oct. 2007): 36–41.

Norwood, Vera. *Made From This Earth: American Women and Nature.* Chapel Hill, NC: U of North Carolina P, 1993.

_____. "Women's Roles in Nature Study and Environmental Protection." *Magazine of History* 10.3 (Spring 1996): 12–17.

Pennisi, Elizabeth. "Where Have All Thoreau's Flowers Gone?" *Science* 321.5885 (04 July 2008): 24–25.

Phillips, Dana. *The Truth of Ecology: Nature, Culture, and Literature in America.* Oxford: Oxford UP, 2003.

Sattelmeyer, Robert. "Depopulation, Deforestation, and the Actual Walden Pond." *Thoreau's Sense of Place: Essays in American Environmental Writing.* Ed. Richard J. Schneider. Iowa City: U of Iowa P, 2000. 235–43.

Thoreau, Henry David. *Walden.* 1854. Ed. William Rossi. New York: Norton, 2008.

Warren, Karen J. *Ecofeminist Philosophy: A Western Perspective on What It Is and Why It Matters.* Lanham: Rowland, 2000.

Weinstein, Josh A. "Susan Cooper's Humble Ecology: Humility and Christian Stewardship in *Rural Hours*." *The Journal of American Culture* 35.1 (March 2012): 65–77.

"A Canticle of My Reaction": Socio-Cultural Criticism in Claude McKay's *A Long Way from Home*

Christopher Allen Varlack

In his 1931 critical text, *The Negro Author: His Development in America to 1900*, widely considered one of the first serious scholarly inquiries into African American literature of its time, Vernon Loggins asserts that "with the exception of his folk songs, the Negro's most valuable contributions to American literature have been in the form of personal memoirs" (4). This is particularly evident through the many slave narratives published in the mid-1800s, instrumental in the development of the African-American autobiographical tradition and in transforming the perceptions of the larger American and global audiences toward the plight of the slave. Frederick Douglass' 1845 memoir, *Narrative of the Life of Frederick Douglass, an American Slave*, for instance, challenged the romanticized image of slavery by describing the very real evils largely absent from the pro-slavery fiction of the anti-abolition South. Detailing incidents from the brutal murder of Demby to Douglass' life-altering interactions with a notorious slave-breaker charged with breaking the stubborn spirit and will of "difficult" slaves, the memoir played a significant role in challenging the plantation myth of happy darkies, wretched freedmen, and contented slaves with a message demanding immediate socio-political change.

Similarly, in her 1861 autobiography, *Incidents in the Life of a Slave Girl*, Harriet Jacobs revealed the relatively unspoken side of American slavery, depicting her experiences resisting sexual abuse and the seven years she spent in hiding in the attic of a nearby shed. Her words, in essence, broke the silence traditionally demanded of female slaves, thus sparking a tradition of African American women writers who utterly refused to die with their voices buried inside them. As Jill Ker Conway contends, Jacob's work, among others, invariably "challenged categories of race, class, and sexuality" while also "expos[ing] Western sentimentality about maternity" in a system where their children were taken and enslaved (43). And in time, like Douglass' work, *Incidents* defied the skewed depiction of slavery perpetuated in the anti-abolition politicking of the pre-Civil War age. Together, these works helped give rise to the African American literary tradition—a body of literature steeped in cultural and political criticism and vital to reshaping the racial landscape through their message of enduring hope in pursuit of their American dream.

While such works have cemented their place in the larger American literary canon taught in colleges and universities nationwide, in the years after, considerably less attention has been given to the growing body of autobiographical literature produced by African-American authors. This excludes major works ranging from Richard Wright's 1945 *Black Boy* to Malcolm X's 1965 autobiography to Maya Angelou's 1969 *I Know Why the Caged Bird Sings,* among a few other select texts.[1] Emphasis, instead, has been placed on the poetry, fiction, plays, and now films that have garnered attention on a more widespread and national stage. This is perhaps most evident in the scholarship of the Harlem Renaissance era—a steady body of criticism traditionally focused on the classics of early twentieth-century African-American literature, such as the poetic works of Langston Hughes, the folk culture novels of Zora Neale Hurston, or the sociological surveys of William Edward Burghardt Du Bois. Though scholarship surrounding these works is certainly vital, the present void in scholarship regarding the African-American autobiography and the general under-appreciation of those "writers who do not fit in the well-worn Harlem Renaissance or New Negro paradigms" cannot be ignored (Thaggert 16).

The minimal scholarship that has, in fact, examined the autobiographical works of the Harlem Renaissance has proven equally flawed. Focusing too heavily on Langston Hughes' 1940 *The Big Sea* and Zora Neale Hurston's 1942 *Dust Tracks on a Road* often at the exclusion of other works, this scholarship across the decades has over-emphasized the perceived failures of the era's nonfiction. Henrietta L. Herod, for example, described *The Big Sea* as "pedestrian and thin both as to content and style"—a text composed "at what may seem a too early age" (96, 94). Similarly, Darwin Turner characterized *Dust Tracks* as a "disappointing blend of artful candor and coy reticence," one he found full of "contradictions and silences" (91). Robert Hemenway expressed parallel observations, citing these works as "discomfiting," revealing far too little information about the authors themselves—a direct contradiction to the traditional expectations of the autobiographical form (283).

Though these criticisms may, at times, certainly have been valid, they seem to point to an overarching failure, not in the literature, but in the criticism itself. The Harlem Renaissance, after all, was a time of widespread creative and cultural revival embraced by authors of color across the United States, not just Hurston and Hughes. Expanding the canon to more fully reflect the breadth of nonfiction works of the post-bellum world is, then, essential to correcting the current void in scholarship. At the same time, scholars must begin to recognize that each work was an experiment in expressing the spectrum of issues and emotions far too long repressed. Even when those experiments faltered and even when those experiments failed, each attempt was one vital step toward unearthing the African American identity. Criticism, moving forward, must then foreground the achievements of these autobiographical works, including overlooked texts, such as Claude McKay's 1937 memoir, *A Long Way from Home*—texts that offer valuable insights into the New Negro movement and the all-important concept of Negritude that eventually became the foundation for the social and cultural criticism of the time.

Self-Discovery and Self-Exploration: The Goal of McKay's *A Long Way from Home*

For the few Harlem Renaissance authors who ever experimented in creative nonfiction, the memoirs, autobiographies, and travelogues they produced throughout the 1900s ultimately enabled them to engage in the types of necessary self-discovery and self-exploration that other literary forms simply could not afford them. Novels of the era often illustrated folk culture, presenting fictional characters representative of what Jill Ker Conway terms, "archetypal life scripts" (7). Here, characters like Ray, from McKay's 1928 novel *Home to Harlem*, struggled to harmonize their intellectual pursuits with the fast-paced, vibrant black culture of Harlem's buffet flats and cabarets—a conflict that spoke to a larger struggle of the African American people to forge their own place in the post-slavery, increasingly Jim Crow world. Poems reflected the multiplicity of explosive events and issues in the changing cultural and political climate. Works, such as his highly anthologized poem, "If We Must Die," catalogued the violence and racial tension of the Red Summer of 1919, adopting the collective voice of a community "pressed to the wall, dying, but fighting back!" (McKay 14). And while the black theater of the era never truly materialized, the few plays produced during the time examined a wide range of complex issues from intra-racial color prejudice to the tragic mulatto condition, many outside of the author's immediate individual experience.

In contrast, nonfiction like *A Long Way from Home*—part memoir, part manifesto—allowed its authors an opportunity to explore the deep interconnections between these issues and the self, where other forms of literary expression were too often detached. As Robert L. Root, Jr. and Michael Steinberg contend in their introduction to *The Fourth Genre: Contemporary Writers of/on Creative Nonfiction*, the subject these works explored then "[became] the catalyst or trigger for some personal journey or inquiry of self interrogation" in a form both public and private and historically central to the burgeoning African-American literary tradition (xxv). In McKay's nonfiction work, largely ignored in criticism, this is no exception. In the opening pages, he describes the vagabond spirit that overtook him, much like Ray in *Home to Harlem*, leaving behind his studies at Kansas State College as well as his Jamaican home to wander the vast American landscape and write. In this spirit, he declares, "I still cherished the urge to creative expression. I desired to achieve something new, something in the spirit and accent of America. Against its mighty throbbing force, its grand energy and power and bigness, its bitterness burning in my black body, I would raise my voice to make a canticle of my reaction" (McKay, *A Long Way* 4).

In these most vital words, McKay expresses not only the overarching motivation behind his desire to write—to use a voice historically silent or silenced for the black community—but also the central impetus behind the African-American autobiographical form—to respond to the social and political factors that inherently impact one's sense of identity and enduring freedom. McKay, too, was frustrated by the pervasive mistreatment of blacks (the segregation of public spaces, the race riots and increased violence against blacks across the United States, etc.) and the resulting divisions that further separated the black community at large. Therefore, like the slave narratives published decades before, he wrote *A Long Way from Home* to offer, in part, his response to the bitterness of America's "mighty throbbing force" that, at a time of heightened racial tension, became an undeniable obstacle to achieving the American dream (McKay, *A Long Way* 4). This theme, after all, was central to his body of literature, also evident in such significant works as his 1921 poem "America," invariably shaped by the Negro problem so heavily contentious in the cultural conversations of blacks and whites alike.

Unlike "America," however, in *A Long Way from Home*, McKay wholeheartedly strives for a different effect. Rather than foreground the need for immediate socio-political change and for the remasculinization of an emasculated people, here, instead, he decentralizes that bitterness in order to participate in the act of *self-interrogation* upon which American creative nonfiction is largely based. For instance, in chapter twenty-one of the memoir, McKay interrogates "the urge that had sent [him] abroad"—an urge he later discovers is based upon a color consciousness that only people of color could truly understand (244). For McKay, constantly labeled as that distant and inferior Other in American society, his drive abroad proves far different from the pressures of white "radicals, esthetes, painters and writers, pseudo-artists, bohemian tourists—all mixed tolerantly and congenially enough together" in what he defines as the pursuit of a ripe European culture, artistic freedom, and uncomplicated sex (243). Therefore, in contrasting his experience and determining the root of his restlessness, he not only examines the social conflict of color, but also reaches a better understanding of self:

Unable to see deep into the profundity of blackness, some [of the white expatriate caravan around him] even thought that [he] might have preferred to be white like them. They couldn't imagine that [he] had no desire merely to exchange [his] black problem for their white problem. For all their knowledge and sophistication, they couldn't understand the instinctive and animal and purely physical pride of a black person resolute in being himself and yet living a simple civilized life like themselves. (245)

This statement has proven controversial in the minimal scholarship surrounding this memoir. In *Color & Culture: Black Writers and the Making of the Modern Intellectual*, for instance, Ross Posnock suggests that the overarching "equanimity of this passage is striking. For it is relatively rare that McKay affirms pride in blackness *within* rather than against 'civilized life'" (240–241). That affirmation of pride within, however, is absolutely vital to the underlying self-discovery of *A Long Way from Home* and to establishing justification for expanding the criticism regarding this significant text.

The memoir, as "a canticle of [his] reaction," by definition presents a hymn or song of praise, in this case celebrating the unique history and culture of an African American people too long dejected and distressed (McKay 4). This perspective, as Posnock claims, largely differs in comparison to the poetic works for which McKay is primarily renowned. At the same time, his unwavering contentment as a black man and pride in a racial heritage too often problematized (hence the controversial phrase, *the Negro problem*, circulating in much of the literature of the Harlem Renaissance itself), are part of the fundamental self-discoveries that McKay reaches through the text. Essentially, what McKay accomplishes in these words is the central goal of creative nonfiction, according to Joseph Epstein: "What one discovers in writing such [works] is where one stands on complex issues, problems, questions, subjects . . . [O]ne tests one's feelings, instincts, thoughts in the crucible of composition" (15). Here, McKay enters into the crucible his thoughts on race and race pride, challenging the misconception of blackness as something to be ashamed of by asserting instead the inherent value "of a black person resolute in being himself" (*A Long Way* 245).

Embracing the Negro Masses: The Message of Negritude in *A Long Way from Home*

For McKay in particular, the nonfiction form is, therefore, vital to the canon of Harlem Renaissance and African American autobiographical works as it afforded him a literary vehicle to explain both his artistic and cultural philosophy—what later became known as the Negritude movement sparked during the 1930s. Essentially concerned with the cultivation of race pride and a return to traditional African and African American cultural values, the movement toward negritude in the United States and abroad was a response to rising prejudice and the perception of black inferiority. As Abiola Irele asserts in "Negritude—Literature and Ideology," Negritude can be viewed as a literary "counter-movement" away from dependence upon the dominant white society—"a symbolic progression from subordination to independence, from alienation, through revolt, to self-affirmation" (499). Accordingly, *A Long Way from Home*, in comparison to McKay's widely discussed poetic and fiction works, is most significant as it serves, in part, as his political manifesto—the one place where he distinctly outlines his perspective on Negritude that later influences the likes of Aimé Césaire, Léopold Sédar Senghor, and others instrumental to the African Negritude movement at large.

This message of Negritude in *A Long Way from Home*, in the spirit of a "canticle of [his] reaction," is then often presented in response to the overwhelming neglect that McKay perceives among the Negro intelligentsia for the Negro masses—a neglect that he claims is destructive to the sense of communal unity that Negritude ultimately intended to evoke (4). As he asserts in his autobiography, the problem is rooted in the increasing number of "educated Negroes who believe that the color line will be dissolved eventually by the light-skinned Negroids 'passing white,' by miscegenation and final assimilation by the white group" (351). Because Negritude, however, essentially rejects assimilation as increased dependence upon the values and culture of the white society, to McKay, such perspectives were historically problematic. They threatened to give rise to a generation of people of color from the jazz and blues clubs of Harlem to the fictional Banana Bottom, who "approximated to the social standards and attitudes of [white society] with little sympathy for the [now] freed blacks and their problems, their struggles for social adjustment" (McKay, *Banana Bottom* 297).[2]

Of all his established works, McKay presents the ideological underpinnings of Negritude most successfully in *A Long Way from Home,* advocating pride among the African American people in their ancestral heritage and demanding an increased awareness (from both blacks and whites alike) of the inherent value in black culture. In reflecting on the achievements and failures of the Harlem Renaissance itself, he thus condemns the Negro intelligentsia, with whom he often had a strained relationship. For instance, he writes, "The Negro intelligentsia cannot hope to get very far if the Negro masses are despised and neglected" (McKay, *A Long Way* 351). The message presented in these words proves fundamental to the literary and cultural ideology at the center of McKay's body of work. Throughout, he embraces the folk—the same Negro masses despised—despite the criticism his works often received. Du Bois, for one, harshly critiqued McKay's *Home to Harlem* and what he perceived as a shameful depiction of the fleeting, hyper sexualized lives of primitive and promiscuous working-class blacks. The novel, he claimed, "nauseates me, and after the dirtiest parts of its filth I feel distinctly like taking a bath" (Du Bois 359).

To McKay, such perspectives seemed to despise the masses and threatened to present an incomplete portrait—"a one-sided idea of [the] life" of the African American people—one that "mistake[s] the art of life for nonsense and tr[ies] to pass propaganda as life in art!" (Cooper 244). In response, in the closing chapter of the memoir, McKay demands increased unity and organization among the entire community of African American people, acknowledging the many valuable contributions the Negro intelligentsia might have to offer, while refusing to ignore the Negro masses too long neglected in the scope of American history. Here, he contends that this unity is necessary to achieve "more important jobs and greater social recognition for Negroes"—part of the social reformation that the progenitors of the Harlem Renaissance ultimately sought to create (McKay, *A Long Way* 352). At the same time, however, he recognizes that "[T]he Negro whom they consider an Uncle Tom among the whites, whose voice is the voice of their white master, cannot [organize the Negro masses], even though he may proclaim himself a radical!" (352). Rather, for McKay, the drive toward Negritude and social change is instead advanced and directed by the common, oppressed, hardworking, vibrant, at times even primitive, unashamedly black people.

Politically-minded, McKay's efforts to infuse socio-cultural criticism into *A Long Way from Home* reflect a common thread in African American autobiography "in which intimate aspects of the autobiographer's personal experience are subordinated to social commentary and reflections upon what it means to be a Negro in a world dominated by white men" (Drake x). Following in the tradition of the slave narratives and post-Reconstruction memoirs published before the Harlem Renaissance era, *A Long Way from Home* thus fulfills the political purpose as George Orwell defines it, also using McKay's travels throughout Soviet Russia, for example, as a platform to shape the perspective of his readers regarding the surrounding world. Expressing his mounting awareness of the commonalities between the Negro and the Soviet as oppressed peoples, McKay moves beyond the microcosm of his individual experience, providing readers necessary glimpses into the larger world he witnesses firsthand as both outsider and participant. And through this, he is able to gain a better understanding of the larger human struggle of which the African-American people are an undeniable part.

Together, these impulses toward Negritude and tracing the role of the African American in a more global context are just some of the reasons the lapse in criticism of the era's memoirs and autobiographies is so disconcerting. The African American autobiography, after all, first emerged to break a tradition of silence and, at times, even complacency; therefore, the silence of criticism in specific eras as vital as this is counterproductive to the ongoing conversation these texts intended to evoke. *A Long Way from Home* is just one core example of an oversight that must be fixed.

As Wayne F. Cooper writes in *Claude McKay: Rebel Sojourner in the Harlem Renaissance*, "Through it all, he portrayed himself as a black man intent upon remaining true to himself, yet accepting, too, the inescapable obligation to write truthfully about those qualities within himself and his race that both set blacks apart as unique and made them one with the rest of mankind" (318). If for no other reasons, McKay's explorations into the racial politics of his time and his demand for unity among the masses are sufficient rationale for increased critical attention of this important, yet under-acknowledged and under-appreciated work.

The Way Home

In the end, with its emphasis on socio-cultural criticism and advancement of the Negritude movement, *A Long Way from Home* should prove one of the Harlem Renaissance era's most noteworthy cultural texts. Here, McKay engages an autobiographical tradition that probes "the entire span of humanistic inquiry about what it means to be human, how the individual is shaped by society, . . . what shapes the imagination, what talents are valued and what misunderstood" (Conway 17). While certainly under-recognized in the canon of American and African American autobiography, the memoir offers another much-needed dimension to the mosaic of American experience: what it means to be black and an intellectual—a subject that McKay only begins to understand in his travels abroad and the self-interrogation of *A Long Way from Home*. As St. Clair Drake acknowledges in the introduction to the 1970 edition, this memoir is perhaps the greatest contribution of the era to this conversation so heavily contentious in the 1960s and beyond, as evidenced in Harold Cruse' 1967 *The Crisis of the Negro Intellectual*, Cornel West's 1985 "The Dilemma of the Black Intellectual," and William M. Banks' 1996 *Black Intellectuals: Race and Responsibility in American Life.* "McKay," however, "came to grips with [these issues] earlier than any of the others, and his autobiography documents the processes of discovery, growth, inner conflict, and disillusionment that all sensitive black intellectuals experience in a world where racism is a pervasive reality" (Drake ix–x).

Though the memoir may never be counted among McKay's greatest works, its overall significance to the African American autobiographical tradition cannot be denied. Representing that consistent push for increased activism, unity, and political change only intensified in later autobiographical works (Eldridge Cleaver's 1968 *Soul on Ice* and Assata Shakur's 1987 *Assata: An Autobiography*, to name a few), *A Long Way from Home* never shies away from the central goal of creative nonfiction. Throughout, it offers an attempt to uncover, to probe, to self-reflect, and to criticize—all features characteristic of the nonfiction essay (derived from Montaigne's use of the term *essai*, to attempt)—while offering a unique perspective of history—a goal traditionally associated with the memoir form. "A mode of thinking and being" as well as "an enactment of the creation of the self," *A Long Way from Home* therefore afforded McKay that crucial opportunity, of which too few Harlem Renaissance authors took advantage, for that necessary self-discovery and self-interrogation upon which nonfiction is heavily based (Lopate xlii, xliv). And while the memoir is often about the self, it is just as much about the community, at times providing a voice for those yet to find their own.

In writing *A Long Way from Home*, however, McKay did not set out "to be the leading spokesman of an oppressed race," as Robert A. Smith inaccurately contends in "Claude McKay: An Essay in Criticism" (273). Rather, he set out to tell a story not fully captured in his previous fiction and poetic works—a story of his travels near and far, a story of his shifting understanding of self. In doing so, McKay engaged that all-important storytelling tradition central to African and African American expression, ultimately building upon the foundation of minority literature established decades prior with Briton Hammon, Olaudah Equiano, and Frederick Douglass' autobiographies. Thus serving the role of a griot of sorts, McKay entered into "the crucible of composition" a tale largely unspoken in the other autobiographical works of his time, these authors were often criticized for masking their individual selves or wandering somewhat aimlessly in the big sea. In contrast, McKay weaves a tale both politically charged and socially demanding, aimed at unifying the African American people in a movement called Negritude, while also addressing the internal and external problems habitually plaguing the black community (Epstein 15). This, after all, was exactly the type of creative revival that the Harlem Renaissance truly sought to unearth.

"Such is my opinion for all it may be worth," writes McKay in the closing paragraph of the memoir (*A Long Way* 354). "I have nothing to give but my singing. All my life I have been a troubadour wanderer, nourishing myself mainly on the poetry of existence. And all I offer here is the distilled poetry of my existence" (354). Though gravely undervalued in the scope of Harlem Renaissance and African American literature, *A Long Way from Home* presents us a beautiful song—one demanding increased attention in order to correct the gaping hole present in existing criticism, while acclimating readers to a black-authored autobiography arguably more successful than the counterparts supposedly flawed (e.g., the memoirs of Hurston and Hughes). And while the Harlem Renaissance is not known for its autobiographies, perhaps it should be. These works ultimately offer us insight into the mind and the spirit of a black community forever working to find its voice, its song. *A Long Way from Home* is one vital chord in this ever-developing string of African American musicality—a chord that cannot simply be deleted or ignored. And for now, it is singing from the shelves of the library, just waiting for when the world is ready to finally listen.

Notes

1. Here Maureen T. Reddy agrees that the overwhelmingly limited scope of criticism regarding the African-American autobiographical tradition across time is problematic. In her 1996 review of *African American Autobiography: A Collection of Critical Essays*, edited by William L. Andrews, she notes, "Although I am delighted to see that African American autobiography is now considered so canonical that a text on its scholarship would be included in a series such as this, the parameters of the series also create certain problems. Predictably enough, none of the essays here focuses on offbeat or lesser known works" (179). Her criticism is certainly valid, citing a very present gap in contemporary criticism of the wide range of

autobiographical texts produced by black authors. Because the topics explored in African American autobiography so greatly differ, this limited scope in criticism too often ignores the valuable contributions of non-canonical texts to expanding our understanding of the human condition.

2.   This theme is vital to the latter works of the Harlem Renaissance era, particularly those works produced after the Stock Market Crash of 1929 that essentially derailed the movement. In *A Long Way from Home*, McKay explores these ideas, in part, as a reflection of Harlem Renaissance society and a critique of figures like Du Bois, whose notions of the talented tenth and strict definition of Negro art (as a source of propaganda) seemed to create a distinct divide between the Negro intelligentsia and the masses McKay strived to represent. The idea that McKay presents here is reminiscent of George Schuyler's 1931 satirical novel, *Black No More*—a novel based upon the false belief that assimilation would solve the Negro problem so volatile in American society. With the invention of Dr. Junius Crookman that promises to alter the pigmentation of black skin, the Negro masses rush to local sanitariums to turn themselves white, driven by an internalized racism and their overarching fatigue with the limited opportunities that "blackness" could afford them. These two texts work in conversation as a critique of this movement toward a raceless society and are, therefore, central, yet drastically under-appreciated, works.

Works Cited

Andrews, William L., ed. *African American Autobiography: A Collection of Critical Essays.* Englewood Cliffs, NJ: Prentice Hall, 1993.

Angelou, Maya. *I Know Why the Caged Bird Sings.* 1969. New York: Ballantine, 2009.

Banks, William M. *Black Intellectuals: Race and Responsibility in American Life.* New York: Norton, 1998.

Cleaver, Eldridge. *Soul on Ice.* 1968. New York: Dell, 1991.

Conway, Jill Ker. *When Memory Speaks: Exploring the Art of Autobiography.* New York: Alfred A. Knopf, 1998.

Cooper, Wayne F. *Claude McKay: Rebel Sojourner in the Harlem Renaissance.* Baton Rouge: Louisiana State UP, 1987.

Cruse, Harold. *The Crisis of the Negro Intellectual.* New York: William Morrow & Company, 1967.

Douglass, Frederick. *Narrative of the Life of Frederick Douglass, an American Slave.* 1845. Lexington, KY: SoHo, 2010.

Drake, St. Clair. Introduction. *A Long Way from Home.* 1937. By Claude McKay. San Diego: Harcourt Brace, 1970. ix–xxi.

Du Bois, W. E. B. Rev. of *Home to Harlem,* by Claude McKay, *Crisis* 35 (1928): 202. Rpt. in *Voices of a Black Nation: Political Journalism in the Harlem Renaissance.* Ed. Theodore Vincent. San Francisco: Rampart, 1973. 359–360.

Epstein, Joseph, ed. "The Personal Essay: A Form of Discovery." *The Norton Book of Personal Essays.* New York: Norton, 1997. 11–24.

Hemenway, Robert. *Zora Neale Hurston.* Champaign-Urbana: U of Illinois P, 1977.

Herod, Henrietta L. Rev. of *The Big Sea,* by Langston Hughes. *Phylon* 2.1 (1941): 94–96. *JSTOR.* Web. 23 June 2014.

Hughes, Langston. *The Big Sea.* 1940. New York: Hill and Wang, 1993.

Hurston, Zora Neale. *Dust Tracks on a Road.* 1942. New York: Library of America, 1995. 561–808.

Irele, Abiola. "Negritude—Literature and Ideology." *The Journal of Modern African Studies* 3.4 (1965): 499–526. *JSTOR.* Web. 28 June 2014.

Jacobs, Harriet. *Incidents in the Life of a Slave Girl.* 1861. New York: Barnes & Noble, 2005.

Loggins, Vernon. *The Negro Author: His Development in American to 1900.* New York: Columbia UP, 1931.

McKay, Claude. *A Long Way from Home.* 1937. San Diego: Harcourt Brace, 1970.

_____. "America." *Selected Poems.* Ed. Joan R. Sherman. Mineola: Dover, 1999. 30.

_____. *Banana Bottom.* 1933. San Diego: Harcourt Brace, 1961.

_____. *Home to Harlem. Classic Fiction of the Harlem Renaissance.* 1928. Ed. William L. Andrews. New York: Oxford UP, 1994. 105–237.

_____. "If We Must Die." *The Portable Harlem Renaissance Reader.* Ed. David Levering Lewis. New York: Penguin, 1994. 290.

Posnock, Ross. *Color & Culture: Black Writers and the Making of the Modern Intellectual.* Cambridge: Harvard UP, 1998.

Reddy, Maureen T. Rev. of *African American Autobiography: A Collection of Critical Essays*, by William L. Andrews. *MELUS* 21.2 (1996): 179–181. *JSTOR.* Web. 25 June 2014.

Root, Robert L., Jr. & Michael Steinberg. "Creative Nonfiction, the Fourth Genre." Introduction. *The Fourth Genre: Contemporary Writers of/ on Creative Nonfiction.* New York: Pearson, 2007. xxiii–xxxiv.

Schuyler, George Samuel. *Black No More.* 1931. Mineola: Dover, 2011.

Shakur, Assata. *Assata: An Autobiography.* 1987. Chicago: Lawrence Hill, 2001.

Smith, Robert A. "Claude McKay: An Essay in Criticism." *Analysis and Assessment, 1940–1979.* Ed. Cary D. Wintz. New York: Garland, 1996. 168–171.

Thaggert, Miriam. *Images of Black Modernism: Verbal and Visual Strategies of the Harlem Renaissance.* Amherst: U of Massachusetts P, 2010.

Turner, Darwin. *In a Minor Chord.* Carbondale: Southern Illinois UP, 1971.

West, Cornel. "The Dilemma of the Black Intellectual." *The Cornel West Reader.* New York: Basic Civitas, 1999. 302–315.

Wright, Richard. *Black Boy: A Record of Childhood and Youth.* 1945. New York: HarperPerennial, 2006.

X, Malcolm & Alex Haley. *The Autobiography of Malcolm X.* 1965. New York: Ballantine, 1992.

"I'm Fighting Because You're Down Here": Small Stories and Big Histories in Shelby Foote's *The Civil War*_____

Christopher Walsh

Epic is an adjective frequently used to praise literary works in both specialist and non-specialist circles. The justification for its use is contested on many occasions, but Shelby Foote's trilogy about the American Civil War is certainly not one of those. Initially intended to be a short history produced by a writer who was already an accomplished novelist, the work became a gargantuan task, comprising over a million and half words, and it ultimately represented a full two decades' work for Foote (Phillips 24).[1] In this opening volume and throughout the trilogy, Foote is skilled at simultaneously offering different perspectives of the same event or events; he provides the point of view of people who may otherwise have been absented, and the narrative has a polyphonic approach, with a multiplicity of voices; there is a fidelity to historical accuracy, but the descriptive and rhetorical range belongs to a practitioner of a different genre. As we shall see, this violates the stylistic and academic protocols of what historical writing does and what it should look like.

   This chapter will provide a brief overview of the history of the trilogy's composition, its relationship to conventional historical writing, and the various stylistic and structural components that ensure its place as an exemplar of creative nonfiction. These include Foote's contrapuntal treatment of events, especially evidenced in key moments in the careers of Jefferson Davis and Abraham Lincoln, and his character descriptions, through which his craft as a novelist shines through, which is also revealed via his use of anecdotes and his depiction of battle scenes. We will also examine Foote's attempts to frame the conflict within larger historical narratives, his hybrid use of sources and his willingness to challenge the established rhetorical and academic practices of historical scholarship.

Beginnings and the "Problem" of History

There is an ironic contrast between Foote's initial conception of the project and what it ended up becoming. Bennett Cerf, Foote's editor at Random House, asked Foote to write a brief history about the war for publication during the centennial celebrations; Foote initially thought that the project seemed easy compared to producing fiction and welcomed switching genres at this point in his career. Ironically, Foote believed the following at the outset of the project; "I figured that I could write about twice as much history per year as I did fiction per year—fiction is hard work; history, I figured, well, there's not much to that" (Phillips 24–5). Volume I is the shortest instalment of the trilogy, and it was published in November 1958; the complete trilogy would eventually take two decades to complete and all three volumes come in at around 1.5 million words (Phillips 159, 26).

What cannot be ignored, and what rankled some traditional historians, is that in the trilogy, Foote privileges the telling and narrative organization over adherence to scholarly practices employed by academic historians. For Wirt Williams, this should be discerned from the subtitle of the work, as it gives a clear indication about Foote's intentions; "The subtitle, *A Narrative*, is a declaration of purpose: this is, manifestly, to present a unified and interesting continuity of what is already known rather than to bring new "facts" to light" (430). A key reference point is the bibliographic note that Foote provides at the end of the volume, where he acknowledges the sources he used during his research, including the 128-volume *War of the Rebellion: a Compilation of the Official Records of the Union and Confederate Armies.* In such sources, Foote claims, "you hear the live men speak" (813). He accomplishes the same in the trilogy, where you hear a range of authentic voices in a prose style that, whilst polished and rhythmical, is never jargonisitc or inaccessible.

The bibliographic note almost resembles a defense of his aesthetic approach rather than a dry record of his research methodology. In it, Foote accepts "the historian's standards without his paraphernalia" (815), and paraphernalia here refers to the rigid academic processes of referencing, footnoting, and documentation that are noticeably absent from Foote's work. One of the ironies of the volume and the trilogy as a whole is that it is intricately plotted and thoroughly researched, but it is not *presented* as history should be. Foote left out footnotes, as he believed they would "detract from the book's narrative quality by intermittently shattering the illusion that the observer is not so much reading a book as sharing an experience…" (815) It is interesting to note that Foote maintained this position over the twenty years it took him to complete the trilogy, and in a 1986 interview, he acknowledged that "…Professional historians resent the hell out of the absence of footnotes, for instance," but he goes on to claim that "footnotes would have totally shattered what I was doing. I didn't want people glancing down at the bottom of the page every other sentence" (Carter 233). Interestingly, Foote also points out the fate that befalls some writers of creative nonfiction as they become victims of their own hybridized and genre-jumping styles. He certainly experienced this, and the claim perhaps reveals a level of disappointment with the formal, academic recognition of his work, especially when it first appeared; "… Professional historians resent it and creative writers don't read it. So I'm falling between two stools, you see." (Carter 233)

Other academic conventions are subverted or absent—a thesis is not dogmatically pursued, and the narrator is never a detached and aloof presence, for example—but what it lacks here it certainly makes up for in terms of fidelity to the experience of events and the organization of their telling. In place of cold rationalism, we have a narrator who is immersed in the action, committed to structure and drawn by character rather than theory; indeed, it is hard to disagree with Robert Phillips' claim that "the narrator is an artist of history" (182). The importance of this was noted by Foote in a letter to his close friend Walker Percy (another fine author from the South) which was composed when Foote was working on the first volume. In the letter in question, Foote explained to his literary friend that, "What I have to do is learn everything possible from all possible sources about a certain phase or campaign, then digest it so it's clear in my own mind, then reproduce it even clearer than it has been to me until I actually begin writing about it... Drama is meaning" (Tolson 111). We can see that the *process*, but perhaps not the execution has much in common with traditional historical scholarship, and a further crucial difference in Foote's version of historical prose is that, for the most part, it is driven by drama and not data.

Aside from the visual academic paraphernalia that Foote dispenses with, readers of conventional historical prose are often surprised by other absences when they start to read, especially as the trilogy is regarded as such an authoritative history of the war. Foote doesn't theorize or interrogate competing historical approaches or interpretations; you don't see the work of other historians analyzed or dissected, nor do you see him propose radical alternatives to established modes of understanding; for him the telling—and the organization of that telling—is everything. As Foote remarked in one of his many candid interviews, the trilogy represented "a gigantic exercise in the handling of plot and I enjoyed it enormously" (Carter 119). Although he was a conservative figure from a conservative region, Foote actually succeeds in pre-empting tenets of some postmodern or post-structural theories about the nature, legitimacy, and assumed objectivity of writing about history. He does this by dismantling the scaffolding of traditional historical writing and hybridizing his style, so that the ideologically powerful and powerless appear side by side (and it's often the latter who have the best lines). Foote didn't actually see too much difference between the craft of the novelist and that of a historian, as for him, a commitment to a higher artistic truth transcends narrow questions about genre. Of course, the very idea of a sovereign, one-size-fits-all notion of truth is a problematic one for many, but this is what Foote is aiming for in the trilogy; "The point I would make is that the novelist and the historian are seeking the same thing: the truth— not a different truth: the same truth—only they reach it, or try to reach it, by different routes . . . they both want to tell us *how it was*" (Foote 815). For Foote, scholarly truth and sophisticated telling are not mutually exclusive, but rather the two are conjoined in order to produce a remarkable narrative.

Contrasts and Descriptions

We've alluded to the intricate structuring of the narrative, and it's now time to turn to the text itself. The opening thirty pages or so of Volume I cover the dissolution of the Union, and it also follows Abraham Lincoln and Jefferson Davis as they simultaneously struggle through the unfolding action. This contrapuntal treatment of events is one of the most successful characteristics of the opening volume, and the early juxtapositioning of the two leaders allows the narrator to articulate the hopes and anxieties of the different sides they were representing. An early, but effective, example of Foote's contrapuntal handling of timelines follows the two presidents as they are about to leave home for their respective capitals. Although Foote holds back from elucidating on the interior processes of those involved, it is made all the more powerful for that, especially as the reader brings their own historical consciousness of the events that were about to unfold to the text. It is symbolic that Davis is tending to his rose garden shortly before leaving home to commence a war whose violence and destruction sharply contrasts with this settled domestic scene; "The day that Davis received the summons in the rose garden was Abraham Lincoln's last full day in Springfield, Illinois. He would be leaving tomorrow for Washington and his inauguration, the same day that Davis left Montgomery and his" (Foote 17).

Foote's narrative approach means that descriptions of characters have a closely focused, novelistic feel to them. Indeed in the opening depictions of Lincoln, the narrator's uncertainty mirrors that of the population at large who "hardly knew what to make of this tall, thin-chested, raw-boned man with the frontier in his voice," who moved with a "shambling western gait" that offended the delicate sensibilities of New Yorkers following a visit to the opera during the early stage of his presidency (Foote 18, 36). The hyphenated descriptions contribute to the overall effect as they encourage readers to immerse themselves in the description, which is central to Foote's approach here and throughout the trilogy. We are implicated in the unfolding narrative; Foote is making us see, as opposed to situating his readers in an evaluative process of weighing points and counterpoints, of delineating competing theoretical interpretations, which characterizes much conventional historical scholarship. Further on in this passage, Foote moves from the physical to the rhetorical, and it is significant that he doesn't ignore Lincoln's oratory. He draws particular attention to his inauguration address where "the mystic chords of memory" phrase stands out (Foote 40). The trilogy itself appeals and adds to the mystic chords of the nation's historical consciousness, and Foote is adept at showing us how Lincoln's use of rhetorical music enabled him to outmaneuver Davis on the linguistic front as well.

It is perhaps tempting to be too Lincoln-centric when discussing Foote's detailed character description, but Davis' treatment is more than fair. Indeed the following example is also emblematic of Foote's style in many respects, and it is worth quoting at length. It describes Davis' inauguration as leader of the Confederacy and its hybridity of perspectives and use of sources is striking. It contains character description, a brief consideration of events from the audience's point of view—indicated only with the use of a pronoun—a treatment of Davis' interiority and then a transition, lacking footnotes or explication, to a primary source (a letter to his wife) that gives Davis' own interpretation of events. The hybrid mix of styles evidenced here, including novelistic description, the considered use and incorporation of primary sources and an almost reportage-like tone, is an exemplar of the style that Foote pursues throughout:

> Charmed by the music of his oratory, the handsomeness of his clear-cut features, the dignity of his manner, they were thankful for the providence of history, which apparently gave every great movement the leader it deserved. Such doubts as he had he kept to himself, or declared them only to his wife still back at Brierfield, writing to her two days after the inauguration: "The audience was large and brilliant. Upon my weary heart were showered smiles, plaudits, and flowers; but beyond them, I saw troubles and thorns innumerable... We are without machinery, without means, and threatened by a powerful opposition..." (Foote 41)

The insightful descriptions of characters are not solely reserved for towering figures, such as Lincoln and Davis. It is notable that they are used throughout as it underpins how Foote's approach here is driven by character and telling rather than data and interpretation. Other memorable character descriptions include that of John Alexander McClernand, a Union general who is described as follows, where his ambition is personified: "McClernand was not tall: not much taller, in fact, than Grant: but he *looked* tall, perhaps because of the height of his aspirations. Thin-faced, crowding fifty, with sunken eyes and a long, knife-blade nose, a glistening full black beard and the genial dignity of an accomplished orator…" (Foote 198–99). Foote's use of punctuation adds to the overall effect here, as he judiciously inserts semi-colons, commas, and hyphenated phrases where he wants our gaze to linger and build up an image of the character being described. Another colorful description, this time from the Confederate side, is that of the charismatic Jeb Stuart, and the detailed description (this time of clothes and apparel) once more privileges the image of the individual over analysis of his military contributions, in what is a memorable passage: "A brigadier at twenty-nine, square built, of average height, with china-blue eyes, a bushy cinnamon beard, and flamboyant clothes—thigh-high boots, yellow sash, elbow-length gauntlets, red-line cape, soft hat with the brim pinned up on one side by a gold star supporting a foot-long ostrich plume […]" (Foote 471). Foote himself acknowledged that such descriptions were a key part of his aesthetic agenda here when he stated that "Nothing flatters me more than to have someone ask me if I made up some scene, because I hope it sounds as if a novelist wrote it… any facts in there are facts, whether it's the weather or the color of somebody's hair and eyes […]" (Carter 183).

Anecdotes

A strategy that makes a crucial contribution to Foote's descriptive rather than interpretive method here is his use of anecdotes. It is another area that evokes the ire of conventional historians, as whilst there's the characteristic fidelity to truth, it's fused with a novelistic use of descriptive details. Foote's use of anecdotes allows him to weave some humor into the narrative, and they also allow him to democratize his use of sources and open the text up to voices that may have otherwise been excluded. An early example of effective anecdotal historiography is when Foote recreates the scene as Davis leaves Washington for the final time before the conflict; "The Senator from Mississippi rose. It was high noon. The occasion was momentous and expected; the galleries were crowded, hoop-skirted ladies and men in broadcloth come to hear him say farewell. He was going home" (Foote 3). In many ways, this brief passage encapsulates Foote's style; the variety of sentence lengths and types build dramatic tension, adjectives are used judiciously but sparingly, and there's historical fidelity to the look and feel of things in terms of dress and appearance, but not to retrospective interpretations of the event itself. In other words, it reads as if we're receiving an oral report of the event immediately after it by someone who was present.

Another striking example of Foote's anecdotal style comes via the story of William Tecumseh Sherman dining with the Louisiana State Military Academy's director of Latin and Greek on the occasion of South Carolina's secession. The passage is emblematic of Foote's use of anecdotes and handling of such situations; Sherman is described so that his physical description is privileged, and the primary source (the conversation itself) is included to add to the narrative flow of events, not to situate it in a comparing and weighing of historical evidence and interpretations. Sherman is described as being "red-bearded, tall and thin, with sunken temples and a fidgety manner" and we learn that "the room had a smell of niter paper, which he burned for his asthma" (Foote 58). With the scene set, the narrator goes on to recount the exchange between the two, in which Sherman harangues his dining companion; "You people of the South don't know what you are doing.... This country will be drenched in blood... It is all folly, madness, a crime against civilization! You people speak so highly of war; you don't know what you're talking about. War is a terrible thing!" (59). Of course dramatic irony is also at play here as readers know what Sherman will do to ensure the country is "soaked in blood," and his warning for the region is contrasted with his later barbarity against it.

Not all of the anecdotes are as apocalyptic, and some have their share of humor. One such example focuses on the elusive Stonewall Jackson's reasons for giving up reading the papers, which he likened to his decision to give up drinking; "Why, sir, because I like the taste of [it], and when I discovered that to be the case I made up my mind to do without [it] altogether" (Foote 458). Comparatively "low" voices also contribute to this polyphonic narrative, and when they do, they get to the heart of the matter at hand and offer the most memorable assessments or interpretations; indeed, it seems as if these analytical vignettes are the ones that Foote regards as the genuine historical record. The example in question came from what the narrator describes as "a ragged Virginia private pounced on by the Northerners in a retreat" (Foote 65). The Northern troops asked him what he was fighting for "as he owned no slaves and seemingly could have little interest in States Rights," and he replied with the following phlegmatic response; "I'm fighting because you're down here" (65).

War Means Fighting—and Attention to Detail

A key reason for the trilogy's enduring popularity is Foote's skill in depicting military campaigns; not just the combat exchanges themselves but the strategizing and frequently anguished deliberations that precede them. Foote extensively researched each campaign, and he frequently visited battle sites to garner a first-hand approach of what occurred in a particular locale. Environmental, geographic, natural, and militaristic details are thus conjoined to create an accurate depiction of events, and from a stylistic point of view, Foote often relies on relatively simple sentences and similes to evoke things as they were for the original participants.

Although not dealing with a particular campaign, there is a remarkable passage in the second section of the first part of the trilogy that foreshadows the barbarity that was to come. In another contrapuntal treatment of events, Foote captures the moment when North and South come to realize that the conflict will not be the quick, clean, and romantic encounter they initially thought it would be. Before the exchanges increase in volume and gruesomeness, the narrator takes a moment to envision Davis and Lincoln looking down the road that connected the two capitals, and he sees them "peering as if across a darkling plain." A few sentences on the narrative consciousness does its own bit of future-gazing as it imagines the agrarian landscape being transformed by battle and made "lurid as the floor of hell itself" (Foote 166). Similes are used effectively elsewhere, such as when plans for Bull Run are imagined as being executed successfully, which would result in the opposing forces meeting "like a pair of dancers clutching each other and twirling to the accompaniment of a cannon" (76), whereas at Wilson's Creek, Kentucky the scene "was more like reciprocal murder" than "panoplied war" (94). A final example comes from the brutal Seven Days when 34,463 soldiers were killed from both sides. The chaotic twenty-mile corridor, where the majority of the fighting took place, witnessed both sides "groping spastically in the general direction of an enemy who fought so savagely when cornered that the whole thing had been rather like playing blind man's bluff with a buzz saw…" (509). As in the Wilson's Creek and Bull Run examples, a simile works here ("like playing blind man's bluff") to capture the chaotic nature of the scene, which is underpinned with the use of the adverb "spastically," which suggests that fear prevailed and neither side had a clear handle on strategy or tactics.

Foote outlined the extensive research he conducted ahead of writing battle scenes in a 1968 interview with Bob Mottley. Foote told Mottley that; "When I write about a battle, I go first to the battlefield in the season of the year when the conflict occurred. I look at the foliage, smell the land, watch the sky. Then I go home and write it up" (Carter 19). This attention to detail, which in turn adds to the dramatic tension and authenticity of the passages, is perhaps best revealed in a section describing conditions prior to events at Fort Donelson, where the narrator sets the following scene: "When dawn came through, luminous and ghostly, the men emerged from their holes to find a wonderland that seemed not made for fighting. The trees wore icy armor, branch and twig, and the countryside was blanketed with white" (Foote 200). The rhythm of the prose mirrors the rhythm of the seasons and landscape, and the juxtaposition between the wonderland depicted here and the bloody scene that is about to unfold is, of course, heightened.

The South

No discussion of the Foote's Civil War trilogy could properly be conducted without a consideration of his treatment of the South. For all its bellicose rhetorical flourishes and contradictory and morally-flawed justifications of its own political philosophies, the region infused the conflict with a tragic poetry of its own. Even in the first volume, which details some of the South's most notable military victories, the seeds of its defeat were evident even to those who believed in the Confederacy's mission with an evangelical zeal. Foote's experience of the South from a contextual viewpoint is also significant, as he lived during a significant transitional phase: "he knew the veterans of the war and watched them die away until there were no more. He watched a generation grow up in the South which was removed from the great tragedy of defeat and inclined increasingly toward the national optimism" (Phillips 158–9)

Foote seeks to legitimize the South's cause by framing it within the American historical experience, at least in mythical terms. He notes that Southerners conceived of the war as "a Second American Revolution, fought for principles no less high, against a tyranny no less harsh.... Southerners saw themselves as the guardians of the American tradition, which included the right to revolt..." (Foote 65). Admirable though this may be, it does smack of an attempt to empirically justify the conflict around a thesis, which is something that Foote eschewed, as we've noted elsewhere. Perhaps surprisingly, he attempts to do some of the drier and more conventional historical work to support this, albeit fused with some mythic intangibles, especially from a Southern perspective. These intangibles included the romantic belief in their supposedly superior morality and culture, which was increasingly hard to justify against prevailing contemporary (and historical) opinion and unavoidable material facts, as evidenced in the following statistic: "The North

had 110,000 manufacturing establishments, the South 18,000—
1,300,000 industrial workers, compared to 110,000—Massachusetts
alone producing over sixty percent more manufactured goods than
the whole Confederacy" (60).

Although doomed to fail militarily, morally, and even empirically
(in terms of the logic of his own text), Foote pursues the Southernist
line. The narrator claims "wars were seldom begun or even waged
according to statistics" and claims that "there were other advantages
not listed in the tables dribbling decimals down the pages. Principal
among these, in the southern mind at any rate, was the worth of the
individual soldier" (Foote 60, 61). A romantic belief in the worth
of individual soldiers will only carry you so far, and eventually, the
"dribbling decimals," a neat alliterative phrase so typical of Foote's
style here, would do the real damage, no matter how fervently a
flawed morality and ideals of regional self-worth were believed in.

This cold empirical materialism is anathema to Foote's
Southern sensibilities, and he counters it at numerous points in
the text with concrete examples of the mythic, romantic South
doing its best to preserve its identity. One such example comes via
P.G.T. Beauregard's reaction to Major General Benjamin Butler's
treatment of the women of New Orleans during his occupation of the
city. Foote counters the material realities of the North's "dribbling
decimals" with Beauregard's impassioned defense of Southern
femininity, which evokes a Walter Scott-inspired Romanticism so
beloved of traditional defenders of the region, even down to its
flowery rhetorical touches:

> "Men of the South! shall our mothers, our wives, our daughters and
> our sisters be thus outraged by the ruffianly soldiers of the North,
> to whom is given the right to treat, at their pleasure, the ladies of
> the South as common harlots? Arouse, friends, and drive back from
> our soil those infamous invaders of our homes and disturbers of our
> family ties!" (534)

From Sources to Story

The fusion of a diverse range of sources is characteristic of much
creative nonfiction. Its fluidity enables the creation of polyphonic

texts that include a range of voices and perspectives; however, this very quality can also provoke the ire of conventional practitioners of a discipline (as we have seen with the reaction of some historians to Foote's work). The opposite is true for Robert Phillips, who maintains "… it is the text itself that substantiates the impression of trustworthiness—the inclusion of resources of all kinds, diaries and, letters, official reports, reports from periodicals, and the written histories." (183)

Foote is especially effective in this regard with his use of letters and newspapers, which help to capture the tenor of the times. Two examples are of interest here, the first from the influential journalist Horace Greely, whose initial enthusiasm for the conflict was dampened so much that he "removed the banner 'Forward to Richmond!' from the masthead of his New York *Tribune*" (Foote 85). Foote pursues this by citing some correspondence between Greely and Lincoln, where the former admits to a succession of sleepless nights and notes that "on every brow [now] sits sullen, scorching, black despair," a turn of phrase that could have come from Foote himself (85). Foote uses similar resources to evoke the darkening mood of Southerners as well, and one such editorial from Georgia reveals the creeping discontent from some corners of the Confederacy with Davis' leadership; "President Davis does not enjoy the confidence of the Southern people…With a cold, icy, iron grasp, [he] has fettered our people, stilled their beating pulses of patriotism, cooled their fiery ardor, […]" (233).

Powerful and powerless, North and South, military and civilian, all are represented here in Foote's polyphonic account. Whilst he does come unstuck when attempting to legitimize the Southern cause, which contradicts his earlier claims to eschew thesis-led arguments, the overall effect of this first volume of the trilogy is indeed remarkable. Foote brings his refined novelistic techniques—especially his ability to vividly construct characters and use anecdotes to illuminate larger historical processes—to capture the unfolding drama of a conflict that has left an indelible mark on the nation's historical consciousness. The voices and views from marginalized figures and absented sources are the very "substance of history" (Phillips 198). They are history as lived and experienced, and above anything else, this is what Foote wanted to capture in his narrative, where telling is everything.

Note

1. The scale of the trilogy means I simply could not do it justice in an essay of this length. For that reason, this chapter will only deal with the first volume of the trilogy.

Works Cited

Carter, William C., ed. *Conversations with Shelby Foote.* Jackson: UP of Mississippi, 1989.

Foote, Shelby. *The Civil War: A Narrative, Vol. 1: Fort Sumter to Perryville.* London: Vintage, 1986.

Phillips, Robert L. Jr. *Shelby Foote: Novelist and Historian.* Jackson: UP of Mississippi, 1992.

Tolson, Jay, ed. *The Correspondence of Shelby Foote and Walker Percy.* New York: Norton, 1997.

Williams, Wirt. "Shelby Foote's *Civil War:* The Novelist as Humanistic Historian." *Mississippi Quarterly* 24.4 (Fall 1971): 429–436.

Medical Humanities and Illness Narratives_____

G. Thomas Couser

In Western literature, a tradition of personal essays about the human body can be traced back as far as Michel Montaigne ("On a Monster Child") and Sir Francis Bacon ("Of Deformity"). These examples predate the establishment of modern medicine and the medical profession. However, in their surprisingly non-prejudicial analysis of abnormal bodies, they not only manifest what we retrospectively think of as Renaissance humanism, but also anticipate the "medical paradigm," which explains ailments and impairments in physical, rather than metaphysical, terms. Thus, after Montaigne describes a child whose body has an undeveloped sibling protruding from its chest, he concludes, "Whatever happens against custom we say is against Nature, yet there is nothing whatsoever that is not in harmony with her" (808). His essay marks a paradigm shift from viewing such anomalies as revelations of divine purpose to regarding them as mere flukes, freaks of nature. Similarly, interpreting the body of a deformed courtier (probably modelled on a cousin), Bacon argues that such bodies are not *signs* of bad character; on the contrary, the derision directed at deformed people may shape their behavior toward extremes, for good *or* for ill. Essays like these made the human body available for open-minded examination in all its shapes and dimensions. Today, when matters once the province of science fiction—test-tube babies, sex-change surgery, cyborgs, for example—have become quite commonplace, the experience of the body provides rich material for creative nonfiction. The field of medical humanities is particularly important in an age when innovations in science and medicine have unprecedented potential to alter human life.

Broadly considered, the medical humanities includes popular accounts of biomedical topics by scientists, like Paul de Kruif (*Microbe Hunters*); by medical writers, like Berton Roueché (*The Medical Detectives*); and by journalists, like Rebecca Skloot

(*The Immortal Life of Henrietta Lacks*). And in the latter half of the twentieth-century, physicians like Lewis Thomas, Richard Selzer, Oliver Sacks, and Sherwin Nuland achieved prominence as writers of personal essays, literary case studies, and long-form science writing. A milepost in this trend was the bestowing of the National Book Award in 1974—in two categories, Sciences *and* Arts and Letters—to Thomas' *The Lives of a Cell*, a volume comprised of essays previously published in the *New England Journal of Medicine*. (In fact, Thomas was later honored by the creation of a prize in his name for science writing, awarded by the Rockefeller Foundation.) As these examples suggest, what distinguishes creative work in the medical humanities is the use of writerly skill and literary devices to render technical matters engaging and accessible to lay readers. For writers from medical or scientific fields, the challenge is to translate, minimize, or decode professional jargon, so as to demystify their often arcane topics. The key for all writers is to highlight the existential implications of biomedical issues.

One successful narrative innovation has been what I call the medical procedural: the biomedical equivalent of the police procedural, a popular mystery genre that tracks the police investigation of a crime, usually murder. Berton Roueché popularized this genre in medical detective stories, many of which were published in *The New Yorker* before being collected in book form. Roueché's narratives focused on mysterious maladies, usually nonfatal (some of which provided material for the popular television series, *House*, starring Hugh Laurie). Abbreviated examples of this genre are found in *The New York Times Sunday Magazine* series, "Think Like a Doctor," by Lisa Sanders, M.D. These third-person narratives begin with the onset of unusual or puzzling symptoms, then follow the testing of various hypotheses in pursuit of correct diagnosis and treatment. The human culprit of the police procedural is replaced by a microbe or pathogen; the police detective, by a physician or researcher. Readers are drawn in by the threat to the afflicted person; following the case to its always successful conclusion, they learn about some obscure illness or ailment. In such narratives, medical professionals play the role of the hero restoring order.

Medical researchers are characterized very differently in Skloot's *Henrietta Lacks*. The Lacks case has a strong hook in the unauthorized use of a black woman's cancer cells after her death: malignant cells from her body were kept alive indefinitely in labs and used repeatedly in medical experiments. Thus, a profession that could not keep Lacks alive as a patient bestowed an odd and somewhat perverse immortality on her as a cell bank. The book is not only an exposé of questionable practices in cancer research, but also a thoughtful account of ethical issues entailed in the use of human tissue. Also, the narrative appeals as the story of the righting of a wrong. But here, the writer, rather than a medical professional, functions as an advocate for the dead woman and her living descendants and as the agent of moral order.

A major aspect of the medical humanities involves the writing doctor. Many modern physicians have had creative lives beyond— and sometimes quite apart from—their clinical practices. Consider the achievements in fiction of Arthur Conan Doyle, Somerset Maugham, A. J. Cronin, Stanislaw Lem, Michael Crichton, Robin Cook, and Walker Percy; in poetry of William Carlos Williams; in drama of Anton Chekhov; and in comedy, theatre, and sculpture of the Renaissance man Jonathan Miller. But a number of physicians have used their clinical experience as material for creative nonfiction. One exemplar of this is the surgeon Richard Selzer—who, like Lewis Thomas, was honored with the creation of an eponymous prize for medical writing. In the 1970s, Selzer made his mark as the author of personal essays about his work as a surgeon: e.g., *Mortal Lessons: Notes on the Art of Surgery* (1976). Selzer used his gifts as a writer to convey the subjective experience of the physician: what is it like to cut open other human beings and handle their organs while they lie unconscious, their lives at risk? Such narratives offer the general reader (and past or future surgery patient) access to the experience of surgery from the doctor's point of view, which is otherwise unavailable.

Perhaps the best known doctor-writer is Oliver Sacks. A neurologist, Sacks has published more than a dozen books, most of them compilations of case studies (many of which appeared first in *The New Yorker*). Sacks' mode is to explore the implications of neurological anomalies—like Tourette syndrome, autism, or prosopagnosia (faceblindness)—that alter their subjects' lives in significant ways. This provides the hook: how does one function with such a condition—e.g., unable to recognize the faces of partners, friends, colleagues, and relatives? Sacks focuses on the existential consequences of the condition for the individual, rather than the neurology behind it. Over the course of his career, his case studies moved out of the clinic into the world; his narratives focused not on institutionalized patients, but on people's daily lives. Whereas clinical case studies are confined to tests, examinations, summaries of symptoms, and implications for research and treatment, Sacks' portraits move toward memoir insofar as they focus on the *experience* of his subjects, with whom he becomes well acquainted, at large in the world. Unlike Selzer's essays, Sacks' are patient-centered. And his rendering of their lives in multi-dimensional narratives appeals to general readers.

By nature, however, neurological conditions are not very amenable to treatment, much less cure; indeed, they may resist definitive diagnosis. So Sacks' cases differ from Roueché's medical procedurals; they are more exploratory and existential. They may lead not to diagnosis and narrative closure, but rather to a sense of wonder at the mysteries of the human mind. Sacks' deep theme is the plasticity of the brain and nervous system. Whereas the various faculties of the normal brain—its six senses, its multiple intelligences—are in balance, those of the abnormal brain may be drastically inconsistent in capability. Limitations in one realm may be balanced, or compensated, by excesses in another, as in the case of the autistic savant. So even while Sacks' subjects' conditions may not "resolve," his narratives often demonstrate that their brains have adapted in some creative way to certain limitations.

Sacks is quite adept at showing the potential value of "neurodiversity." What his work lacks, however, is a developed disability awareness. For all his interest in neurological plasticity, his work seems totally invested in the medical paradigm, which focuses on the body's variation from a norm, rather than the social paradigm, which addresses the lack of fit between anomalous bodies and restrictive or hostile features of their environment—architectural, attitudinal, legal, and so on. (In the standard illustration, the paraplegic's *impairment*—his paralysis—prevents him from walking, but his *disability*—his existential disadvantage—is a function of an environment devoid of ramps or elevators.) Sacks does not seem interested in norms as social constructs rather than facts of nature. Nor does he attend to the collective interests of people with disabilities as a class subject to exclusion, stigmatization, and oppression.

So while Sacks' work is more patient-oriented than Selzer's, it retains the hierarchy of the clinical encounter, in which the physician is the active observer and interpreter, while the subject is quite passive. A new development in the medical humanities is to present the physician-patient relationship in more egalitarian terms, as something of a partnership or collaboration. This is, at least, the promise of work like Danielle Ofri's *Medicine in Translation: Journeys with My Patients* and Lauren Slater's *Welcome to My Country*, in which the clinician-authors offer narratives of working with patients to make them well. This reflects a paradigm shift in medicine from an authoritarian and paternalistic model ("doctor knows best") to one that acknowledges patients' rights and autonomy, their agency in their own illness narratives. The therapeutic stance of "narrative medicine" is also representative of this new paradigm. According to Rita Charon, its primary expositor and advocate, narrative medicine elicits "accounts of self . . . that include emotional, familial, aspirational, creative aspects of the self" ("Listening"). With this medical ethos, a physician's relation to her patients moves closer to that of a psychotherapist. This should serve the patients' interests; that is the aim (and claim) of narrative medicine. But there is some danger in this stance as well: Dr. Charon herself has acknowledged that rather than empowering patients, narrative medicine may serve to amplify the power of clinicians because they know more than conventional physicians do about their patients' private lives, their hopes and fears ("Listening"). This puts them in a position to write case narratives that may seem intrusive or exploitative to their subjects (even if their identities are disguised, as medical ethics requires).

The areas surveyed above continue to be fertile ground for writers in the medical humanities. Most notable since the 1990s, however, has been the proliferation of first-person illness and disability narratives by writers who are not medical professionals. Witness the success of memoirs of mental illness (e.g., William Styron's *Darkness Visible*, Susannah Kaysen's *Girl, Interrupted*, Kay Redfield Jamison's *An Unquiet Mind*), facial disfigurement (Lucy Grealy's *Autobiography of a Face*), and countless memoirs of breast cancer, HIV/AIDS, and autism. Especially striking is the emergence of autobiographical narratives of conditions one might think would preclude memoir: e.g., locked-in syndrome (Jean-Dominique Bauby's *The Diving Bell and the Butterfly*), early Alzheimer's (Thomas DeBaggio's *Losing My Mind*), and even amnesia (David Stuart MacLean's *The Answer to the Riddle Is Me*).

In surveying this phenomenon in *Recovering Bodies: Illness, Disability, and Life Writing*, I coined a term to denominate such personal testimony, "autopathography," which seemed preferable to phrases like "first-person narrative of illness and disability." But I abandoned the term after being reminded that the "patho" root is not so suitable for impairment, as distinct from illness. This is an important distinction: disabilities are not the same as diseases, and people with impairments are not sick. Because such conditions are generally not correctable or curable, however, their narratives do not lend themselves to the happy ending considered desirable in memoir. This preference, "the tyranny of the comic plot," favors memoirs of illness over those of impairment—and narratives of acute illness over those of chronic illness. The result is an imbalance in the literary representation of illness and disability, the exclusion of those whose stories do not match the publishers' notion of the appealing memoir.

Overall, the proliferation of narratives of illness and impairment, which we can more neutrally refer to as "autosomatographies" (self-body-writing), involves two distinct, but related, phenomena. One is that a few conditions have generated many narratives; the other is that many other conditions have each generated a few. The most obvious examples of the first kind are HIV/AIDS (among communicable illnesses); breast cancer (among malignancies), depression (among mental illnesses), and autism and Aspergers (among neurological differences). Only in the case of HIV/AIDS was the upsurge of narratives a function of a sudden epidemic. But it takes more than a rise in incidence to create an upsurge in narratives. And the emergence of the HIV/AIDS narrative demonstrates the complex interplay between disease and cultural representation. For one thing, it demonstrates the difficulty of narrating a condition that cannot be cured. At the beginning of the epidemic, it was not possible to write of surviving AIDS, and the preference for narratives with a happy ending meant that AIDS narratives were slow to appear. In the early years of the epidemic, when the disease was always fatal, AIDS memoirs were composed not by those afflicted, but by their family members or partners—almost always posthumously. That changed as new drug regimens rendered the condition survivable. But the gradual emergence of a significant number of AIDS memoirs should also be seen against the cultural backdrop of homophobia (in the developed world, gay men were prominent early victims) and reaction against it. Thus, the rise of the HIV/AIDS narrative was as much a function of the gay rights movement as of a sudden deadly epidemic.

Herein is a key to a larger phenomenon. The proliferation of breast cancer narratives was not a function of the spread of that disease, but rather of cultural developments, most obviously women's liberation and patients' rights. Breast cancer is not the primary killer of women. (It is not even confined to women; a small number of men get it.) But cancer of the mammary gland raises issues not just of personal survival, but also of gender and identity; thus it is an apt prompt for memoir in a period of unprecedented opportunities and power for women. And as patients demanded and were granted more autonomy, women took more assertive roles not only in their own treatment options, but also in telling their own stories.

Agency and self-narration are also important with regard to the rise of autism memoirs. Mere decades ago, it was thought that autism and autobiography were inconsistent; autistics were thought totally incapable of self-narrative. As with HIV/AIDS, then, but for very different reasons, the first wave of autism narratives came from parents and caregivers. The situation has changed dramatically with the advent of narratives composed by autistics themselves. As with breast cancer narratives, then, the rapid rise in the incidence of autism memoirs is not a function of a surge in the frequency of the condition. Rather, greater awareness of autism and recognition of self-expressive capability in some autistics have supported the publication of first-person narratives. Indeed, these have become so common that they've been given their own name, "autiebiographies." This proliferation has coincided with, and helped to promote, an appreciation of neurodiversity, part of a trend toward acceptance and inclusion of anomalous bodies (and minds) in an age of disability rights.

Another condition generating large numbers of narratives at the turn of the twenty-first century is Alzheimer's disease. With the aging of the American population, the incidence of dementia *is* on the rise, and the care of people with dementia consumes more and more time, effort, and money. A few of these narratives, as observed above, are first-person accounts by individuals in the early stages, when the composition of a retrospective account is itself a benefit to the afflicted person. But because of the cognitive deficits inherent in Alzheimer's, most memoirs are written by caregivers, often after their subjects have died. However, although Alzheimer's is more common in women than in men (mostly because of their greater longevity), the preponderance of Alzheimer's memoirs features demented fathers; reflecting the gendering of caregiving in a patriarchal society, they are typically written by wives or daughters.

Complementing the conditions that have generated many narratives are the many conditions that have generated a few memoirs.

Since becoming interested in autosomatography in the 1990s, I have accumulated a long and growing list of these. Among them are—in alphabetical order—agoraphobia, amputation, amyotrophic lateral sclerosis (or Lou Gehrig's disease), anorexia, anxiety, aphasia, asthma, bipolar syndrome, bulimia, cerebral palsy, chronic fatigue syndrome, cystic fibrosis, deformity, diabetes, epilepsy, multiple sclerosis, Munchausen syndrome by proxy, obesity, obsessive-compulsive disorder, Parkinson's disease, schizophrenia, stroke, stuttering, Tourette's, and vitiligo. It would seem that, at least in the United States, illness narrative has become a kind of literary epidemic and that having a niche disorder, even an orphan disease (one affecting so few people that it attracts little research funding), can be an asset for a prospective memoirist.

Still, as in the memoir marketplace generally, there is a two-tiered system: in the competition for agents and publishers, somebodies do better than nobodies. And celebrities with diseases, like Michael J. Fox with Parkinson's, are catnip to publishers. Nevertheless, in recent decades, the literary marketplace has been surprisingly accessible to nobodies with odd or anomalous physical conditions, especially those who have MFAs and/or literary talent. Consider the success of Lucy Grealy's *Autobiography of a Face* and Lauren Slater's *Prozac Diary*. Indeed, one could argue that the rise of what I call the "some body memoir" (an account of living with an anomalous somatic condition, an illness or disability) was a significant aspect of the memoir boom around the turn of the twenty-first century.

A significant feature of autosomatographies is that they often challenge the authority of medical discourse and seek to destigmatize the conditions in question. So, for example, in *Girl, Interrupted,* rather than reconstruct her life leading up to her diagnosis of borderline personality syndrome—as she presumably was encouraged to do in therapy at McLean Hospital—Kaysen focuses almost exclusively on her sojourn in the institution. Moreover, she embeds and contextualizes excerpts from her medical records (her "chart") in her narrative in such a way as to undermine her diagnosis, eroding the authority of her physicians. Similarly, she co-opts standard scientific terms—viscosity, velocity, topography, and etiology—to characterize her experience in an unscientific (or mock scientific) mode, and she invents a technical-sounding term, "stigmatography," to characterize the prejudicial social response to mental illness. One short chapter ("Etiology") takes the form of a multiple-choice sentence completion quiz that begins: "This person is (pick one)." The possible answers span responses to mental illness from the moral ("a witch") through the clinical ("ill") to the sociological ("a victim of society's low tolerance for deviant behavior")—a capsule narrative of cultural constructions of insanity from the medieval to the modern. Thus, Kaysen invites her readers to understand her experience in other than clinical psychiatric terms. She writes back *against* medical discourse.

Recent illness and disability narratives have been counterdiscursive in another way: in their resistance to the cultural preference for the inspirational story—of triumph over physical affliction, whether through cure, recovery, or "overcoming." A preference for narratives with happy resolutions may seem common-sensical and harmless. But when enforced by agents, editors, and publishers, it threatens to eclipse stories of chronic illness and of impairment that can't be fixed. The result is that, overall, published accounts *mis*represent the general experience of illness and disability.

In the disability community, triumphal narratives are disparaged as "inspiration porn," their protagonists as "super-crips." The hostility to these stories has to do in part with their focusing on individuals (usually privileged to begin with) who achieve an unlikely goal, like climbing a mountain on prosthetic legs. While such accomplishments are undeniably impressive, it is usually the nondisabled who find them most inspiring. What seems inspirational to the nondisabled may seem oppressive to the disabled, indicting them for failure to be exceptional. In any case, the narrative of triumph distinguishes the super-crip from others with the disability in question—leaving the stigma in place. A related problem has to do with the distinction between the medical and the social paradigm: the narrative of overcoming foregrounds impairment (the deficit in the body, which is miraculously transcended by the super-crip), overlooking obstacles in the environment for the disabled population at large.

In contrast to—and reaction against—inspiration narratives, a generation of activists and academics has begun to tell stories that focus on the problems accruing from a culture that oppresses and marginalizes those with different bodies. Examples would be Simi Linton's *My Body Politic*, Harriet McBryde Johnson's *Too Late To Die Young*, and Harilyn Rousso's *Don't Call Me Inspirational*. And a new subgenre of disability memoir is the coming-out story, which narrates the process of accepting and embracing the identity of being disabled. This usually involves individuals with impairments, like low vision or hearing loss, which can be concealed in order to pass as nondisabled. But in some cases, it involves very visible impairments that may be denied rather than disguised. (The analogy with gay life writing should be clear.) In her memoir, *Sight Unseen*, Georgina Kleege announces, "Writing this book made me blind." By this, she does not mean that she lost her vision straining to write the book, but rather that the process of reconstructing her life brought her to a new self-consciousness as a blind person. In writing, she came to own blindness as a major aspect of her identity and life. Similarly, Stephen Kuusisto organizes his memoir *Planet of the Blind* around his adoption of visible signs of his blindness—first a white cane and ultimately a service dog.

The emergence of the disability narrative can be seen as manifesting a more general phenomenon in which memoir works to grant visibility and audibility to a hitherto marginalized or oppressed population. This can be seen in the slave narrative in the nineteenth-century United States, memoirs of Eastern European immigrants around the turn of the twentieth century, in the African American memoirs published during the civil rights movement, and so on.

Perhaps the aspect of the memoir boom that registered most visibly in the mass media was a spate of frauds that accompanied it. Most of these involved stories in which authors assumed the identity of members of oppressed groups. The most obvious of these targets is the dwindling population of Holocaust survivors, and the most notorious of the fraudulent Holocaust memoirs was Misha

Defonseca's *Surviving with Wolves*. Investigation revealed that the author (whose real name was Monique de Wael) wasn't Jewish and that she hadn't been a Holocaust survivor, much less been "rescued" by a wolf pack. Other cases of fraudulent memoirs involved faking ethnic or racial minority identity. Although there have been cases of impersonating cancer victims, for example, in on-line support groups (sometimes for financial gain, sometimes for less venal reasons), there have not been, to my knowledge, any published fraudulent memoirs of disability or illness.

But that does not mean that the narration of disability is without ethical dangers. One difference between groups marginalized on the basis of ethnicity, gender, sexual orientation, and race, on the one hand, and people with disabilities, on the other, is that disability can inhibit or preclude authorship in quite direct ways. As suggested earlier, some conditions are not as disabling in this regard, as they had been thought—autism being the prime example. But when unassisted first-person narration is impossible, collaboration is sometimes used to generate narrative. There is always a risk of exploitation or expropriation in these scenarios. It is possible that the "writer" will take too much liberty with the "subject's" experience. And there are hard questions to be asked about who has the right to tell the story of an individual too impaired to tell it single-handedly. In the past, parents have often assumed this right: care-giving and stewardship have been presumed to authorize authorship. In most cases, the motives are benign and the results are beneficial, a kind of public advocacy. But a condition that precludes authorship may compromise the ability to give informed consent. In many cases, the subject's minority status is also an obstacle to meaningful consent. And benign motives may not guarantee ethical practice. It is no favor to one's child to hold him up as the personification of a condition so terrible it should be prevented at all cost, as I argue Michael Dorris did with his son "Adam" and fetal-alcohol syndrome in *The Broken Cord* (*Vulnerable Subjects*, ch. 4)

Scenarios involving siblings are likely to be less problematic, especially if the disabled one is capable of understanding what is involved. That seems to be the case with Rachel Simon's *Riding the*

Bus with My Sister, a memoir of her cognitively disabled sister Beth, who spends most of her waking hours riding buses in her home town, chatting up the drivers and sometimes annoying other riders with her volubility. After a period of being somewhat distant, Rachel offered to ride with her sister regularly for a year. In the process, the two grew closer; Rachel came to appreciate the pleasure Beth took in what might seem to outsiders a monotonous and empty life— literally pointless, since she wasn't "going anywhere." The memoir offers a sympathetic glimpse into a life with its own gratification and meaning. (And Beth seems to have endorsed it.)

Disability is different from other minority statuses, also, in that it is the one into which everyone can fall as a result of injury or illness. And that makes it especially threatening to the nondisabled, who estimate the quality of life of disabled people as quite low. By contrast, people with disabilities report their quality of life nearly as high as nondisabled people. One explanation for this is that nondisabled people can only imagine the immediate and negative consequences of not being able to see, or hear, or walk. The value of first-person testimony is that it renders the life of the impaired person holistically, with an appreciation of what can still be performed. So perhaps the best way to understand these narratives is as "quality-of-life" writing that resists the devaluation of the lives of disabled people.

Contemporary biomedicine offers much in the way of promise for human ills and ailments, but the same science has potential for harm to the vulnerable. Because the decoding of the human genome will expose "harmful" genes before it supports prevention, treatment, or cure for genetic anomalies, it will place ever more of the human population in the category of the anomalous, at risk of illness and or disability. In various forms and genres, the role of the medical humanities is to render medicine accessible to the public and to advocate on behalf of humane care.

Works Cited

Bacon, Francis. "Of Deformity." *The Essayes or Counsels, Civill and Morall.* Ed. Michael Kiernan. Cambridge, MA: Harvard UP, 1985. 133–34.

Bauby, Jean-Dominque. *The Diving Bell and the Butterfly.* Trans. Jeremy Leggatt. New York: Knopf, 1997.

Charon, Rita. "Listening, Telling, Suffering, and Carrying On: Reflexive Practice or Health Imperialism?" MLA paper. 2011.

_____. *Narrative Medicine: Honoring the Stories of Illness.* New York: Oxford, 2008.

Couser, G. Thomas. *Recovering Bodies: Illness, Disability, and Life Writing.* Madison: U of Wisconsin P, 1997.

_____. *Signifying Bodies: Disability in Contemporary Life Writing.* Ann Arbor: U of Michigan P, 2004.

_____. *Vulnerable Subjects: Ethics and Life Writing.* Ithaca, NY: Cornell UP, 2004.

DeBaggio, Thomas. *Losing My Mind.* New York: Touchstone, 2003.

Defonseca, Misha. (Monique de Wael.) *Surviving with Wolves.* New York: Portrait, 2005.

De Kruif, Paul. *Microbe Hunters.* New York: Harcourt, Brace, 1926.

Dorris, Michael. *The Broken Cord.* New York: Harper and Row, 1989.

Grealy, Lucy. *Autobiography of a Face.* Boston: Houghton Mifflin, 1994.

Redfield Jamison, Kay. *An Unquiet Mind.* New York: Knopf, 1995.

Kaysen, Susanna. *Girl, Interrupted.* New York: Turtle Bay Books, 1993.

Kleege, Georgina. *Sight Unseen.* New Haven: Yale UP, 1999.

Kuusisto, Stephen. *Planet of the Blind.* New York: Dial, 1997.

Linton, Simi. *My Body Politic.* Ann Arbor: U of Michigan P, 2005.

MacLean, David Stuart. *The Answer to the Riddle Is Me: A Memoir of Amnesia.* Boston: Houghton Mifflin Harcourt, 2014.

McBryde Johnson, Harriet. *Too Late To Die Young: Nearly True Tales from a Life.* New York: Holt, 2005.

Montaigne, Michel de. "On a Monster Child." *The Essays of Michel de Montaigne.* Trans. & Ed. M. A. Screech. London: Allen Lane, 1991. 807–08.

Nuland, Sherwin. *How We Die: Reflections on Life's Final Chapter.* New York: Knopf, 1994.

Ofri, Danielle. *Medicine in Translation: Journeys with My Patients.* Boston: Beacon, 2010.

Roueché, Berton. *Annals of Medical Detection*. New York: Victor Gollanz, 1954.

Rousso, Harilyn. *Don't Call Me Inspirational: A Disabled Feminist Talks Back*. Philadelphia: Temple UP, 2005.

Sacks, Oliver. *An Anthropologist on Mars: Seven Paradoxical Tales*. New York: Knopf, 1995.

Sander, Lisa, M.D. "Think Like a Doctor." *New York Times Sunday Magazine*.

Selzer, Richard. *Mortal Lessons: Notes on the Art of Surgery*. New York: Simon & Schuster, 1976.

Simon, Rachel. *Riding the Bus with My Sister: A True Life Journey*. New York: Plume, 2003.

Skloot, Rebecca. *The Immortal Life of Henrietta Lacks*. New York: Crown, 2010.

Slater, Lauren. *Prozac Diary*. New York: Random House, 1998.

_____. *Welcome to My Country*. New York: Random House, 1998.

Styron, William. *Darkness Visible: A Memoir of Madness*. New York: Random, 1991.

Thomas, Lewis. *Lives of a Cell: Notes of a Biology Watcher*. New York: Viking, 1974.

The Grand Memoir: Temple Grandin and Autism

Katherine Lashley

As a graduate student working on my master's project on autism, I read several books by Temple Grandin: *Emergence* (1986), *Thinking in Pictures* (1995), and *Animals in Translation* (2005). Temple Grandin is the foremost advocate of autism awareness because of her personal experience and research. I read her to see how she wrote about her autism and if I could imitate her style in writing about my older sister, who also has autism. Grandin's organizational scheme of focusing on topics instead of strictly adhering to chronological order encouraged me to do the same in writing about my sister. Once I read Grandin and others, I was finally ready to address autism in my own life. The timing was right: the years 2007 to the present have seen a large influx of autism memoirs. Now that there are so many autistic writings, the scholarly and literary communities should support and accelerate autism's emergence into literary genres and criticism.

There is little critical material within literary studies and disability studies about Grandin and her writings on autism. This needs to change, as indicated by the amount of writing on autism and the several books that Grandin has published. Literary critics can use what can be termed an "autism criticism" that would focus on different thought processes, the use of language, the use of therapies, and the focus on ability. To illustrate autism criticism, Temple Grandin breaks through the stereotypes and concerns that critics often harbor concerning memoirs written by autistics, and she also breaks away from typical personal narrative in order to contribute to the positive views of autism culture. Through joining together personal narrative and technical writing about autism and animal psychology, she creates her own writing style that verifies her as an individual, an autistic person, and a writer.

The past thirty years have seen an increase in writings on autism, including memoirs written by those on the autism spectrum. G. Thomas Couser discusses the growing amount of autobiographies by autistics: "A dramatic example of the generation of autobiographical literature devoted to a particular condition is the advance of autobiographies by people with autism (sometimes referred to as 'autiebiographies'). Before 1985, these were virtually nonexistent; since 1985, nearly one hundred have been produced. (This number does not include the many narratives written by parents of autistic children)" (Couser, "Disability" 457). Couser provides these numbers in 2013, indicating the significant growth in memoirs written by autistics in recent years. Other memoirs by autistics come to mind, such as *Nobody Nowhere* (1992) by Donna Williams, *Born on a Blue Day* (2006) by Daniel Tammet, and *Look Me in the Eye: My Life with Asperger's* (2007) by John Elder Robison. While other autism memoirs should also be studied, this chapter will focus on Grandin's books in particular because of the new territory of life-narrative writing she has accomplished in her various books.

While Couser notices the higher publication numbers of autistic autobiographies, Joseph N. Straus also comments upon the body of literature: "Despite the necessity, in at least some cases, for 'some level of intervention,' the sheer number of autism memoirs now available, and the qualities they almost universally share, make it possible to treat them both as a coherent body of literature and as one that expresses a reliably authentic autistic world view" (470). Straus' term "body of literature" is appropriate for the growth of autistic memoirs, and Grandin's books are included, even to the extent of forming the base and structure of autism memoirs. Actually, a scholar would be considered remiss if he or she would not mention Grandin in an article, since her books and insights on autism are considered one of the foundations of autism literature.

Even Grandin admits that she enjoys reading the autism literature, noting how much she learns: "When I read autism literature I gain great insight from both personal accounts of people on the autism spectrum and neuroscience research" (*The Way I See It* 76). Throughout her later works, she mentions other autistics who have written memoirs. She also compares herself to them, illustrating for her readers that, among autistics, there are different thought processes: "I myself have been guilty of moving too fast for other autistic people. Daniel Tammet wrote that when he and I met, I quizzed him too quickly" (Grandin, *Autistic Brain* 85). By referencing other autistics and their writings, she verifies their life narratives, and she includes them in her autism culture, recognizing that she is not alone in her autism. The paradox of autism—a physiological disorder, which causes an autistic to be consumed within oneself—is growing into a culture, a body of people joining together their experiences and voices, and a body of literature that will inform the language-oriented and typical American society of the growing autism culture that is taking shape and demanding attention for equal treatment within school, the workplace, and society.

In the midst of this growing body of autism literature, some critics are concerned with the writing style itself, particularly the role of collaboration in producing these autism memoirs. Straus also mentions an important aspect of autistic writing that concerns several critics, and it is one that Couser addresses as well: the issue of collaboration. Couser writes: "If a disability is such that it requires collaboration in the production of an autobiography, questions arise as to the agency, authority, voice, and authenticity of the self-representation" ("Conflicting" 79). It is easy even with Grandin's writings to question the influence of collaboration on her books: what is and is not revealed, how certain parts are written, and how much influence the collaborator has on the book. Grandin had a coauthor for *Emergence*: Margaret M. Scariano. *The Autistic Brain,* coauthored with Richard Panek, provides more insights into the writing process. Grandin explains their combined writing style:

> I'm always saying to Richard, 'You're the structure guy'—meaning that his strength in organizing the concepts in the book compensates for my weakness in that area.... When he tells me that a particular concept we've been chewing over belongs in chapter 6, I say, 'Okay'.... The strengths I bring to the collaboration are strengths that belong to my kind of autistic brain—the quick associations, the long-term memory, the focus on details. (199)

When it comes to organization, Grandin is like other writers—many authors have trouble with organization. Nevertheless, readers know with confidence that her coauthor, Richard Panek, did not write the book for her; instead, he helped with structure and in gathering and organizing ideas.

Even in reading *Emergence*, when it is not entirely clear how much of it is Grandin and how much is by Scariano, readers can be put at ease when they read about the different experiences and thoughts Grandin had, especially those in her journal entries. Her journal entries throughout *Emergence* and even *Thinking in Pictures,* which does not have a coauthor, are vital in enforcing Grandin's writing style and capabilities. She recounts that for years in grade school and college she kept journals. Even her journal entries from when she was in high school read clearly; she adequately describes her feelings and she has a smooth, descriptive writing style: "The Crow's Nest is like a holy place. Being there, I appreciate the beauty of nature. When I look out the window of the Crow's Nest, I feel something more. I must conquer my fears and not let them block my way" (Grandin, *Emergence* 81). Occasionally, a few words or a phrase may seem awkward, or even poetic: "I have put all my fears anxieties about other people on the door" (Grandin, *Thinking in Pictures* 94). These journals reinforce her ability with language. In *Emergence*, she even provides for the reader her graduation speech from high school. Her long history of giving speeches at autism meetings and the several videos of her presentations reinforce her language abilities.

Related to the issue of collaboration and life writing is the self-report: the report an autistic can give to someone relaying how they feel or why they are acting the way they are. Grandin notes both the problems and the benefits of using more self-reports in working with the autistic person, whether it is a parent, a therapist, or a medical professional attempting to understand the autistic's behaviors. Ultimately, she favors the use and encouragement of self-reports, and her comments are worth quoting at length:

> Researchers routinely disparage self-reports, saying they're not open to scientific verification because they're subjective…. But the

person suffering from sensory overload is the only one who can tell us what it's really like....The problem in eliciting self-reports from this population is obvious. If a sensory problem totally disorganizes a person's way of thinking, then he'll have trouble describing the problem. If a person is nonverbal, then another means of expression, like typing or pointing, has to be used. In the most extreme cases, however, even that goal would be unrealistic. And unfortunately, wrist-supported writing produces unreliable information; the facilitator might be moving the hand without realizing it, as one would with the planchette on a Ouija board. (Grandin, *Autistic Brain* 76–7)

She insists that self-reports are the ideal; however, she also recognizes that there are items that hinder this: if an autistic is so severely autistic that he or she cannot communicate in any way, and the fact that even facilitated communication, such as wrist-supported writing, can produce errors.

Although Grandin does not analyze her own writings in relation to self-reports, Couser does mention the value in reading self-reports: "Yet one can see why autobiography is a particularly important form of life writing about disability: written from inside the experience in question, it involves self-representation by definition and thus offers the best-case scenario for revaluation of that condition" (Couser, "Disability" 458). When Grandin provides instances from her childhood of fighting, temper tantrums, being mesmerized, and seeking comfort, she explains why she did these things and what she was thinking. She takes her actions, which to some people appeared erratic and without cause, and she explains her thoughts and feelings, that her actions were rooted in actual causes. In her books, she provides large, thorough self-reports on her childhood, adolescent, teen, and adult years, explaining how she viewed the events around her and how she reacted.

Her self-reports, both with and without collaborators, reveal that an autistic person's explanation of experiences are vital to broader understanding of the perspectives of those with autism so that others may help and accept them. A good example of this includes instances of physical affection from Grandin's childhood:

she could not stand being touched or hugged, even by her mother. Her mother, of course, for a time believed that Grandin did not love her, yet Grandin, through her writings, explains that although she craved hugs, her body was sensitive to the pressure, and this caused her to pull away. Thus, because Grandin explains why she pulled away from physical affection, she reassures those around her that it was not a lack of love, but a sensory issue that, for a long time, she could not control.

In addition to the value of self-reports, some critics, such as Marla Carlson, take a more positive and accepting approach to autistics writing memoir: "The many autographical accounts written by individuals with high-functioning autism or Asperger syndrome convey a vivid sense of their cognitive styles and struggles to communicate" (205). Not only is there a growing body of literature written solely by autistics and Aspergians, but Grandin herself has written two books in particular (*Emergence* and *Thinking in Pictures*), which are very memoir-like, and several more books, which are a combination of memoir and technical information: *Animals in Translation* (2005), *The Way I See It* (2011), and *The Autistic Brain* (2013). She has not written about autism once and then left the subject alone. Instead, she writes about it repeatedly— autism experts would call this a perseveration; however, other scholars write numerous books on similar subjects and are dubbed experts. Therefore, Grandin, in writing and publishing several books about autism does what other scholars do: publish in one's fields of interest and expertise. Thus, her publications and speeches have made her an expert on autism.

In connection with Grandin's writing style is her use of language and her thoughts on language: that she thinks in pictures and that she is also stronger in written language than in spoken language. Kari Weil notes that "Grandin's work is compelling especially for the way she turns her linguistic disability into a special ability or gift. She claims, for instance, that her autism has given her special insight into the minds of nonhuman animals, cattle in particular" (88). Grandin certainly does discuss her language ability, which is connected with her thinking abilities. Because she thinks in pictures and not in language, she sees the world differently, and she is able to place herself within a cow's perspective and to see the cattle chute as the cow would see it. In the beginning of *Thinking in Pictures*, Grandin directly confronts the reader: "I think in pictures. Words are like a second language to me. I translate both spoken and written words into full-color movies, complete with sound, which run like a VCR tape in my head" (19). In order to convey to the reader what thinking in pictures means, she provides the previous explanation and even more details and examples throughout her text. She reiterates her pictorial way of thinking because she recognizes that there are many people who think primarily with language and words. While the books explain through language how Grandin thinks visually, the movie *Temple Grandin* (2010), about her life, visually shows her thought processes. When she thinks of a door, she sees every door she has ever seen; when she thinks of shoes, she sees every pair of shoes she has ever worn and even shoes she has seen advertised. The images flash quickly on the screen, one right after another. In her recent publications and presentations, Grandin has verified that the movie is accurate in depicting how she thinks because she worked with the director, Mick Jackson, who is also autistic and also thinks in pictures.

Another way she startles the reader into acknowledging her visual thinking is by stating bluntly: "When I invent things, I do not use language" (Grandin, *Thinking in Pictures* 27). Later in the same text, she describes how she manages to see like a cow by imagining herself in the cow's position, seeing and hearing as a cow would. "It is the ultimate virtual reality system, but I also draw on the emphatic feelings of gentleness and kindness I have developed so that my simulation is more than a robotic computer model" (143). She directly challenges the reader's assumptions about rational thought: she reiterates her ability to think in pictures without language. She emphasizes the fact that she does not use language, and one can assume that language would hinder her ability to create cattle chutes. The contradiction in her explanation of thinking in pictures comes through the fact that, in order for her to explain this to the reader, she must use written language, which is oftentimes also read aloud.

However, Grandin also explains that written language, surprisingly enough, is easier for her and other autistics to grasp than spoken language. In *Emergence*, she summarizes several research studies that she has read: "Another study reports that autistics often process written language better than spoken" (135). She supports this study and its claim by telling the reader about writing in her journals: "I could write my thoughts and often, while visiting the Crow's Nest [a small area where construction was being done in her school], I wrote my feelings in a diary" (85). By telling the reader that she often wrote her thoughts in her diary reinforces her strengths in writing and not in verbal communication.

A number of critics focus on the writing styles of autistics because their writings tend to be characterized with certain features, such as private meanings, repetition, and audience awareness. Indeed, Grandin certainly has her own writing style, which is characterized by straight-forward directness in her words and meanings and a reiteration of her main concerns within autism and animal awareness.

Narrative cohesion includes the writing style and the content that is included in the memoir. Straus states that there is little narrative cohesion in memoirs by autistics: "In these memoirs, and allowing for considerable individual variation, the features of autistic consciousness discussed above—local coherence, fixity of focus, and private meanings—strongly shape the style of the writing. They often lack narrative cohesion, preferring to string together brief episodes." (470). In a number of Grandin's books, she does this: her fixity of focus includes several topics: autism, her squeeze machines, and cattle psychology. When it comes to autism, she emphasizes the importance of physical sensitivities, using herself as a prime example, since she has experience with sensitivities. She shares that her skin cannot tolerate itchy fabrics, such as wool. She describes that certain, sudden loud sounds scared her and gave her headaches, such as the foghorn on a ferry boat or the sound of a balloon popping. In her later books, she expands on information about her sensitivities, explaining that, in 2013, autism researchers still do not study sensitivities, and they do not put much effort or attention into it. She persistently argues against this scientific inattention, even observing that severe, debilitating sensitivities keep some who are labeled as severely autistic from being able to communicate because they are so caught up in their discomfort. By her repetition of analysis and examples of sensitivities, one recognizes that this topic within autism is important to her and that she wants her audience to also recognize how vital it is for autistics who suffer from various sensitivities.

Although the squeeze machine is related to her autism, it deserves its own section because she writes so much about it—this is one of her fixed, repetitive interests. The squeeze machine is a long, narrow box that holds the body still. The person inside the box uses a lever or button (depending on how it is constructed) to inflate the plush sides of the inside of the box. When an autistic does this, he or she controls how much pressure is put on the body. Grandin created this because she craved the feeling of strong pressure encompassing her total body. This machine helped to calm her. She also wanted to be hugged, although she could not tolerate the physical act of hugging another person. Before constructing the squeeze machine, she hypothesized that experiencing the pressure in the machine would help her body to adjust and tolerate being hugged. And her hypothesis was correct. Her machine has helped her feel comforted and it has opened the way for her to experience more typical physical contact, such as being hugged by another person, or even shaking someone's hand. Although Grandin's insights into autism have immensely helped parents, teachers, autistics, and many in the autism community, her squeeze machine holds a special distinction because she has had her design patented. Other squeeze machines have been made and used with other therapies— the people conducting these experiments reported that, for the most part, it appears that the squeeze machine helps.

Another writing motif that Grandin uses that illustrates Straus' "private meanings" is the symbol of a door. She explains that for her, a door means a change—leaving one place and going to the next. Her symbol of the door became literal when she would find an actual door that would symbolize her experience of graduating high school and going to college, and then graduating college to go on to graduate school. Even Straus analyzes the importance of the door symbol, thus making the private symbol and meaning for Grandin an important one to study as a reader and as someone attempting to understand autism: "Much more commonly, we find a metaphors (sic) of doors ... and glass. Both involve an idea of separation—the autistic world and the normate world are distinct—but the boundary between them permits people on both sides to see through... and possibly move through as well" (Straus 471). When Grandin explains how she walks through the doors to make graduation real for herself and how she walks through the sliding glass door at the supermarket where the door is see-through, providing no privacy, yet still a barrier, she makes these transitions more realistic for herself. When she moves through these doors, she symbolizes and concretizes for herself and for others that she can move through the boundaries of autism and into the typical world, while still being autistic.

Due to several reasons—including private meanings and repetition—several scholars focus on the autistic's audience awareness in writing and telling stories. Jennifer L. Barnes and Simon Baron-Cohen state that autistics are not always aware of their audience when telling a story: "Because telling a story requires taking into account the informational needs of the audience, it has been suggested that individuals with ASC, who have difficulties appreciating others' thoughts, may also have difficulties grounding their stories in an understanding of what their audience needs to know" (1557). Although this may be true for some autistic autobiography writers, it is not true for Temple Grandin, as she is very aware of her various audiences. In her sections that are more memoir, she writes primarily for a general audience, yet it has indications of being written to help parents understand autism. When she clarifies her thought processes and feelings, her audiences include parents and scientists, particularly psychologists or therapists. There are times when she will directly speak to one audience, making it clear that certain information is for teachers or therapists. That Grandin is aware of her audience indicates that she knows that certain information will be more pertinent to others. In her 2011 book, *The Way I See It*, Grandin explains that, "I created things taking into consideration the thoughts and preferences of others in my environment. The end result was positive recognition for my work" (71). Although she refers to the various carpentry and cattle projects she worked on, this awareness of others' "thoughts and preferences" has spilled into her writing. She breaks from the stereotypes of autistic writers by being mindful of her audiences: she even changes her writing style. When she writes for scientists, she provides research, whereas when she writes to parents and teachers, she uses more personal experience and a less academic voice. Her tailoring information to specific audiences shows her awareness of them and a higher level of categorizing information for audiences. Thus, Grandin shows that autistics can be aware of audiences, which adds more support to the argument that some autistics can communicate effectively about their own experiences.

Although Grandin is aware of her various audiences, Couser notices a recurring trope among disability memoirs: the story of triumph over adversity, which not only reflects upon Grandin, but also involves the audience. Couser explains that,

> This paradigm nominates as the representative disabled person the Supercrip, who is by definition atypical. These may be 'true stories,' but they are not truly representative lives. This rhetoric tends to remove the stigma of disability from the author, leaving it in place for other individuals with the condition in question. ("Conflicting" 80)

Grandin is a supercrip within the autism community, and her books support this identification. She describes learning how to talk, yet those with severe ASD may never learn to talk. She recounts her school experiences, even up through graduate school, yet many people with ASD do not attend college, let alone graduate. She tells of the different jobs she has and how she learned from them, yet some people with ASD do not have jobs because they are not capable of work. A number of them who can work need a job coach—someone who is on the job with them, helping them to perform the job and interact with other people. Grandin also reinforces her savant skill, which has led her to many jobs, an international reputation in stockyards, and a PhD in animal psychology: visualizing, troubleshooting, and designing cattle chutes. She even asserts that most people with ASD are not like her: they do not have a savant skill, and they may not be as successful as she is.

Although she is a supercrip and is not representative of a typical autistic person, she provides hope for parents and those working with children, teens, and adults with ASD. She repeatedly reminds her audiences that "One thing many people do not realize about people on the autism spectrum is that they never stop growing and developing" (*The Way I See It* 75). Among several of the explanations and examples she provides of herself in becoming better at communicating, writing, and working, she also broadens the prospects of both improving with autism and recognizing that it will never leave the individual with ASD: "I also want to emphasize that as therapy helps a child improve, a diagnosis is sometimes changed, and in some cases, children can make such progress that they lose their label. However, autism or Asperger's syndrome is a lifelong condition arising from biomedical, brain-based origins; it never goes away" (*The Way I See It* 8). Here, she emphasizes that even though she is a supercrip, and she has improved so much with her autism, she still has autism and some of the difficulties it adds to her life, such as being sensitive to unpredictable, uncontrollable sounds and certain fabrics and having issues communicating with others when there are many distractions. She aptly notes that autism is a contradiction in improvements and lingering issues that causes some to remain severely autistic and others to have high-functioning autism.

In *Emergence*, Grandin includes a final exam essay she wrote in college that discusses her purpose in life: "My purpose for being on this planet is to build a device or develop a method that can be used to teach people how to look at themselves and to be gentle and caring" (112). Grandin has repeatedly accomplished her purpose through the creation of the squeeze machine and through her writings on thinking in pictures and the beneficial treatments of autism. Her memoirs instruct readers to acknowledge that not everyone thinks in the same way. Her writings also explain autistic behaviors, such as sensitivities, and she promotes autism culture by asserting that therapies are necessary, but that people should also accept and promote the abilities within an autistic person. By writing so much on autism, Grandin adapts the creative nonfiction genre to suit her needs in communicating autism to others. She reinforces the advances in autism that have been made, and she challenges us to be more accepting and to learn more about autism so that it can become a manageable ability with skills that will benefit everyone.

Works Cited

Barnes, Jennifer L. & Simon Baron-Cohen. "The Big Pictures: Storytelling Ability in Adults with Autism Spectrum Conditions." *J Autism Dev Discord* 42 (2012): 1557–65. Web. 10 May 2014.

Berube, Clair T. "Autism and the Artistic Imagination: The Link Between Visual Thinking and Intelligence." *TEACHING Exceptional Children Plus* 3.5 (2007). Web. 10 May 2014.

Carey, Jessica L. W. "'The Paradox of My Work': Making Sense of the Factory Farm with Temple Grandin." *CR: The New Centennial Review* 11.2 (2011): 169–192. Web. 11 May 2014.

Carlson, Marla. "Furry Cartography: Performing Species." *Theatre Journal* 63.2 (2011): 191–208. *ProjectMUSE.* Web. 10 May 2014.

Couser, G. Thomas. "Conflicting Paradigms: The Rhetorics of Disability Memoir." *Embodied Rhetorics: Disability in Language and Culture.* Eds. James C. Wilson & Cynthia Lewiecki-Wilson. Carbondale: Southern Illinois UP, 2001. 78–91.

_____. "Disability, Life Narrative, and Representation." *The Disability Studies Reader.* Ed. Lennard J. Davis. 4th ed. New York: Routledge, 2013.

_____. "Signifying Bodies Life Writing and Disability Studies." *Disability Studies: Enabling the Humanities.* Eds. Sharon L. Snyder, Brenda Jo Brueggemann, & Rosemarie Garland-Thomson. New York: MLA, 2002. 109–17.

Grandin, Temple. *Different...Not Less: Inspiring Stories of Achievement and Successful Employment from Adults with Autism, Asperger's, and ADHD.* Arlington, VA: Future Horizons, 2012.

_____. *Thinking in Pictures: And Other Reports from My Life with Autism*. New York: Doubleday, 1995.

_____. *The Way I See It: A Personal Look at Autism & Asperger's*. 2nd. ed. Arlington, VA: Future Horizons, 2011.

_____ & Catherine Johnson. *Animals in Translation: Using the Mysteries of Autism to Decode Animal Behavior*. New York: Harcourt, 2005.

_____ & Margaret M. Scariano. *Emergence: Labeled Autistic*. Novato, CA: Arena Press, 1986.

_____ & Richard Panek. *The Autistic Brain: Helping Different Kinds of Mind Succeed*. Boston: Mariner, 2013.

Straus, Joseph N. "Autism as Culture." *The Disability Studies Reader*. Ed. Lennard J. Davis. 4th ed. New York: Routledge, 2013. 460–84.

Temple Grandin. Dir. Mick Jackson. *HBO*, 2010. Film.

Weil, Kari. "Killing Them Softly: Animal Death, Linguistic Disability, and the Struggle for Ethics." *Configurations* 14.1 (2006): 87–96. Web. 10 May 2014.

Stories of the Self in Cinema: Autobiography and the Documentary Image_____

Shira Segal

How does one tell the story of one's self through cinema? In what ways does the cinematic apparatus lend itself to the representation of a subjective and complex self? What is the relationship between autobiography, images, and embodiment on-screen, not only for filmmakers and film subjects, but for film audiences as well? Given the rich and ongoing tradition of personal cinema in film history that includes a wide range of first person image-makers across experimental and documentary film, this chapter focuses on the dynamic between interior and exterior in two recent films that demonstrate a creative interplay between subjectivity and objectivity in cinema. Both *Stories We Tell* (Polley, 2012), and *Out-Takes from the Life of a Happy Man* (Mekas, 2012) actively grapple with internal, subjective experiences of being and memory alongside external, pro-filmic realities of the physical and photographable world. In content and form, these documentary films raise pertinent questions about the state of representation itself and the many uses of the image for personal and public explorations of the self.

To begin, the very term *documentary* in popular culture historically, but mistakenly, implies an assumption of undeniable truth assigned to the image. In its depiction of real people, places, and events rooted in a historical past, the documentary project is inextricably bound with the desire to provide what Jane M. Gaines and Michael Renov call "visible evidence" or "referentiality" of pro-filmic realities and truths (5). "As viewers," Bill Nichols points out, "we expect that what occurred in front of the camera has undergone little or no modification in order to be recorded" (*Representing* 27). The documentary or archival image functions primarily as an indexical signifier of the pro-filmic world, or what Roland Barthes describes as the "has been there" quality of the photographed object and its presumed honesty or authenticity regarding the physical world (76). Indeed, the first of the four fundamental tendencies of documentary film outlined by Michael Renov is to "record, reveal, or preserve" (25), and we rely on this function primarily.

And yet, all images—and cinematic images in particular, including those of documentary, amateur home movies, un/ official archives, news sources, or even surveillance footage— are ultimately mediations and interpretations of the real and of the filmmaker. Representation simply cannot equal or stand in for reality, as it remains one step removed from actual experience and presented through a nuanced point of view. Most overt in cinemas of persuasion, or what Nichols calls the expository mode of documentary filmmaking (*Introduction to* 167), propaganda's explicit aim to persuade audiences toward an ideological position illustrates this sentiment in its fullest. Even in films that aim to "analyze or interrogate" (documentary's third fundamental tendency [Renov 30]) or those that presumably and "simply" observe (such as *cinema vérité* within the observational mode) are undoubtedly structured by the privileged stance of the filmmaker, the authorial weight we assign those with access to the modes of production, and the reinforcement of a particular set of visual conventions deemed transparent and, hence, trustworthy. The fact that all images are ultimately constructed for us often gets overlooked. The truth is that all images are culturally and technologically situated and are received within a particular social/historical context that is also in itself in flux.

Beyond documentary's ability to record, persuade, or analyze, Renov arrives at the fourth fundamental tendency of documentary film: to express (32). This tendency is epitomized by experimental filmmaker Stan Brakhage, whose dictum to capture "the emotional truth and the spiritual truth" of perception and being ("60th Birthday" 145) illustrates lyrical filmmaking practices and a deep investment in cinema as a mode of personal expression. From Brakhage's hand-held camera-work and rhythmically clustered editing techniques to his hand-painted films that consist entirely of light and color moving in time, the film form itself becomes an externalizing medium for

---

filmmakers like Brakhage. "I could not get a camera inside my head," he tells fellow filmmaker Hollis Frampton, "so I painted on film to get as near an equivalent I could of things ... I have to search for equivalents that will give something of the quality of what I'm seeing" ("Stan and Jane" 186). Such visual poetics aptly constitute documentary's poetic mode of filmmaking that emphasizes "visual associations" as well as "tonal or rhythmic qualities" of the image (Nichols, *Introduction to* 31). Nichols further describes how this mode "stresses mood, tone, and affect" over information or persuasion because "We learn in this case by affect or feeling, by gaining a sense of what it feels like to see and experience the world in a particular, poetic way" (*Introduction to* 162). It is not merely what we see (content), but how we see it (form, structure, style) that creates meaning within this mode in particular.

The desire for cinema to externalize an otherwise subjective or interior experience occurs in both poetic and performative modes of documentary. In the former, visual poetics demonstrate John Grierson's early definition of documentary as "the creative treatment of actuality" (8) with an acute emphasis on the creative aspects of representation. In the latter, the cinematic apparatus allows the filmmaker to "perform" oneself for the camera and imagined audience, emphasizing what Nichols describes as "the emotional intensities of embodied experience and knowledge" and "the subjective qualities of experience and memory" for filmmaker and viewer (*Introduction to* 202–203). This highly personalized representation of the self, in which filmmaker becomes film subject (either directly on-screen or indirectly via voice-over narration), illustrates Stella Bruzzi's understanding of documentaries as "performative acts whose truth come into being only at the moment of filming" (7). The combination of auteur, apparatus, and anticipated audience provides this documentary mode's overarching faith in the image to reveal some aspect of "truth" about oneself or others, even as that very image is pointedly constructed and subjective. Such autobiographical reflexivity and apparatus/audience awareness sets the stage for fictional and nonfictional representations of the self by blending the interior, subjective experience of the world or oneself with the exterior physicality of the material and historical world. This dynamic is at the heart of creative nonfiction on screen.

I, therefore, turn to the creative nonfictions of Sarah Polley and Jonas Mekas as contemporary examples that actively grapple with these nuances within the documentary genre itself. Whether it is Polley's use of talking head interviews, home movie re-enactments, or the strategic evocation of the aesthetics of realism as dictated by the tenets of the observational mode, or be it Mekas' long-standing visual style of the shaky, hand-held camera in conjunction with his use of voice-over narrations as ongoing structuring devices across his lifetime of diary films, these filmmakers interrogate and use the cinematic image, simultaneously constructing and deconstructing it in the same breath. From the very titles of each film—*Stories We Tell* and *Out-Takes from the Life of a Happy Man*—these filmmakers point to the storied nature of representation, from the stories we construct for one another as well as ourselves to the outtakes that are worthy of re-examination. Whereas Polley frames the collective, cinematic telling of her family on film as an "interrogation process" (*Stories*) to point to the unreliability and intersections of "the stories we tell" about the past and each other, Mekas turns to sixty years worth of "outtakes" to demonstrate his conviction of the image's contained reality, even as he pointedly constructs it for us. These reflexive, yet strategic, uses of the cinematic image and its apparatus rely on a variety of documentary aesthetic traditions, while also creating new ways of seeing, experiencing, and telling stories.

While each filmmaker arrives at different conclusions regarding memory and the nature of representation, the insistence on a nuanced documentary image echoes alternative documentary philosophies that refuse preliminary claims of objectivity. For instance, Frederick Wiseman argues that documentaries are not and cannot be unbiased, that the possibility of objectivity gained through the cinematic image is, in fact, illusory: "Any documentary, mine or anyone else's, made in no matter what style, is arbitrary, biased, prejudiced, compressed and subjective" (4). Carolyn Anderson and Thomas W. Benson point out that Wiseman even calls documentaries "reality fictions" or "reality dreams" due to their rootedness in the auteur's imagination and the role of editing in creating meaning (41). Wiseman explains,

> your imagination is working in the way you see the thematic relationships between various disparate events being photographed, and cutting a documentary is like putting together a "reality dream," because the events in it are all true, except really they have no meaning except insofar as you impose a form on them and that form is imposed in large measure, of course, in the editing. (Graham 32)

For Wiseman, the imagination of the auteur gets asserted in the editing process, during which the filmmaker "imposes" his or her interpretations and intentions onto the material itself. In addition to the many choices made during production, including shot duration, subject matter, and visual style (Wiseman 4), editing as a structural device functions as an overarching framework for creating meaning. "[I]n that framework," Wiseman argues, "you can make a variety of movies, and it's the way you think through your relationship to the material that produces the final form of the film" (Graham 32). The film's formal elements and the filmmaker's mind together shape nonfictional material into a constructed fiction for both auteur and audience, "You are creating a fiction based on non-fiction material that these things are related to each other, but they may be related to each other only in your mind" (Halberstadt 22). Editing is, therefore, a key tool for externalization.

The subjectivity and mind of the filmmaker shapes nonfictional material into a type of fiction for the auteur and audience and can be seen in the final cuts by Polley and Mekas. If meaning is primarily created through the imposition of form and influence of an auteur's intentions onto the material, the interplay between film form and content for these filmmakers is revealing. Various formal choices (cinematography, camera-work, composition, editing, and sound) also involve issues of visual style, authoritative voice, and the relationship(s) between filmmakers and film subjects. Whether or not to shoot on film, invite the film subject to directly engage with the camera, rely on a polished aesthetic of pre-planned fictional or documentary cinema, utilize on-location or post-production sound, or unapologetically include one's own vision or narrative—each choice determines the extent to which a film fulfills an autobiographically poetic or performative function.

At the same time, both filmmakers evoke the reflexive mode of documentary filmmaking, in which the cinematic apparatus *is* or becomes the film subject, featuring the very medium that enables the process of image-making to occur (alongside the filmmaker's choices surrounding its use) within the image itself. "Instead of *seeing through* documentaries to the world beyond them," Nichols argues, "reflexive documentaries ask us to *see documentary* for what it is: a construct or representation" (*Introduction to* 194, emphasis original). The reflexive mode draws attention to the medium itself and the constructedness of the film's representation of reality, functioning as an internal commentary on the image, apparatus, and auteur, while simultaneously making an effort to include the audience in these aspects. In fact, Nichols describes "the process of negotiation between filmmaker and viewer" as a key focal point for this documentary mode (*Introduction to* 194). This type of interactive cinema intimately evokes audience awareness of the apparatus and the auteur's manipulation or use of that apparatus in the service of a (highly constructed) image that is both upheld and deconstructed simultaneously. The reflexive mode assists our understanding of the filmmakers of this chapter due to their multifaceted engagement with the cinematic image and their creative envisioning of new types of storytelling—visually and emotionally—for themselves and their audiences.

For Mekas, this combination of documentary modes comes through in *Out-Takes from the Life of a Happy Man* in the visual style of the film's aesthetics (found in the shaky hand-held camera; rhythmic in-camera editing, due to alternating short and shorter shot durations; and the inclusion of a wide range of intentional imperfections that mark an amateur or avant-garde aesthetic, such as over- and under-exposures, flash-frames, jump cuts, or creative superimpositions) as well as in the film's content and internal structuring devices. In terms of content, for instance, Mekas' film participants, including himself, often glance directly into the camera lens, hold their own cameras, or turn their own lenses back onto the filmmaker. Additionally, this film is structured by the recurring visual motif of the very process of editing the 16mm "outtakes" of his life. Such images assert particular authorial weight, as they are also accompanied by "real time" diegetic sound unlike the other shots of the film, whose sound consists of music, narration, or ambient nature sounds added in post-production. In fact, *Out-Takes* not only begins and ends with Mekas working with the footage at his editing table, but also gets punctuated throughout by the visual and aural revisiting of the 16mm rewind wheels spinning, film moving through the viewfinder, and Mekas' hands as they manually cut, glue, and splice various shots and strips of film. Furthermore, Mekas' intermittent voice-over narration internally structures the film's images by intermittently addressing the acts of filming, editing, viewing, and thinking about the cinematic image and what it means to him as the lonely filmmaker working late into the night.

Also evident in Polley's work, the reflexive documentary mode and its particular ability to highlight the intersections between image, apparatus, and auteur can be seen in one of the opening sequences of *Stories We Tell*, in which family members are pre-filmed as they get situated for the camera. This staging (of Polley's siblings in particular) strategically intercuts to an archival reel of Polley's now-deceased mother Diane similarly getting situated for a past musical performance. From the outset, the film acknowledges the staged aspects of talking-head interviews within the documentary genre and integrates past archival images to complete the family roster, despite Diane's twenty-year absence. Since this film is about origins and absence—not only surrounding Diane but also the secret she kept regarding Polley's true biological father—Polley's evocation of the reflexive mode offers a visual repairing of the family's collective loss as well as a self-aware filmic space for the reconstruction of memory and meaning through cinematic devices. Thus, *Stories We Tell* highlights the processes of image-making precisely because that unique interplay of the many different types of cinematic images– and the very fact of mediation itself—constitute Polley's visualization of this story on film. Formal interviews co-exist with home movies, which seamlessly intercut with re-enactments either from the nostalgic past or the not-so-distant past, which then also relate to multi-camera depictions of the present. The many cameras of the film participate in this story's telling and eventually become part of the story as well as its agency of vision, fantasy, memory, and suture.

The mediation of memory gets further perpetuated in *Stories We Tell* by the fact that we are misdirected into assuming that all of the home movie footage is authentically tied to the Polley family's visual history, whereas approximately half is eventually revealed to have been staged re-creations directed by Polley herself. Actors, costumes, make-up, and set design in combination with the amateur or home movie aesthetic have undeniably tricked us, calling into question the historical status of the image and the viewer's own relationship to representation. The image cannot be fully trusted, and yet through the cinematic image one can imagine the past and share that vision with others, even if that vision is, as Amelie Hastie points out, "necessarily a fantasy" that Polley "imagines and enacts in the course of her film" (60). Such imaginings occur on multiple levels: visually, aurally, and narratively. Visually, the hand-held Super 8 film camera and its grainy, rough visual style makes its appearance throughout the film, not only in the home movie images of the nostalgic past (real or retroactively fabricated), but also as an internal, additional gaze that functions as a contemporizing "home movie" of the documentary as it is being made. These images initially point to the documentary's staging and later remind us of Polley's editorial hand and the resulting underlying fictional quality of the re-created and imagined family archival image.

Not limited as a visual artifact of Polley's creative treatment of her family history, this film's story is heard and narratively situated by an auteur who frequently appears on-screen, but participates in the telling of this story quite differently than her siblings, father(s), and family friends. While she refuses to assert her authorial voice either through a monolithic voice-of-god narration or a formal interview process, Polley's voice is featured off-screen and always in relation to her film subjects. For instance, Polley remains heard, but not seen, in her opening questions to various family members, in which she asks them to tell the whole story from beginning to end in their own words, "as though you're telling a story to someone." This early strategy that points to the questions asked of her interviewees as well as their responses gets reiterated and transformed throughout the film—she goes on to ask her participants what they think of the documentary being made and the way in which it is being made, in which they are free to tell her candidly "I don't like it" (as her biological father Harry admits) or to ask her what *she* thinks the documentary is about. Other times, Polley's voice is featured as a voice-over narration that reads aloud past correspondences between herself and her father(s). In one such case, she reads an email addressed to Harry,

> One of the main focuses in the documentary are the discrepancies in the stories. All of us—you, me, dad, my siblings, my mother's friends, etc.—have similar stories with large and small details that vary. I'm interested in the way we tell stories about our lives, about the fact that the truth about the past is often ephemeral and difficult to pin down, and many of our stories, when we don't take proper time to do research about our pasts (which is almost always the case), end up with shifts and fictions in them, mostly unintended. (Polley, *Stories*)

The status of the film as a "documentary memoir," as Celia Lambert calls it (16), resides in the creative interplay between fact and fiction, objectivity and subjectivity, the individual and the collective. While based on real memories, events, and interpretations by family members and friends, Polley's vision is inclusively polyvocal even as it is at times admittedly fictionalized. The film's driving principles is, therefore, one of multiplicity, or what Leah Anderst calls "choral autobiography" that "makes visible a uniquely collaborative process" (n.p.). The film's collectivity manages to both uphold and undermine each individual perspective at once, providing a "medley" of narratives, to borrow a phrase from Polley's half-sister Susy, leaving Polley as the reluctant organizing principle of the film as both filmmaker and primary family member.

The differences in each person's story may, at times, be quite minute (the paternity test reads a 99.997 percent probability of a DNA match, whereas various storytellers claim 99.9997 percent or 99.97 percent), while, in other instances, it may be glaringly overt. For instance, Polley's half-brother Johnny accounts his mother's feelings surrounding her fifth pregnancy as something new and exciting ("She just loved new. New was what she was all about"), whereas a friend of Diane emphatically insists, "I don't think your mother was elated that she was pregnant. I do not think so. No, I do not think so. I do *not*. I do *not*." Whether it is Harry asserting that his love affair with Diane "was a pretty open thing because you need … witnesses which sort of confirm you" or others claiming it was not common knowledge, or Polley's half-brother Johnny asking the filmmaker what *she* remembers him saying because "I trust you more than I trust myself," *Stories We Tell* indeed points to the illusory nature of knowledge and what Polley's father Michael calls the "vagaries of truth" and the "unreliability of memory" (Polley, *Stories*).

However, rather than point to the unreliability of memory or the inability to "touch bottom," as argued by Polley's biological father Harry as a weakness in her approach, Polley seems less concerned about arriving at an absolute truth than evoking the spirit of her absent mother. In response to her half-brother's question regarding what she thinks the documentary is about, an off-screen Polley mentions memory and "the way we tell the stories of our lives. I think in many ways it's like trying to bring someone to life through people's stories of them." And yet she has her doubts, as illustrated in a letter to her father Michael, Polley wonders, "Have I totally lost my mind, trying to reconstruct the past from other people's words, trying to form her? Is this the tsunami she unleashed when she went, and all of us still flailing in her wake, trying to put her together in the wreckage, and her slipping away from us, over and over again, just as we begin to see her face?" (Polley, *Stories*). Given that this is undeniably a search for origins story, Diane's absence and inability to tell her side of the story forms the very reason these other stories—all of them—become necessary. The film creates a memory space in which to honor (albeit expose) Diane and, as such, fulfills an imaginary function rather than an indexical one. Home movies—fabricated, real, and contemporized—along with creative intercutting and the inclusion of multiple perspectives all point to the unreliability and imagination of the visual and the verbal, as well as the construction of each in the film. The constructedness of the image and the stories it contains allows Polley to insert her mother—both real and re-enacted—into everyone else's imaginings and on film.

Mekas, on the other hand, utilizes (and, in many ways, establishes within the postwar American avant-garde film community) an amateur home movie aesthetic not necessarily to point to the constructedness of the cinematic image, but rather to assert its legitimacy as an indexical signifier of the past. The reminiscent tone of his heavily accented and slow-paced narration offers a dreamy insistence on the legitimacy of the image, "This is all real what you see. Every image, every detail. Everything is *real*." He goes on,

> Memories are gone but the images are here, and they're *real*. What you see— every second of what you see here is *real*. Right there, in front of your eyes. What you see—it's real. There, in front of you. Yes, on that screen. It's all real… And it's there! And I'm happy that it's there, that I did it, that I managed to capture some of the beauty, some of the happiness, some of the beauty. That's all I care, all I care to catch—some of the beauty around. (Mekas, spoken emphasis original)

The film's overarching insistence on the reality of the image simultaneously foregrounds that image as mediated. Mekas champions what Maya Deren calls the art of the "controlled accident" (155), evidenced in his body of work that he continues to re-work well into his nineties as he "strives to make art out of fragments of everyday life," as noted by Jeffrey K. Ruoff, "through a collage of images and sounds" (8). And yet, in this particular film, Mekas evokes these images and their creative visual treatment on film in order to comment on the ontological conditions of being and representation. The goal throughout his life's work, including

Out-Takes, is to share a visual and emotional experience of the past through its depiction in the present.

Out-Takes from the Life of a Happy Man, therefore, functions as an invitation to witness and participate in a shared sense of wonder and connection to Mekas' life and world. Paul Bower concurs that "the filmmaker is attempting to find genuinely timeless moment from his life" and argues that "We never get the sense that he's trying to re-capture the past so much as find a present appreciation for what's been" (n.p.). For Manohla Dargis, "what's been" before the camera consists of light itself and its interplay amongst the subjects and objects of Mekas' everyday life,

> In tone, mood and image quality, it is suffused with light. At times, it is brightened by sunshine that poured through windows of the SoHo loft in which, once upon a Manhattan time, Mr. Mekas lived with his young family, several cats, a lot of plants, many more books and stacks and stacks of film cans and boxes. (Dargis n.p.)

Dargis goes on to describe how "The streaming sun turned hair into halos and illuminated faces and rooms. It also flowed through Mr. Mekas' camera, inscribing shadow images of these children, those plants, the dancing cats, that smiling woman, on the loops of film he has now returned to" (Dargis n.p.). Objects, light, autobiography, family, the city, the seasons, and an intense desire to share experience and vision shapes Mekas' creative treatment of the cinematic image as evidence of an indexical truth that is also emotionally infused. This comes through in his use of intertitles as well, "Who in this city of light and sadness is searching for salvation, truth, final answers? Is there anyone who doesn't sleep nights thinking about the meaning of the city, the night, the sadness, and oneself?" (Mekas). Both the visual and verbal poetics of *Out-Takes* illustrate the interplay between the internal and the external that is the mark of creative nonfiction in documentary and avant-garde cinema.

The desire for cinema to take on an externalizing function in the visualization process of an otherwise invisible or imagined state of being, emotion, or experience is at the heart of my understanding of first-person filmmakers like Polley and Mekas who manage to honestly depict themselves and their families on film. In combination with the performative aspects of an autobiographical self that gets asserted through the creative use of the cinematic apparatus, the visually-reflexive works by both filmmakers effectively point out the nuances within Ellen Maccarone's definition of documentary:

> a film that attempts to tell a true story as it happened, often from a particular perspective, that tries to elicit in us a feeling of what the real event or person was like, relying little on the obvious manipulation of images and sound in its recording yet at the same time displaying some degree of artistry. (196)

Here, Maccarone takes Grierson's early definition of documentary as "the creative treatment of actuality" (Grierson 8) a step further in order to point out elements of perspective, affective qualities of the image, and artistry amidst the underlying premise of documentary "truth." The question then becomes *how* to tell a "true" story and with what limits (if any) on the degree of any artistic assumptions embedded within the cinematic image. For documentary filmmakers like Werner Herzog, the premise of artistic license is instrumental to the realization of a "deeper strata of truth in cinema," or what he calls a "poetic, ecstatic truth" that can only be reached "through fabrication and imagination and stylization" (Herzog n.p.). To borrow from Eric Ames, Herzog (like Polley and Mekas, I argue) thus "blurs the distinction[s]" (Ames 5) not only between fact and fiction, but also between inside/outside and imagination/actuality in order to visually realize the full range of poetic possibilities on film for both auteur and anticipated audience. Across Maccarone, Grierson, and Herzog's understandings of the very definition of documentary, there exists a shared, recurring notion of the importance of both auteur and artistry via the cinematic apparatus in the representation of experience and relationships. Ames describes Herzog's use of the term *stylization* as "a term that encompasses the aesthetic effects of filmmaking, the translation of a director's perspective on the world, and his involvement with the film's subject as well" (Ames 5), and we can see echoes of this sentiment and use of the image in the autobiographical documentaries of Polley and Mekas as well.

Both *Stories We Tell* and *Out-Takes from the Life of a Happy Man* demonstrate the nuances of depicting a complex, autobiographical self in relation to each filmmaker's belief in the image to reveal a deeper truth about the internal and external conditions of existence and relationships. To do this, Polley relies on multiple cameras, staged interviews with family members, as well as authentic and recreated home movies in order to evoke the presence of her mother, while also uncovering the truth about her biological father. Mekas uses the hand-held camera, short shot duration, rhythmic in-camera editing, intertitles, voice-over narration, and music from his wedding in order to evoke the presence of a past that he insists is "real," very much alive, and evidentiary of life as it is experienced, recorded, and received in the present tense. On the one hand, Polley collects and deconstructs each family member's story, never "touching bottom" as Harry believes, ultimately pointing to the elusive nature of knowledge, experience, and image all at once. On the other hand, Mekas utterly insists on the legitimacy of the cinematic image, even as his use of a home movie visual style foregrounds his perspective and many interventions of reality through the acts of filming, editing, and creating a narrative arc for the viewer. Through form, content, visual style, and narration, each filmmaker interrogates the parameters of what constitutes *creative nonfiction* in cinema and manages to uphold, undermine, and ultimately insist upon the cinematic image as an instrument for exploring and representing the complex self and others on screen.

Works Cited

Ames, Eric. *Ferocious Reality: Documentary According to Werner Herzog*. Minneapolis: U of Minnesota P, 2012.

Anderson, Carolyn & Thomas W. Benson. *Documentary Dilemmas: Frederick Wiseman's Titicut Follies*. Carbondale: Southern Illinois UP, 1991.

Anderst, Leah. "Memory's Chorus: *Stories We Tell* and Sarah Polley's Theory of Autobiography." *Senses of Cinema* 69 (December 2013): n.p. Web. 01 June 2014.

Barthes, Roland. *Camera Lucida: Reflections on Photography*. Trans. Richard Howard. New York: Hill and Wang, 1981.

Bower, Paul. "Outtakes From the Life of a Happy Man." *TinyMixTapes. com*. Tiny Mix Tapes, 26 Apr. 2013. Web. 01 June 2014.

Brakhage, Stan. "Stan Brakhage: The 60th Birthday Interview" Interview with Suranjan Ganguly. 1994. *Experimental Cinema: The Film Reader*. Ed. Wheeler Winston Dixon & Gwendolyn Audrey Foster. New York: Routledge, 2002. 139–162.

_____. "Stan and Jane Brakhage (and Hollis Frampton) Talking" (Jan. 1973, *Artforum*). *Brakhage Scrapbook: Collected Writings 1964–1980*. Ed. Robert A. Haller. New York: Documentext, 1982. 169–189.

Bruzzi, Stella. *New Documentary: A Critical Introduction*. NY: Routledge, 2000.

Dargis, Manohla. "Luminous Time Capsule, Bobbing Alongside the Present." ny*times.com*. New York Times Company, 24 Apr. 2013. Web. 01 June 2014.

Deren, Maya. "Cinematography: The Creative Use of Reality." *Daedalus* 89.1 The Visual Arts Today (Winter 1960): 150–167.

Gaines, Jane M. & Michael Renov, eds. *Collecting Visible Evidence*. Minneapolis: U of Minnesota P, 1999.

Graham, John. "How Far Can You Go: A Conversation with Fred Wiseman." *Contempora* 1.2 (Oct./Nov. 1970): 30–33.

Grierson, John. "The Documentary Producer." *Cinema Quarterly* 2.1 (Autumn 1932): 6–10.

Halberstadt, Ira. "An Interview with Frederick Wiseman." *Filmmaker's Newsletter* 7.4 (1974): 19–25.

Hastie, Amelie. "The Vulnerable Spectator: Vagaries of Memory, Verities of Form." *Film Quarterly* 67.2 (Winter 2013): 59–61.

Herzog, Werner. "The Minnesota Declaration: Truth and Fact in Documentary Cinema." *WernerHerzog.com*. Werner Herzog, Walker Art Center. 30 Apr. 1999. Web. 01 June 2014.

Lambert, Celia. "Sweet Little Lies: Truth and Fiction in *Stories We Tell*." *Screen Education* 73 (Mar. 2014): 16–21. Web. 01 June 2014.

Maccarone, Ellen M. "Ethical Responsibilities to Subjects and Documentary Filmmaking." *Journal of Mass Media Ethics* 25 (2010): 192–206.

Mekas, Jonas. *Out-Takes from the Happy Life of a Man*. Anthology Film Archives, 2012. Film.

Nichols, Bill. *Introduction to Documentary.* 2nd ed. Bloomington: Indiana UP, 2010.

_____. *Representing Reality: Issues and Concepts in Documentary*. Bloomington: Indiana UP, 1991.

Polley, Sarah. *Stories We Tell.* National Film Board of Canada, 2012. Film.

Renov, Michael, ed. "Toward a Poetics of Documentary." *Theorizing Documentary*. New York: Routledge, 1993. 12–36.

Ruoff, Jeffrey K. "Home Movies of the Avant-Garde: Jonas Mekas and the New York Art World." *Cinema Journal* 30.3 (Spring 1991): 6–28.

Wiseman, Frederick. "Editing as a Four-Way Conversation." *Dox: Documentary Film Quarterly* 1 (Spring 1994): 4–6.

One Life Transformed: Natalie Goldberg's Writing, Art, and Religion_____

Beth Walker

As a Zen Buddhist who sees the interconnectedness of all things, Natalie Goldberg recycles personal stories to reinforce those connections between her teaching, her religion, and her creative work, both written and visual. Indeed, Goldberg writes repeatedly about the same real-life events across genres—as memoir (*Long Quiet Highway* and *The Great Failure*), poetry (*Top of My Lungs*), fiction (her novel *Banana Rose*), and anecdotal material for her many bestselling books about the writing process, beginning with *Writing Down the Bones*. While the parallels between Goldberg's artistic life and spiritual life suggest that they are one and the same, switching genres entails making critical choices about detail, structure, and theme—all while retaining fidelity to the facts of the real-life events. Regardless of the genre, Goldberg's books are built from short chapters and scenes that emphasize personal anecdotes and Zen teaching stories, called koans. Often, these koans feature a father figure, whether literal or spiritual. This overview of Goldberg's ten books uses the idea of switching genres as way of critiquing her artistry, not just her life. Comparing her artistic choices for similar subjects across multiple genres illuminates how Natalie Goldberg transforms one life into art.

Goldberg as Teacher

Writing Down the Bones, the book Goldberg is most acclaimed for, has sold more than a million copies since its appearance in 1986 and has been translated into fourteen languages (*Old Friend* 311), attesting to its accessibility as a "how-to-write" manual. Although Goldberg had few publishing credits when she decided to write this book about the writing process, she had valuable teaching experience leading hands-on workshops in which participants write and read their work aloud instead of listening to lectures or to success stories about getting

---

published. With *Writing Down the Bones* to promote these workshops, Goldberg has become a nationally-recognized teaching guru.

Goldberg jokes that *Bones* influenced an entire generation in the self-help decade of the 1990s to quit their jobs and embrace the freewriting process as a way of defining their lives: "Vice presidents of insurance agencies, factory workers in Nebraska, quarry diggers in Missouri, lawyers, doctors, housewives, all with secret, tender hearts yearning to step forward and speak, were sending me fan letters" (*The Great Failure* 79). Those fan letters indicate that *Bones* is more than a book about the writing process. In a scene in *Wild Mind*, her second book about writing, a writer-friend tells Goldberg that *Bones* "should be very successful. When you are done with it, you know the author better. That's all a reader really wants.... Even if it's a novel, they want to know the author" (*Wild Mind* xvi). In other words, even a book about the writing process is really about the writer *doing* writing. Her friend's comment suggests that readers want a personality behind the piece of paper more than "what happened next"; they want to read about people doing and saying things in places that they can see. Such is the challenge of the creative nonfiction writer: to put his or her personality on paper even when the writing is about something else.

Not a textbook of rules, *Bones* offers inspiration to "burn through to your first thoughts" (*Bones* 8) as well as short, easy-to-read advice about getting words onto paper. Indeed, what Goldberg says about the writing process is not complicated. Instead of repeating the well-worn advice to flesh out the details—in other words, to put some meat on those bones—she emphasizes the basics, the bones themselves. Most importantly, she advocates the "practice" of writing (*Bones* 11): write without stopping, crossing out, or correcting for timed intervals, usually ten minutes (*Bones* 8). Writing non-stop helps to cut through resistance to say what you want to say. Timed intervals also provide a natural structure—"the basic unit" (*Bones* 8)—resulting in vignettes, or short self-contained pieces of writing.

Goldberg's techniques work. As evidence, most of her books about the writing process are structured from those very vignettes she practices with her students. *Bones* and *Wild Mind* especially show their origins as compilations of fifty to sixty chapters of two to four pages apiece. In this way, the advice remains simple and to the point. The chapters can be read in any order, reinforcing her observation that "There is no logical A-to-B-to-C way to be a good writer" (*Bones* 3).

As a way to begin, Goldberg starts with the phrase "I remember" (*Bones* 20) or "I am thinking of" (*Wild Mind* 10). Two basic elements of creative nonfiction—memory and reflection—get pride of place with her emphasis upon the self (the "I" pronoun). Thus, instead of opening with a rule about writing, almost every chapter in *Bones* opens with an anecdote, a brief story used to illustrate a point. This story is almost always about Goldberg herself, and the point of the chapter, of course, is related to the writing process. Here is an example from the very beginning of the book: "I was a goody-two-shoes all through school. I wanted my teachers to like me. I learned commas, colons, semicolons. I wrote compositions with clear sentences that were dull and boring" (*Bones* 1). Right away, *Bones* signals that this will be no typical writing textbook: it will not be "dull and boring"; rather, it will be about how to avoid being dull and boring. To do so, Goldberg places herself in scenes—whether in cafés or camping on Taos Mountain—actually doing writing practice or teaching a class. The immediacy of these scenes reveals as much about herself as a writer and as a person as about the techniques she advocates.

This basic structure of *Bones*—the anecdotal vignette—proved to be so useful and engaging that it has become the genre Goldberg is most closely associated with. More striking, however, is that she has modeled this structure upon an even more ancient genre—the spiritual teachings of Zen masters called *koans*.

Goldberg as Zen Buddhist
Goldberg's writing life is an extension of her spiritual life as a practicing Zen Buddhist. The first of her two books about her mentor, Katagiri Roshi, is a spiritual memoir called *Long Quiet Highway.* Roshi taught Goldberg that writing was her true path, a form of Zen

unto itself: "'Make writing your practice,' Roshi had told me…. 'If you commit to it, writing will take you as deep as Zen'" (*Long Quiet Highway* 183). Later, she observes that she had started and failed to write *Bones* several times until Zen provided her the structure she craved (*Thunder and Lightning* 22).

Zen is about showing up and waking up. Specifically, Goldberg practices a Zen form of meditation called *zazen*, or sitting without thought for timed intervals (*Wild Mind* 216–17). By not second-guessing herself in timed vignettes, she applies that discipline of simply being in the moment to her own writing practice. Transplanted from Zen, practice and timed structure became the "bones" not only for her advice about writing, but also for her subjects. Her writing prompts, for example, are borrowed from Zen, especially in the use of opposites, such as "I know/don't know" and "I want/don't want" (*Wild Mind* 10). Indeed, the subjects of many of Goldberg's chapters are borrowed from well-known sayings and concepts from Zen Buddhism, such as "don't marry the fly" and "the ordinary and the extraordinary" (*Bones* 55, 74).

Specifically, Goldberg's anecdotes are based on *koans*, which are pithy stories about teachable moments with the ancient Zen masters. Part of her spiritual training, "Zen koans [are] short interchanges between teachers and students from eighth- and ninth-century China that cut through conditioned ways of seeing, enabling a person to experience one's true nature" (*The Great Failure* 8–9). Often making no literal sense and having no real answers, koans are designed to "wake up" the student and to encourage original thinking. One of Zen's most familiar koans, for example, is "What is the sound of one hand clapping?" The best koan from *Bones* is about a yogi who eats a car part by part, which illustrates a point about metaphor (34–35). Elsewhere, Roshi tells Goldberg another about a father and son fishing in a rowboat. At the moment the father falls overboard, the son experiences a great longing to enter a monastery, so he rows to shore (*Wild Mind* 175). Ironically, Goldberg's struggle to understand this koan parallels her own struggles to follow her true path, regardless of all other considerations—especially those of her two "fathers." In her later books, following the writing path often requires re-assessing her father's Jewish traditions and coming to terms with her Zen mentor's influence.

The koan is so important in Goldberg's work that she uses it to structure the major sections of her memoirs. The introduction to *Long Quiet Highway* contains a koan about a woman who wanted to enter a monastery (xi), which echoes Goldberg's own desire to study with Roshi, a character she does not introduce until a hundred pages into the memoir. Likewise, in *The Great Failure*, Goldberg tells the story of losing the interest of seven hundred people who had come to hear her lecture about the writing process: she told them a koan instead (9). Her failure to connect the point of this koan to a teachable moment drives the structure and theme of the memoir; she re-introduces the koan when she switches from describing her failure to communicate with her father in Part I to her failure to recognize the fallibilities of her beloved Zen master, whom (again) she does not introduce until halfway through the book. The koan is even set off in italics to stress its importance (*Great Failure* 155, 176).

As a structural and thematic device in her memoirs, the koan further demonstrates a concept that Goldberg teaches in her workshops called, simply, "The Third Thing." Sometimes, Goldberg explains, writers cannot approach the topic head on; sometimes it is best to first explore its opposite, what she calls the "essential conflict" (*True Secret* 133). Thus, to write about Roshi, she begins *The Great Failure* by writing about her father, just as she begins *Long Quiet Highway* by writing about other teachers. The third thing, the story of failing to explain a koan to her audience, bridges the two great subjects into one cohesive book-length narrative and gives *The Great Failure* its theme. In this way, the smaller self-contained structures of the koan and the anecdote continue within the larger framework of memoir, with its extended dialogue scenes and its emphasis upon conflict and cause and effect.

Goldberg as Creative Writer

Although memoir and the anecdotal vignette have provided her the most recognition, Goldberg turned to creative writing after publishing *Long Quiet Highway*: "I couldn't let go, and I couldn't go on," she says of the success of that book (*The Great Failure* 89). Upon learning, after its publication, that her beloved Zen master had affairs with his students, she set aside memoir to finish the poems that would become *Top of My Lungs* and to labor over a novel, *Banana Rose*, a thinly disguised account of her marriage and divorce. The greatest accomplishment of *Banana Rose* is that it provides an extended example of how not to write a novel. Goldberg frankly discusses the struggles with and ultimate failure of this book in her later work, especially in *Thunder and Lightning*, a book about structure and revision.

Ironically, the same techniques and real-life material that became the bones of her first memoir and her books about the writing process also appear in her novel; indeed, some real-life anecdotes get recycled as fictional scenes. The novel is so obviously autobiographical that the copyright page provides a disclaimer in the form of an "Author's Note": "Though there are certain similarities between Nell Schwartz's life and my own, and I've set this novel in familiar locations, *Banana Rose* remains a work of fiction. All of the characters are the product of my imagination, and their actions, motivations, thoughts, and conversations are solely my creation." In other words, casting real-life material into an extended fictional form effects a fundamental change in fidelity to fact.

In real life, Goldberg's mentorship with Roshi was evolving while her marriage was disintegrating. Yet Roshi does not appear in the novel, perhaps in as a way to shorten and more tightly focus the plot on the marriage relationship. Unfortunately, omitting this real-life fact eliminates two key elements of narrative—character motivation and conflict. As a result, the remaining anecdotal vignettes that govern the structure of *Bones* and *Wild Mind* read in the novel as a series of unrelated episodes instead of as a unified plot governed by cause and effect. In fact, her editor warned her that her novel's first draft had "no narrative drive" (*Thunder and Lightning* 54), which Goldberg later comes to understand as a reason to keep turning the page (55). Overlong at three-hundred-seventy-three pages and fifty-five chapters, only Goldberg's most interested fans would keep turning those pages.

Nevertheless, the same material that appears in *Banana* Rose also becomes poems for *Top of My Lungs*. It is likely that many of the poems were drafted well before the publication of the 1995 novel; in fact, Goldberg says that she turned to finishing *Bones* because she had a poetry manuscript that "no one wanted" (*Thunder and Lightning* 21). However, it was not until 2002 that she published that manuscript as *Top of My Lungs*.

Ironically, what does not work as scenes in the novel does indeed read better as poetic fragments, musings, metaphors, and epiphanies. For example, Goldberg's literal description of despair over being an outsider in her husband's world, the Midwest, turns into a metaphor in "I Tried to Marry America": "I tried to make a wedding band of wheat" (line 18). Her tried-and-true topic starter, "I want," begins the poem "Coming Together": "I want to do it in different rooms/ I want us to turn out all the lights" (lines 1–2), and she goes on to imagine elephants "making love under the African sky" and "whales rising/ out of the center of the Atlantic/ coming together on the surface of water" (lines 19–22). These images are more tasteful than the ones that describe lovemaking in *Banana Rose*: "When Gauguin poured himself into me, I pictured beaver swimming upstream" (288–89). Perhaps Banana Rose, as the narrator dubs herself, is not supposed to be a poet.

Fortunately, the narrator of *Top of My Lungs* is more sympathetic than Banana. Whereas Banana seems cold, removed, and silent in the scene in which a judge dissolves her marriage—"I was no longer human. I had become a robot, drained of emotion" (300)—the poem "November 30" reveals that the speaker is thinking of New Mexico, where she had fallen in love, as the judge is speaking. The speaker wants the judge to know: "I would have liked us to keep loving / to find some peace in the morning light ..." (lines 16–17) in New Mexico. In these poems, the marital relationship is described through metonyms, figures of speech in which something very closely associated with a thing or idea acts as its stand-in—hence the wedding band, wheat, and New Mexico landscape. Whereas Banana's motivation to return to New Mexico seems selfish at the expense of her marriage, the speaker of the poems longs to return to the earlier happiness of that marriage. Ultimately, Goldberg's stylistic tendencies toward figures of speech and toward descriptions of the landscape, as well as her emphasis upon the interior life of the first-person narrator rather than upon plot, lend themselves more naturally to the genre of poetry than fiction.

Goldberg as Painter

After the publication of *Long Quiet Highway* in 1993, not only did Goldberg switch to creative writing, she also publically acknowledged another facet of her artistic life, painting. *Banana Rose* is a type of novel known as a *künstlerroman*, a German word used to describe the development of an artist. One of its major conflicts is Banana's growing commitment to her painting at the expense of her personal relationships. Until this work of fiction allowed her to do so, Goldberg had not mentioned her paintings in her published work. But thereafter, many of the novel's scenes in which Banana Rose is working on a canvas are repeated in other books, especially in the book about painting, *Living Color*. Beautifully printed on glossy stock, Goldberg's paintings are featured in both *Top of My Lungs* and *Living Color*. These paintings are the visual equivalent of her anecdotal vignettes.

As with her writing style, Goldberg's painting style keeps to the basics. Her mantra is to work with "whatever's in front of you" (*Bones* 29). Following her own writing practice rule to "keep your hand moving" (*Bones* 8), she does not obsess over brush technique or correcting errors: "The rule I created: Let the original form have its own integrity" (*Living Color* 150). Thus, simple everyday objects, such as chairs and trucks, and favorite landscape scenes, such as those visible from the window of a café or hotel room, are rendered in bold, shaky outline, as if done for speed rather than for correctness; these are filled in with a child's palette of primary colors, particularly red and yellow, bordering between playful and gaudy. Her idiosyncrasy is her use of perspective: like a child's cartoony drawings, her work is slightly off-kilter. Floors, walls, and windows refuse to angle toward a vanishing point. Proportions are exaggerated, particularly in textile patterns on shirts, couches, and linoleums. The boldness of Cézanne, the color of Matisse, and the whimsy of Chagall are stronger influences than Zen restraint upon her style.

Instead, Goldberg's Zen training appears yet again as the koan, which informs both the process of her paintings as well as the structure of her book: "What I didn't realize at the time was [that] the process of me attempting to understand and respond to the koans was a similar process to what I was doing with the paintings.... Similarly, with painting...I had to go under, inside out, find my way beyond normal perception" (*Living Color* 150). At first appearing amateurish or even childish, those lop-sided chairs, crooked sidewalks, and gaudy patterns are the result of pushing past that layer of "normal perception" into "the bones of seeing," a phrase that becomes the subtitle to *Living Color*. As in her earlier books about the writing process, there is no chronology to follow; the anecdotal essays about art lessons, her visits to museums, and her conversations with other artists can be read in any order. The revised edition of *Living Color* even includes exercises for writing vignettes and rendering them into their visual equivalents.

Goldberg as Memoirist: Revisiting an Old Friend
After writing three books in the 1990s that explored fiction, poetry, and painting, in the new millennium, Goldberg returned to writing memoir with *The Great Failure* and with teaching memoir in *Old Friend from Far Away* and *The True Secret of Writing*, two books based on her workshops. Goldberg refers to memoir as "an old friend from far away." This phrase comes from Confucius: "To have an old friend visit/ from far away—/ what a delight!" (*Old Friend* xix). Her most obvious "old friend," Roshi, not only provided Goldberg with her greatest subject but also provided her with a way to write: "For me, the structure was Katagiri Roshi. I learned it all from him.... Structure had saved my life, given me a foundation ..." (*The Great Failure* 97). Unfortunately, that foundation upon which Goldberg had built several books "was cracking" (97).

The cracks appeared not so much in the structure of Goldberg's work as in her faith in her content. Whereas before she had focused on metaphorical truths found in koans, she now focused on telling the literal truth of her personal life. *The Great Failure* is about not realizing the truth and, consequently, not telling the whole truth about Roshi, a man whom she had revered in *Long Quiet Highway* as her guru, but who secretly had been having affairs with his students. *Long Quiet Highway* is only a part of the truth—not a lie, but not complete.

The Great Failure faced hostile reviews upon airing Roshi's dirty laundry, yet its chapters are prefaced with quotations that reveal the book's purpose is to understand, not to malign. One of these quotes is from Roshi himself: "Don't worry if you write the truth. It doesn't hurt people, it helps them" (*Great Failure* 5). Herein lies the memoirist's dilemma: how to retain fidelity to the facts without embarrassing loved-ones. Goldberg explains that she had "to be faithful to the legacy he gave me: to write honestly," even if it "causes trouble" (*The Great Failure* 123). More than merely writing down the facts themselves, more than simply reporting the way it really happened, writing the truth is a process.

Ultimately, this is why Goldberg re-uses material. A life worth examining is worth returning to again and again. The same moment can have multiple meanings, both metaphorical and literal, in different contexts. In *The Great Failure*, for instance, a memoir of her two fathers, she re-cycles a scene from *Living Color* in which she and her parents visit an art museum. The two scenes are so similar that she repeats her father's jokes and even observes that she "was in the process of writing a book about painting" (*The Great Failure* 52). Her father's failure to appreciate art, an important part of Goldberg's life, acts as a synecdoche for the failure of his relationship with his daughter in general. (A synecdoche is a figure of speech in which a part represents the whole.) The scene works because failure is the theme of the memoir: ironically, the Goldbergs are visiting the museum as a way of changing the subject, for Goldberg has been trying to get her father to open up about her childhood for the first fifty pages of the book. However, the point of this same scene in *Living Color* is not to reflect upon the failure of a personal relationship but simply to explain how to appreciate that "This is art?" (142); thus, Goldberg omits the personal tension that builds up to the visit. Here, the omission is not a lie; it simply serves a different purpose. Overall, Goldberg's various retellings reinforce the idea that there is a difference between reporting or repeating facts and discovering the truth, between telling the truth of what really happened and recalling memories of those same events, and between trusting the author's memory and making the story believable for its readers.

So often, beginning writers are encouraged to write what they know. When the story then sounds unbelievable or boring, they try to explain, "But that's the way it really happened." In creative nonfiction, however, what really happened—the nonfiction part—is not as important as the selection and arrangement of details—the creative part. Then, too, plot and characterization—the two primary elements of fiction—are often secondary to the memoirist's persona. As Goldberg's work demonstrates, the art of the novel can be a challenge for the creative nonfiction writer, for memory owes no fidelity to fact, and facts do not necessarily lend themselves logically to cause and effect. Through the short, self-contained structures of the anecdotal vignette and the koan, however, Goldberg bridges memoir, teaching, and her creative work, so that her published works do not sound repetitious. Instead of writing the same book over and over again, Goldberg writes what she knows, what really happened, one teachable moment at a time.

The American writer, teacher, and Zen Buddhist monk Natalie Goldberg provides an opportunity to explore how one life becomes transformed—not once or twice, but multiple times—into art. In her near-thirty-year publishing career, she has repeatedly transplanted "real-life" details into various genres—not only in the memoirs *Long Quiet Highway* and *The Great Failure*, but also into the poetry collection *Top of My Lungs*, the autobiographical novel *Banana Rose*, and anecdotal material for her popular books about the writing process and creativity, beginning in 1986 with her bestselling *Writing Down the Bones* and most recently continuing in 2013 with *The True Secret of Writing: Connecting Life with Language* and *Living Color: Painting, Writing, and the Bones of Seeing*. Although she tells the same stories over and over again, her selection and arrangement of those real-life details demonstrate that genre itself not only provides structure, but, more importantly, it determines the reason for the telling, or the author's purpose. The remark made by Goldberg's friend that all the reader wants is to get to know the writer a little better suggests that the best writing has, as its foundation, details from the writer's life, but genre provides the structure, or "bones," for that life.

Works Cited

Goldberg, Natalie. *Banana Rose.* 1995. New York: Bantam, 1996.

_____. *The Great Failure: A Bartender, a Monk, and My Unlikely Path to Truth.* New York: Harper San Francisco, 2004.

_____. *Living Color: Painting, Writing, and the Bones of Seeing.* New York: STC Craft, 2014.

_____. *Long Quiet Highway: Waking Up in America.* 1993. New York: Bantam, 1994.

_____. *Old Friend from Far Away: The Practice of Writing Memoir.* New York: Free P, 2007.

_____. *Thunder and Lightning: Cracking Open the Writer's Craft.* New York: Bantam, 2000.

_____. *Top of My Lungs.* Woodstock: Overlook P, 2002.

_____. *The True Secret of Writing: Connecting Life with Language.* New York: Atria, 2013. Kindle.

_____. *Wild Mind: Living the Writer's Life.* New York: Bantam, 1990.

_____. *Writing Down the Bones: Freeing the Writer Within.* Boston: Shambhala, 1986.

David Foster Wallace and the Ethical Potential of Creative Nonfiction_____

Brandon Benevento

". . . the common denominator of all we see is always, transparently, shamelessly the implacable 'I'"

(Joan Didion)

Like many authors, David Foster Wallace managed to raise some questions about the veracity of his work. Personally, I'm quite comfortable with writers altering and exaggerating in pieces labeled "nonfiction."[1] The central ethical issue of creative nonfiction—the question of 'true' representation of others—remains important, but far more so as a question than a set of answers about what really happened. By displaying the question, Wallace's work reveals what I call the ethical potential of the genre.

Portrayal of other people by individual writers contains instructive value—demonstrating a situation we all face, whether we write or not. The question, 'Am I *really* seeing or seeing what I want to see?' should arise from our activities in a busy world where judgments flow from every gaze. Our interactions thus create an ethical moment at which we must, as Wallace puts it, "*choose* what [we] pay attention to and . . . *choose* how [we] construct meaning from experience" (*Water* 54, original emphasis). The moment we reflect on and re-present something (or someone) is the ethical moment; by displaying it, creative nonfiction models the tools necessary for mitigating self-enclosure.

In *This Is Water*, Wallace's most directly moralizing work, he describes the human "default setting," as the "deep belief that I am the absolute center of the universe, the realest, most vivid and important person in existence" (38, 36). Put in general and somewhat hyperbolic terms, this "default setting" recalls Didion's implacable 'I,' and indicates what Lynn Bloom calls the creative nonfiction writer's "single ethical standard, to render faithfully... '*how it felt to be me*'" (278, original emphasis). I like Didion and don't believe she really wrote this way because, as both readers and writers know, works focusing on "how it felt to be me" are boring. The successful story investigates how it feels to be us.

Self, of course, remains fundamental. Creative nonfiction rests upon layered representation of selves: a narrative voice speaks, presenting the story of a characterized self moving around in real places full of real people. Highlighting self-reflection, creative nonfiction weds individuality to human interconnection—indeed, at its best, it uses the former to display the latter. The genre can thus clarify something often imbedded in literature: "the horror of being isolated in a personality" as Brian Philips puts it (676). This he labels Wallace's moral project; while Philips focuses on his fiction, I argue his nonfiction, and creative nonfiction itself, can display the individual's role in witnessing and generating the connectivity of human beings. Wallace describes individualism as "the freedom to all be lords of our tiny skull-sized kingdoms, alone at the center of all creation" (*Water* 117). To write from this lonely location demands the best qualities: judgments based on attention, an attempt to see other's perspectives: the use of the self to get past the self.[2]

Rich in implacable 'I' subjectivity, Wallace's nonfiction carries strong opinions and harsh judgments. Describing actor Balthazar Getty in "David Lynch Keeps His Head," Wallace writes:

> [I]t's almost impossible for me to separate predictions about how good Balthazar Getty's going to be in *Lost Highway* from my impressions of him as a human being around the set, which latter impressions were so uniformly negative that it's probably better not to say too much about it. For just one thing, he'd annoy the hell out of everybody between takes by running around trying to borrow everybody's cellular phone for an "emergency." I'll confess that I eavesdropped on some of his emergency cellular phone conversations, and in one of them he said to somebody "But what did she say about *me?*" three times in a row. For another thing.... (175)

On one hand, Wallace demonstrates the ethical handwringing of the writer: the attempt "to be frank" meeting the need to "not say too much about it." But, as readers expect, he does judge—he does say "it"—and says quite a lot. He criticizes Getty for solipsism—a disingenuous use of other people to reinforce self-centeredness. Though Wallace draws attention to the pull of his own "impressions," noting that he, too, can't get past himself, the passage shows these impressions stem from judgments about Getty's relation to others. Most importantly, Wallace situates himself as an observer. Although eavesdropping on conversations may lack a certain ethical high-ground, doing so adds the necessary ingredient to the profile's judgments: attention.[3] Wallace attends to his subject and focuses on that subject's attention to others.

Another subject of Wallace's scorn, John Updike's *Toward the End of Time*, reviewed in 1998, similarly invokes charges of solipsism. Of the main character, Wallace writes, "he persists in the bizarre, adolescent belief that getting to have sex with whomever one wants whenever one wants to is a cure for human despair" ("Certainly" 59). His criticism extends beyond the character: the "author, so far as I can figure out, believes it too" (59). Before delivering his judgment, Wallace explains the appeal of Updike's position, writing that "for the young educated adults of the sixties and seventies, for whom the ultimate horror was the hypocritical conformity and repression of their own parents' generation, Updike's evection of the libidinous self appeared refreshing and even heroic" ("Certainly" 54). Attempting to understand the origins of such solipsism, he locates his criticism of Updike in a larger cultural problem: the deterioration of "this brave new individualism and sexual freedom . . . into the joyless and anomic self-indulgence of the Me Generation" (54). Here, as with Getty, Wallace indicates his own "figuring out" as the location from which the judgment comes. Open about his lack of objectivity, he sets harsh judgment about Updike's generation against a sympathetic attempt to understand it.

Combining sympathy and judgment, Wallace's basic method attends to others in a way neither one-sided nor impossibly objective.

For example, in the well-known "A Supposedly Fun Thing I'll Never Do Again"—about a luxury Caribbean cruise—he writes:

> In response to some dogged journalistic querying, Celebrity [Cruises]'s PR firm's press liaison (the charming Debra Winger-voiced Ms. Wiessen) had this explanation for the cheery service: "The people on board—the staff—are really part of one big family. . . . [t]hey really love what they're doing and love serving people, and they pay attention to what everybody wants and needs"
>
> This is not what I myself observed. What I myself observed was that the *Nadir* was one very tight ship, run by a cadre of very hard-ass Greek officers and supervisors. (266)

Here, two sides of the creative nonfiction coin—the prominent I-voice and the observant "journalistic querying"—each work to show something hidden to readers. Not removing his subjectivity, Wallace employs it to create trustworthiness, and sarcastic humor, and to provide a context for his observations. Notably, he targets mass-consumerism, which frequently pushes us to view others as surfaces—cheery ones, in this case. Suspicious of the official line, Wallace shows a hierarchy motivating workers. And while the word "charming" may indicate the sirens' call aspect of such service-loving dogma, Wallace manages to humanize a spokesperson for dehumanizing mass-consumption.

As he writes in *This Is Water*, by extending individuality to others when making judgments, we "can choose to look differently at this fat, dead-eyed, over-made-up lady who just screamed at her kid in the checkout line—maybe she's not usually like this..." (89). This approach uses individual perspective to offer 'strangers' the justifications and explanations we automatically give ourselves—an inclusive gesture, which allows broader perception to come *through* subjectivity, with "through" meaning both "beyond" and "by way of." Fundamental to creative nonfiction, such use of perspective is the very thing writers point to when claiming reinterpretive rights. Wallace's nonfiction draws attention to the self-directedness of this process. He writes, "the only thing that's capital-T True is that you get to *decide* how you're going to try to see it"—"it" meaning a site of mass-consumption like a cruise or a traffic jam, and the people there encountered (Wallace, *Water* 94, original emphasis). Of course, Wallace writes not about generating nonfiction, but about constructing understanding in general. As such, the writing models broader ethical activity.

If the self is (to cite an unlikely source) "the decider," seeing oneself thus precedes understanding/representing others. Following the "creative" conventions of the genre, Wallace never fails to locate himself in his work. Using the example of traffic, he suggests people can break from the self-centered position that rages, "who the fuck are all these people in my way?" by simply (though not easily) switching the perspective: perhaps "it is actually *I* who am in *his* way" (Wallace, *Water* 77, 85, original emphasis). This maintains attention on the self, but in a way that comes through consideration of others. Paul John Eakins writes that "because we live our lives in relation to others, our privacies are largely shared, making it hard to demarcate the boundary where one life leaves off and another begins" (8). On one hand, this raises the ethical problems of writing about others: following one's authentic vision bumps against representing people justly, and different truths overlap. But this overlap generates the very context of "ethics"—a context well-emblemized by a traffic jam. Like the car itself, privacy becomes inescapable, yet—since traffic is basically a herd—completely illusory. Violations of gaze and personal space proliferate; the demands of the self loom. "Shared" privacy indeed gives rise to boundary problems—the actions (even the very presence) of others often registers superficially—i.e., I am quick to find a bunch of assholes in my way. But, alone on an empty freeway, one would not need ethics. Wallace points out that "the traffic jams and crowded aisles and long checkout lines give me time to think" (*Water* 77). Public space provides opportunity—the potential to see our similarities to others.

Attention to Work as a Method of Ethical Nonfiction

We inhabit a landscape of hidden labor, in which we constantly encounter consumable surfaces—food packages, television shows, smart phones, suburbs: all, like the cruise-ship, hide their human origins. Writing about the "ethics of maintenance and repair," Matthew Crawford notes this "creeping concealedness" and suggests it generates "an affable complaisance," which reconfirms self-centeredness and reinscribes long-term capitalist trends (6, 2, 9). Because the products from which we build our lives entail construction (and maintenance, delivery, decoration, etc.) by people, attention to constructedness reveals interdependence and allows the lives of others to register as not-Other, or at least as less so. And since "work" denotes locations and activities involving human interaction, investigating the large systems and small commodities that surround us, looking at how things are made and the people who make them, offers greater connective potential than aiming to explain "how it felt to be me."

From the sewage system on the *Nadir* to the making of *Lost Highway* to John McCain's own construction via cameraman and campaigner-organizer in the 2000 election primary, Wallace often focuses on work and workers. In "The View From Mrs. Thomson's," Wallace deconstructs the September 12, 2001 newspaper, noting "a half-page photo of a student . . . saying a rosary in response to the Horror, which means that some staff photographer came in and popped a flash in the face of a traumatized kid at prayer" (132). By reflecting on the work that made the picture, Wallace's sardonic and disgusted self operates as a vehicle to display what transpires beneath the surface.

The attention on constructedness bespeaks the ethics of agency over that of self-reliance. While the latter denotes individual separation from the crowd, the former retains the importance of individuality, but not in a vacuum. Crawford explains that "the idea of agency . . . is activity [which must, I think, include writing] directed toward some end that is affirmed as good by the actor, but this affirmation is not something arbitrary and private. Rather, it flows from an apprehension of real features in the world"—such as the likelihood that lobsters feel pain when boiled alive, or that few people really regard service-work with love (206). Agency, in this sense, links objective truth with the "affirmations"—the judgments—of a single actor. As a genre that unites sub- and objectivity in transparent and central ways, creative nonfiction embodies the type of agency Crawford imagines; still, in case there is any doubt, I think Wallace excels at this interactive process.

In the midst of his investigation about how television works (on mechanical, historical, social, and emotional levels) Wallace links seeing the constructedness of television programming with the development of self-reflexivity. Citing "Reagan's lame F.C.C. chairman Mark Fowler [who] professed to see [TV] in 1981 as 'just another appliance, a toaster with pictures,'" Wallace writes:

> I knew it was a "vast wasteland" way before I knew who Newton Minow [who coined this phase] and Mark Fowler were. And it really is fun to laugh cynically at television—at the way the laughter from sitcoms' "live studio audiences" is always suspiciously constant in pitch and duration, or at the way travel is depicted on *The Flintstones* by having the exact same cut-rate cartoon tree, rock, and house go by four times. ("E Unibas" 27)

Wallace suggests that seeing the constructedness of television, a medium foisting surfaces and promoting individualism like no other, allows reflection—cynical in this case, but also full of "pleasure"— on that very constructedness. The "I" voice that tells what it "knew" speaks from the moment he saw the flaws and seams in the programming. If seeing constructedness has ethical value, a strong case can be made for the importance of flaws. "Seams" equates to "flaws" imperfectly, but both describe the imperfect places where parts of things meet. The word "fault"—denoting both flaws and, as in "fault-lines," seams—serves to unite them. In the process of learning about something, seeing faults brings understanding: tailors have a keen eye for the less-smooth spot where sleeve meets body; bakers a taste for raw ingredients in a finished dish; critical readers an eye for tropes, allusions, subtexts. Knowledge and agency come from an ability to discern the various parts of something, a skill aided—at least in early stages of learning—when the fit is particularly rough. Karl Marx—a champion of work and workers, to understate the case—also noted the humanizing potential of faults, writing,

It is by their imperfections that the means of production in any process bring to our attention their character of being products of past labour. A knife which fails to cut, a piece of thread which keeps on snapping, forcibly remind us of Mr A, the cutler, or Mr B, the spinner [sic]. In a successful product, the role played by past labour in mediating its useful properties has been extinguished. (289)

Searching out the flaws, the seams, the imprint of human hands makes for a great investigative method. In one of my favorite examples, Wallace, waiting to be "herded via megaphone" onto the *Nadir*, receives "a little plastic card with a number on it.... [t]he cards are by no means brand new, and mine has the vestigial whorls of a chocolate thumb print in one corner" ("Supposedly Fun" 271). This detail—related by an individual likely grossed-out by the remnants—serves to display, via a finger-print flaw, a shared experience underneath. Pushing beyond the revelation of hidden labor as a method of visualizing human interconnection, here Wallace reveals hidden consumption. He also uses the shared, very familiar experience of waiting with a number to converse with people around him.

Similar to "E Unibus Pluram"'s suggestion that seeing TV's constructedness mitigates its mind-numbing effects, "A Supposedly Fun Thing," implies that seeing "a whole battalion of wiry little Third World guys who went around the ship in navy-blue jumpsuits scanning for decay to overcome" allows consumers to ourselves overcome at least some isolating and solipsistic effects of our culture (263). Seeing that real people act to make and maintain the products and services surrounding us generates sympathy, connection, and (fingers crossed) solidarity. And what about flaws in people? Seeing the self-centeredness of, for example, Balthazar Getty, allows reflection on self-centeredness itself. Revealing faults entails judgment, which creative nonfiction, by presenting its own constructedness, both models and promotes. Good creative nonfiction will display its own faults.[4]

Investigating work and seeking out faults does not guarantee interconnection—and can result in the opposite. For example, in "A Fire on the Moon,"—which delves into the work of the moon shot—

Norman Mailer rails against the type of sterilization enacted by consumer culture. He describes the plastic subdivisions developing around the NASA Center in late '60s Houston as "without flavor or odor" (27). The people who live in them are the same. He writes:

> [I]f we honor or fear the presence of odors because they are a root to the past and an indication of the future, are indeed our very marriage to time and mortality, why then it is no accident that the Wasps were in the view of [Mailer], at least, the most Faustian, barbaric, draconian, progress-oriented, and root destroying people on earth. They had divorced themselves from odor in order to dominate time, and thereby see if they were able to deliver themselves from death. (27)

In one sense, Wallace echoes this point of view. Openly skeptical about the 'realness' of the locations of mass consumption, he, too, connects elimination of smell with concealment of human nature. Of his "odorless" cruise-ship cabin and its bathroom's vacuum toilet—"both scary and strangely comforting [because] your waste seems less removed than *hurled* from you"—he writes:

> It's pretty hard not to see connections between the exhaust fan and the toilet's vacuums—an almost Final Solution-like eradication of animal wastes and odors (wastes and odors that are by all rights a natural consequence of Henry VIII-like meals and unlimited free Cabin Service and fruit baskets)—and the death-denial/-transcendence fantasies that the [cruise]...is trying to enable. ("Supposedly Fun" 305)

Like Mailer, Wallace sees a lack of honesty in our cultural paradigms and sees that covering up undesirable effects enables the perpetuation of consumption. But Wallace, while affronted, doesn't draw me-vs.-them lines like Mailer does by attributing the problem to "Wasps." Mailer looks and sees "them"; Wallace—even hiding out in his cabin writing about his toilet—sees us. An investigation of the ship's sewage system ensues, sewage systems in general well-display our hidden interconnections.

Attention to Extremes as a Method of Ethical Nonfiction

In a 2004 interview, Wallace explains that nonfiction "is very very hard for me" because "there is just so much freakin' real stuff in any scene." His biographer D.T. Max writes that "what always amazed Wallace about real life was the overload of information. He did not see how anyone could really capture what went on in a single moment" (244). Yet he tried, often approaching a subject in a bi (or multi-) polar way capable of both "capturing" the moment and displaying the "overload" of info. While a binary approach may seem reductive, revealing polar extremes provides a way to navigate between the pull of individual perspective and the responsibility to consider other viewpoints. To affect a more comprehensive "capture," Wallace frequently mixes irony with earnestness, scorn with respect, jest with sentiment, and especially, isolation with connection.

Of living in Bloomington, Illinois, he writes that people don't "go meet each other face to face in public places. There don't really tend to be parties or mixers per se so much here—what you do in Bloomington is all get together at somebody's house and watch something" ("Mrs. Thomson's" 134). TV-less himself, Wallace becomes "a perpetual guest of folks who can't quite understand why somebody wouldn't own a TV but are totally respectful of your need to watch TV, and who will offer you access to their TV in the same instinctive way they'd bend to offer a hand if you fell down in the street" (134). Depicting his neighbors' allegiance to television as compulsive, Wallace displays scorn and cynicism toward a group he most definitely divides himself from.[5] But the depiction of "folks" in Bloomington is also kind and respectful. He shows them welcoming him, a TV-less weirdo, into their homes. While giving readers his view, Wallace invites a reversal of perspective—we see him through them. This delivers the anxiety of social interaction, but also the release of that anxiety, as the group of people he'd convinced us are Other embrace him. Through such fluctuation, Wallace captures both the connection and the isolation of the moment.

Similarly, in his review "Greatly Exaggerated," Wallace represents critical theory in extremes of complexity and simplicity.

Praising H. L. Hix's *Morte D'Author: An Autopsy,* Wallace writes that the author "has a rare gift for the neat assembly of different sides of questions" (144). Wallace appreciates this skill—the (if not *neat*) *clear* presentation of opposing "sides." Juxtaposition of extreme differences in perspective allows Wallace to achieve such "assembly." Thus a long section of "A Supposedly Fun Thing," which details a crowd of people's absurdness—a "thirteen-year-old kid with [a] toupee"—and general sameness—"close to a dozen confirmed sightings of J. Redfield's *The Celestine Prophecy*"—a long section describing fully Othered people provided by an outsider watching and writing from a corner, finally ends with Wallace saying "a little kid right near me is wearing the same exact kind of hat I am, which I might as well admit right now is a full-color Spiderman cap" (274). He is, he shows readers, *in* the crowd, a part of the weirdness as much as the sameness.

Wallace's prose style also incorporates extremes—particularly between clarity and complexity. Franze describes his writing as full of "crackling precision," which at first seems like wrong terminology for some very dense prose (164). But his style does show an almost obsessive desire to *make clear* for readers. Consider the following from "Big Red Son," which covers a 1998 porn-industry awards ceremony. Describing a speaker as "a porn icon," he writes, "[Al Goldstein] drinks in the applause and loves it and is hard not to sort of almost actually like. He's clearly an avatar of contemporary porn's *unabashedness,* its modern Yeah-OK-I'm-Scum-but-Underneath-All-Your-Hypocrasy-So-Are-You-and-at-Least-I-Have-the-Guts-to-Admit-it-and-Have-a-Good-Time persona" (44, original emphasis). Whatever you think of the porn industry, or of a construction like "sort of almost actually," it's hard to deny the 27-word compound's "cracklingly precise" job of summing up the helpfully-italicized word *unabashedness.* Such a sentence is for readers. Though dense, the style lends clarity—often of complexity itself.

Depicting the barrenness of American consumer culture and the alienated inhabitants thereof, inhabitants maneuvering from TV set to dinner plate to car seat and back again, Wallace nevertheless returns to a wholly traditional type of human sympathy—positing, for example, the idea that a "consumer-hell-type situation" might allow access to "the subsurface unity of all things" (*Water* 93). That such peace-love-and-understanding comes from the least likely source—an artist rooted in the ironies of postmodernism and infinitely obsessed with the superficiality of American life—has a Nixon-China effect, a trustworthiness created by revealing a flawed and highly-judgmental self, capable of widely diffuse feelings about a single subject, just like you.

So, when Wallace writes in "E Unibus Pluram" that "irony, irreverence, and rebellion come to be not liberating but enfeebling," I believe him, because he has quite clearly plumbed the shallows of irony, irreverence, and rebellion (76). He offers criticism of American culture, yet refuses impermeable us vs. them lines. Again from "E Unibus Pluram": "I'm not saying television is vulgar and dumb because the people who compose Audience are vulgar and dumb. Television is the way it is simply because people tend to be extremely similar in their vulgar and prurient and dumb interests and wildly different in their refined and aesthetic and noble interests" (37). Here Wallace draws lines not between individual people—not between us and them—but between aspects of all of us. Note "E Unibus Pluram"'s description of "Joe Briefcase . . . an average US male, relatively unlonely, adjusted, married, blessed with 2.3 apple-cheeked issue, utterly normal, home from hard work at 5:30, starting his average six-hour stint in front of the television" (39). Rare in a composite of American normality, Wallace provides Joe Briefcase a high degree of self-reflexivity.[6] He writes "surely, deep down, Joe was uncomfortable with being one part of the biggest crowd in human history watching images that suggest that life's meaning consists in standing visibly apart from the crowd" ("E Unibus" 58). Graciously, Wallace makes distaste for the norm normal, suggesting that everyone in the crowd feels pretty much the same way about the crowd as I do.

Combining discussion of his writing, his depression, his interest in individual fame and success, Wallace described himself on Charlie Rose in 1997 as "not substantively different" from other people;

indeed his experience "is very very average." I celebrate this—our culture has promoted individualism for some time, pushing us to view and display ourselves as unique and exceptional. And, like Wallace, we are. But that is only half the story—we are also quite similar and interdependent. Creative nonfiction, using a unique self to tell a true story accessible to others, models the interplay of these two truths, presenting ethical potential by displaying *someone* looking *out*. It can, as in Wallace's work, show a person trying to see through the "implacable I"; if it fails to make this attempt, the work slips into adolescence, telling instead a self-invested non-story about me, me, me.

Notes

1. Were I the subject of a piece taking liberties with factualness, I might be less comfortable, as were some subjects of Wallace's writing. As it turned out, the trueness of his fiction occasioned more criticism than the falseness of his nonfiction; as his sister puts it, the family "quietly agreed that his nonfiction was fanciful and his fiction was what you had to look out for" (Max 318). Only after his suicide in 2008 did the autobiographical extent of his fiction—particularly *Infinite Jest*—become clear.

2. Knowing only his work, I don't wish to dwell on Wallace's personal biography; still it seems important to note that Wallace failed in this attempt as much as he succeeded. Reflecting on his death— "calculated to inflict maximum pain on those he loved most"— and the mental illness preceding it, fellow novelist Jonathan Franzen calls his "beloved dead friend" David Wallace "a lifelong prisoner on the island of himself" ("Farther" 38, 48, 40).

3. Underscoring the importance of observation and attention, Wallace describes his nonfiction method as "basically an enormous eyeball floating around something, reporting what it sees" (Max 228). His sister calls him "the best listener I ever met" ("Amy Wallace Speaks")

4. This might, in part, explain the prominence of self-deprecating humor in creative nonfiction, Wallace's included.

5. As an example of Wallace's departure's from strict fact, the neighbors and church friends in this piece were actually members of his substance abuse recovery group—a quite justifiable change in light

of needed anonymity (Max 263). Less immediately understandable—and treading towards fictional territory—other nonfiction works reinvent his hometown, relate unlikely weather events, and seem to make up both childhood and adult experiences (Max 186).

6. With "Joe," he also constructs a transparently fictional character to drive a piece of nonfiction.

Works Cited

"Amy Wallace speaks about her brother David Foster Wallace." Interview by Anne Strainchamps. *To the Best of Our Knowledge*. PRI. WPR, 23 Aug. 2009. *YouTube*. Web. 4 Aug. 2014.

Bloom, Lynn Z. "Living to Tell the Tale: The Complicated Ethics of Creative Nonfiction." *College English* 65.3 (2003): 276-89. *JSTOR*. Web. 25 Sept. 2013.

Crawford, Matthew B. *Shop Class as Soul Craft: An Inquiry into the Value of Work*. New York: Penguin, 2009.

"David Foster Wallace—Conversation (San Francisco 2004)." Interview by David Kipen. *City Arts Lectures*. 89.3 KPCC. SCPR. *YouTube*. Web. 4 Aug. 2014.

"DFW." Interview by Charlie Rose. *Charlie Rose*. PBS. WGBH, Boston, 27 Mar. 1997. *YouTube*. Web. 4 Aug. 2014.

Didion, Joan. "On Keeping a Notebook." 1961. *We Tell Ourselves Stories in Order to Live*. New York: Knopf, 2006. 101–8.

Eakin, Paul John, ed. *The Ethics of Life Writing*. Ithaca, NY: Cornell UP, 2004.

Franzen, Jonathan. "David Foster Wallace." *Farther Away*. New York: Farrar, Straus & Giroux, 2012. 161–168.

Mailer, Norman. "Fire on the Moon Part I." *Life* (29 Aug. 1969): 25–40.

Marx, Karl. *Capital Volume I*. 1886. New York: Penguin, 1990.

Max, D.T. *Every Love Story is a Ghost Story: A Life of David Foster Wallace*. New York: Penguin, 2012.

Philips, Brian. "The Negative Style of David Foster Wallace." *The Hudson Review* 57.4 (2005): 675–82. *JSTOR*. Web. 25 Sept. 2013.

Wallace, David Foster. "Big Red Son." 1998. *Consider the Lobster*. New York: Backbay, 2007. 3–50.

_____. "Certainly the End of *Something* or Other, One Would Sort of Have To Think." 1998. *Consider the Lobster*. New York: Backbay, 2007. 51–9.

_____. "David Lynch Keeps His Head." 1996. *A Supposedly Fun Thing I'll Never Do Again*. New York: Backbay, 1997. 138–212.

_____. "E Unibus Pluram." 1993. *A Supposedly Fun Thing I'll Never Do Again*. New York: Backbay, 1997. 21–82.

_____. "Greatly Exaggerated." 1992. *A Supposedly Fun Thing I'll Never Do Again*. New York: Backbay, 1997. 138–45.

_____. "A Supposedly Fun Thing I'll Never Do Again." 1996. *A Supposedly Fun Thing I'll Never Do Again*. New York: Backbay, 1997. 256–353.

_____. "The View From Mrs. Thompson's." 2001. *Consider the Lobster*. New York: Backbay, 2007. 128–40.

_____. *This Is Water*. New York: Little, Brown & Company, 2009.

Choreographing Time: Art Spiegelman's Present, Past(s) and The Craft of Creative Nonfiction Comics_____

David Bahr

In 1991, when Art Spiegelman's *Maus II* was published, it made the *New York Times'* bestseller's list—as fiction. In response, Spiegelman wrote to the newspaper that finding "a carefully researched work based closely on" his "father's memories of life in Hitler's Europe and in the death camps classified as fiction" made him "a bit queasy" (Spiegelman, *MetaMaus* 150). Spiegelman added that the "borderland between fiction and nonfiction has been fertile territory for some of the most potent contemporary writing," but "I believe I might have lopped several years off the 13 I devoted to my two-volume project if I could only have taken a novelist's license while searching for a novelistic structure" (150).

Although readers now may be surprised to learn that Spiegelman's Pulitzer Prize-winning graphic memoir initially had been categorized as fiction by the "paper of record," comics is still not readily recognized as a mode of creative nonfiction.[1] Part of the problem is that comics continues to be misperceived as a genre and not a medium (Chute, "Comics" 452). In America, "comics" has long been associated with superheroes and talking animals, not typically the stuff of high-brow literature, much less creative nonfiction. Throughout most of the twentieth century in America, illustrated narratives—or "picture books"—were largely marketed to, and seen as the province of, children and the less-educated (Sabin 15–79). In the late 1960s and early 1970s, the American comics landscape expanded with the emergence of "underground comix," driven by a politically charged youth culture and the era's reaction to the 1955 comics code, which prohibited references to sex, "excessive violence," and "challenges to authority" (Sabin 68; Nyberg; Hatfield 164–65). "Underground" artists like Spiegelman challenged not only the code, but also assumptions about comics' audience, producing mature, autobiographical works that addressed sex, war, and mental illness, to name a few controversial topics. Hilary Chute states how, in the hands of Spiegelman and other cartoonists, including but not limited to later nonfiction practitioners Joe Sacco, Marjane Satrapi, and Alison Bechdel, "the form confronts the default assumption that drawing as a system is inherently more fictional than prose and gives a new cast to what we consider fiction and nonfiction" ("Comics" 453).

Comics' tendency toward abstraction, exemplified by Spiegelman's use of anthropomorphism in *Maus*, has contributed to resistance in viewing comics as a form of creative nonfiction. Spiegelman recounts learning of one editor's determined opposition to listing *Maus* as nonfiction:

> Because I have friends who worked at the *Times*, I was told of a remarkable exchange that happened after the editors got my letter and were debating about whether to move my book over to the nonfiction list or not. [. . .] But one editor was furious at the idea, saying, "Well look, let's go out to Spiegelman's house and if a giant mouse answers the door, we'll move it to the nonfiction side of the list!" (Spiegelman, *MetaMaus* 150)

Of course, resistance to *Maus'* visual metaphors overlooks experiments in form and representation in creative nonfiction prose. Further, a bias towards prose disregards the symbolic and rhetorical constructs that constitute all written, not only visual, language. Nonetheless, as Chute contends, it is out of the underground culture, of which Spiegelman was a key figure, that "today's most enduring graphic narratives took shape—serious, imaginative works that explored social and political realities by stretching the boundaries of a historically mass medium" ("Comics" 456).

Spiegelman's decision to anthropomorphize the story of his parents' experience as Holocaust survivors dates back to the early 1970s, when a group of his cartoonist colleagues proposed an animal-themed comic, *Funny Animals*. Then a non-matriculating student, Spiegelman visited an introduction to cinema class, during which the instructor screened several clips of early animation, including a series with African-Americans "cheerfully represented as subhuman, monkeylike creatures with giant minstrel lips" (Spiegelman, *MetaMaus* 112) and some "Farmer Gray cartoons" (112). "I think he might have even shown 'Steamboat Willie'—the first sound cartoon by Walt Disney," Spiegelman recalls. "'Steamboat Willie' had come right in the wake of *The Jazz Singer* and essentially what we're looking at here is a jazzy Mickey Mouse" (112). This lead to what the cartoonist identifies as his "Eureka moment" (112). For his contribution to *Funny Animals*, he thought about countering such racist imagery with a comic featuring "Ku Klux Kats"; however, he soon abandoned the idea in favor of a short strip about his parents' story, featuring mice and cats. Although Spiegelman did not immediately recognize it, the concept would resonate both with Nazi propaganda that depicted Jews as rats and with the Bird's Head Haggadah (the earliest Ashkenazi illuminated Passover text), which portrayed human characters as animals to comply with religious proscriptions against desecrating God's image. As Spiegelman notes, whereas the Bird's Head Haggadah portrays something "too sacred to show," the choice of using mice would be interpreted by some critics as representing that which is "too profane for depiction" (Spiegelman, *MetaMaus* 117). For Spiegelman, anthropomorphism has roots in "the junk culture I'd actually grown up with" (117) and an underground comix climate valuing experimentation and play. This early, three-page version of "Maus" appeared in *Funny Animals* in 1972.

In 1973, Spiegelman continued to mine his life for material. He published "Don't Get Around Much Anymore" (subtitled "To Be Read to the Accompaniment of a Dripping Faucet, Slowly") and "Prisoner on The Hell Planet," two short, autobiographical strips that deal with depression and mental illness. A single page of fourteen panels, "Don't Get Around Much Anymore" involves a sequence of close ups of mostly inanimate objects, including a stack of magazines, an empty refrigerator, a television with no functioning sound, and a sink. The claustrophobic images are presented as ten non-sequitur and two pairs of moment-to-moment panels, conveying disconnection, stasis, and repetition.[2] The protagonist only appears in the first frame (and in a zoom-in, duplicate shot within the title panel): seated, he stares at images on a mute television as a phonograph plays. The only other human, aside from the frozen figures of several magazines and the fragmented female face on a television, is a boy—outside a window and bouncing a "ball for hours" (Spiegelman, *MetaMaus* 169)—who appears as inanimate as the objects within the room. The comic masterfully conveys the phenomenology of despair. Spiegelman recalls: "It was a hard-won page, one I remain inordinately proud of, trying to find a new way of using these words and pictures together to indicate the languor and timeless depression I still remain prone to: the feeling that 'Oh, here I am again, trapped, and I ain't never gonna be anywhere else'" (168–69). A visual staccato that engages the reader with its busy, condensed, yet clean and uncomplicated cartoons, "Don't Get Around Much Anymore" could only work as graphic. It visually conveys the energy expended in the paralysis of despondency. It communicates depression's temporality.

Working with the same themes of emotional stasis and psychological entrapment as "Don't Get Around Much," "Prisoner on the Hell Planet" concerns Spiegelman's paralytic response to his mother's suicide soon after his release from a mental hospital at age twenty. As with "Don't Get Around Much," "Prisoner" reveals what may be comics' strength as a medium: its unique ability, as Spiegelman puts it, to "choreograph and shape time" (Spiegelman, "Ephmera" 4; Chute, "Comics" 452). Chute explains: "The form of comics always hinges on the way temporality can be traced in complex, often nonlinear paths across the space of the page; largely this registers in both words and images, although it doesn't always have to" ("Comics" 452). Comics' capacity to "choreograph and shape time" can be valuable in creative nonfiction works of history and autobiography, where the "problem" of time, as it relates to memory and testimony, can be portrayed in compelling, innovative ways.

In this regard, "Prisoner" is a compact comics masterwork, a skillful demonstration of the form's possibilities and strengths. (It is the first comic, after Scott McCloud's pedagogic primer

Understanding Comics, that I teach in my graphic narrative course.) Originally published in *Short Order Comix #1*, the four-page graphic is comprised of thirty-six panels. It reappears, re-contextualized, in *Maus I: My Father Bleeds History*, when the protagonist, Artie, holds the 1973 zine after learning that his father Vladek has just discovered it, years after publication (Spiegelman, *Maus* 101). It is to this version of "Prisoner"—as it appears in *The Complete Maus*—that I will refer because its re-contextualization amplifies Spiegelman's rich handling of temporality. Following an overhead "shot" of the rodent Artie holding the 1973 comic, Spiegelman zooms in on the text, exactly as it appeared in *Short Order Comix*, except for the pagination layout and a hand, at the bottom left, holding the zine, with the bottom and sides of the "original" pages framed by what the cartoonist calls a "funereal border" (Chute, "Shadow" 207).[3] As Chute notes, "Prisoner" does "not seamlessly become part of the fabric of the larger narrative but rather maintains its alterity" (207). Mostly rendered in the coarse, scratchy style of a woodcut print, the strip and its human figures disrupt the "rough and utilitarian" (Wolk 343) felt-pen illustrations of *Maus'* anthropomorphic memoir. Chute writes that the "heavy German Expressionist style [of "Prisoner"] is an unsubtle analog to the angry emotional content of the strip" ("Shadow" 207). Unlike with typeset prose, the variability of the hand-drawn line in comics can be used to aesthetic effect to convey shifts in mood, setting, and time. Chute notes, with comics, the "subjective presence of the maker is not retranslated through type, but, rather, the bodily mark of handwriting both provides a visual quality and texture and is also extrasemantic" (*Graphic* 11). She adds that comics "differs from the novel, an obvious influence, not only because of its visual-verbal hybridity but also because of its composition in handwriting" (11).

The contrast in visual style is immediately apparent in the opening frame of "Prisoner," which includes a hand holding a reprint of a 1958 photograph of Artie's mother, Anja, looking robust and standing beside a smiling ten-year-old Spiegelman. In position and angle, this hand mirrors the one on the bottom left that emerges from the "funereal border," and which represents that narrative world of *Maus*. Although more realistically drawn than the lower cartoonish hand, the hand within "Prisoner" does not match the verisimilitude of the reproduced photograph; it remains an illustration. The three different styles on the first page communicate three distinct temporal realms: a photo-document of Spiegelman's childhood; a comix artifact produced while the cartoonist was in his mid-twenties; and the anthropomorphic *Maus* project of a man approaching middle age. Further, the illustrated title, "PRISONER ON THE HELL PLANET: A CASE HISTORY"—with "prisoner," "on the," and "planet" rendered in white block "3D" lettering, and "hell" drawn in the shape of a flame, all against a black outer-space background—evokes the playful visuals of a children's comic. The innocent, juvenile mood is in tension with the top row's second and only other panel, which shows a relatively realistic illustration of a somber Artie, wearing a concentration camp uniform, in a prison mugshot. The accompanying word balloon narrates: "In 1968, when I was 20, my mother killed herself. She left no note!" (Spiegelman, *Maus* 102). The next frame, beginning the three-panel second row, is a cartoonish drawing of a skeletal Vladek, discovering Anja in a bath, her arm draped over a tub, with a puddle of what appears to be blood on the floor. The caption in the overhanging gutter states, "my father found her when he got home from work . . . her wrists slashed and an empty bottle of pills nearby . . . "; Vladek's word balloon contains the dramatic and almost comical "oy gott!" (102).

The following two panels portray a more realistic woodcut depiction of a zombie Artie, in his prison uniform, exiting the subway (before the bare, ghostly outline of two passing pedestrians) and walking down the street, respectively. The floating caption in the gutter of the middle frame says, "I was living with my parents as I agreed to do on my release from the state mental hospital 3 months before" (Spiegelman, *Maus* 102). The final and sixth panel of the page encompasses the entire last row and reveals a close-up of Artie in profile, observing the crowd in front of his parents' home. A couple stare at Artie, the woman pointing in his direction. The caption in the above gutter says, "I suppose that if I had gotten home when expected, **I** would have found her body" (102; bold in original). The longest panel of the strip suggests a momentary cessation of time, which could be interpreted as expressing shock and/or paralysis. As McCloud notes, "the panel shape can actually make a **difference** in our **perception** of time" and that "a wider panel has the **feeling** of greater length" (101; bold in original). It demonstrates what Thierry Groensteen calls the "expressive function" of the frame (53). Groensteen writes that "the ultimate signification of a comics panel does not reside in itself but in the totality of relations in the network that it maintains with the interdependent panels"; when used expressively, the panel "acts upon the layout [. . .] to draw attention to a rupture in the level of enunciation regarding the status of the image" (53).

In the second page of "Prisoner," the visual style becomes more varied, mixing realism with the abstract woodcut graphics of a horror comic. The first of a the top three panels shows a cartoonish, moon-faced man with his arm around Artie, as a line of glowing jack-o'-lanterns, signifying the staring crowd, hover above them. The floating caption reads, "A cousin herded me away from the scene" (Spiegelman, *Maus* 103), and the cousin's word balloon states, "come to the doctor's. . . your mother is—ah—sick! . . . he will explain" (103). A narrower frame follows, which contains the broad rendering of a doctor with a Hitler mustache and round glasses that depict empty white sockets for eyes. The final frame of the triad returns to the size of the initial panel, and the doctor is seen in close-up. He has morphed into a greater caricature: his shoulders are pointed, and his hands posed in the exaggerated tepee gesture of a detached "shrink." The surrounding room—comprised of the rigid lines of a wall, bookshelf, and desk—has collapses askew, communicating a phenomenological shift in perspective, as the doctor bluntly announces in a word balloon: "you're mother killed herself—she's **dead!**" (103; bold in original). As with the rest of strip, the three frames reveal how, as Chute writes, "textured in its narrative scaffolding, comics doesn't blend the visual and the verbal—or use one simply to illustrate the other—but is rather prone to present the two nonsynchronously" ("Comics" 452). The asynchronous dynamic of comics—the ability to convey simultaneously two or more settings, events, or affective states—allows the medium to portray the paradox, conflict, and heterogeneity of an experience more readily than text alone. We can read (i.e., "hear") the words of the unsympathetic doctor and see (i.e., "feel") the turmoil of Artie's situation.

In the following five frames, which begin the second row, Spiegelman effectively employs frame and illustration to express Artie's internal state upon being informed of his mother's suicide. The floating text in the gutter above panels ten through fourteen states: "I could avoid the truth no longer—the doctor's words clattered inside me. . . . I felt confused; I felt angry; I felt numb! . . . I didn't exactly feel like crying. But I figured I should! . . . ." (Spiegelman, *Maus* 103). (See Figure 1.) As I have written in "Labile Lines," an essay about comics and mental illness:

> The third and center panel transforms the already cartoonish face of the doctor delivering the news into a ghostly skull, lurid and frightening, his open palms out (the right hand bleeding into the adjacent panel), as if unveiling a magic trick. Inside the center frame, above the spectral doctor, appear the boldface graphics, a searing abracadabra to accompany this sleight of hand: "She's dead! A suicide!" Bookending this ghastly image are two pairs of panels: four fairly realistic portraits of Artie's hangdog face. His right hand extended beyond the border, the doctor appears to reach out toward the reader; he pushes the frames of Artie aside like vertical blinds. Artie is compressed, as if his skull is being squeezed for whatever tears can be bled, conveying the claustrophobia of emotional overload. (Bahr 7)

In "Labile Lines," my previous analysis of these frames focused on the phenomenological effects of comics to communicate physiological states that often defy language. But here, I am concerned with how the series portrays a single event as an asynchronous experience. The doctor's hands reaching "out toward reader," pushing "the frames of Artie aside" and squeezing him dry, convey the tension between two competing styles representing distinct points of view: the world as it may objectively appear versus how it is subjectively experienced. Frank Cioffi has noted how the "word-image gestalt" in *Maus* shows readers that "images can be used to create a world both believable and fantastic, linked to actual historicity but at the same time part of another realm or dimension altogether" (121). In panels ten through fourteen of "Prisoner," the overhanging narration straddles five frames, effectively producing a single, fractured

Figure 1. Panels 10 through 14; *The Complete Maus*, p. 103 by Art Spiegelman
© Penguin Random House LLC (print); © Wiley Agency (electronic). Printed with permission.

panel, simultaneously expressing the disconnect between Artie's internal and external worlds. Emotionally numb, Artie performs what he believes is the expected reaction, while the expressionistic rendering of the ghoulish doctor and the pig-faced uncle reveal a surreal encounter that matches Artie's traumatized subjectivity.

Cathy Caruth defines trauma as the "structure of" a received experience, in which an extreme and overwhelming event "is not assimilated or experienced fully at the time, but only belatedly" (4). Marianne Hirsch observes how *Maus* "performs an aesthetics of trauma" in that "it is fragmentary, composed of small boxes that cannot contain the material, which exceeds their frames and the structure of the page" (1213). If trauma is the inability to integrate past and present, "Prisoner" orchestrates these contending temporalities in unique ways through the medium of comics. In the third and

Critical Insights

fourth pages of the strip, Spiegelman employs several other comics-specific techniques to illustrate the ever-present past. Frames 20–24 recount Anja's funeral, beginning with an establishing shot of the funeral home. Below that frame is another panel in which we see her casket and Vladek, beside a stunned Artie, praying in Hebrew. Together, these two frames, twenty and twenty-one, are the same height as the adjacent panels (to the left, Vladek clutches Artie on the floor the night before the service; to the right, a pan shot of father and son standing behind their mother's coffin), evoking, in cinematic terms, a split screen. As with the sequence involving the doctor's news of Anja's suicide, the effect is to present a series of panels as a single, fractured frame. The top, establishing shot shows a funeral home as another building on an uneventful street; beneath, hidden from view of passersby, is Anja's funeral, and the site of an operatic scene. The next row consists of only two frames. Panel twenty-three shows Vladek throwing himself on his wife's casket, screaming her name—"Anna Anna Anna Anna" (Spiegelman, *Maus* 122)—which, iconically illustrated, becomes part of the panel and continues into the neighboring frame, connecting them. Panel twenty-four is a close-up of a dazed Artie, his wailing father having receded to the background, with the above caption: "It was too much—I had to leave . . ." (122). Once again, Spiegelman violates the borders as the coffin from panel twenty-three encroaches on twenty-four. As with the hand of the wraith-faced doctor delivering the news of Anja's death, the coffin breaks the "fourth wall" of the comic, shooting out like a missile, or gun barrel, toward the head of Artie, and the reader. Death impinges on the present.

The last row of the third page consists of three panels. In the first, Artie weeps in the hall of the funeral home, as he is scolded by a family friend: "**Now you cry!** Better you cried when your mother was still alive!" (Spiegelman, *Maus* 122; bold in original). He then stumbles out the door, and, finally, in the last frame, onto the street, as a kaleidoscope of icons from the avenue collapse around Artie, who covers his face with his arm, as if to protect himself from falling debris. The illustrations become increasingly skewed, like a fun house mirror, as the narration above the last two frames states: "I felt nauseous . . . the guilt was overwhelming!" (122). The sequence is not a visual illustration of the verbal, per se, but a graphic amplification that appeals to the senses. As McCloud argues, "the power of the line, shape and color to suggest the inner state of the artist and provoke the five senses" (123) has long been acknowledged in the fine arts, but not readily acknowledged in the "'low' art of comics" (123). Spiegelman, however, is clearly aware of the sophisticated, synesthetic capacities of comics' line and form. The frames' progressive claustrophobia and wonky imagery culminates in the compelling graphics of panels twenty-eight through thirty. The first, twenty-eight, shows Artie hunched in the right corner, as a man and woman with black-socket eyes gaze down at him. The floating caption states: "The next week we spent in mourning . . . my father's friends all offered me hostility mixed in with their condolences . . ." (Spiegelman, *Maus* 123). In a word balloon, the woman states "Arthur—we're **so** sorry" (123; bold in original), while the thought bubbles connected to the man and Artie state, respectively: "It's his fault—the punk!" and "They think it's my fault!!" (123). Artie's self-perception of public guilt is in tension with the performed conventions of mourning.

This internal conflict leads to the arresting density of panel twenty-nine, which represents his private angst, as the self-condemnation of the prior scene is visually depicted beneath the caption, ". . . but for the most part, I was left alone with my thoughts . . ." (Spiegelman, *Maus* 123). (See Figure 2). Unlike the busy frames twenty-seven and twenty-eight, this one illustrates five distinct historical moments simultaneously, four of which, as Chute notes in her formative reading, are "criss-crossed by text that alternates sentiments corresponding with the frame's accreted temporalities" ("Shadow" 207–8). On the bottom right, beneath the weight of past memories, Artie crouches in the same position as in the preceding panel, although he leans in further, his head against his hand. To the left, Anja slits her wrists, sandwiched by the bold black lettering of "Bitch," and, above, "Mommy!"; the latter acts as a caption for Anja reading to Artie as a child, dressed like his adult self, in a prison camp uniform. At the upper right is a pile of corpses, a swastika, and

...BUT, FOR THE MOST PART, I WAS LEFT ALONE WITH MY THOUGHTS...

Figure 2. Panel 29; *The Complete Maus*, p. 105 by Art Spiegelman © Penguin Random House LLC (print); © Wiley Agency (electronic). Printed with permission.

"Hitler Did It!" Topping it all is an image of Anja's naked corpse in a bathtub of black bloody water, and "Menopausal D e p r e s s i o n" ceremoniously draped below. The entire frame effectively functions as five separate narratives that are inextricably connected, resulting in a fusion of past and present. Chute writes: "Approaching the past and the present together is typical for someone considering narratives of causality, but here Spiegelman obsessively layers several temporalities in one tiny frame, understood by the conventions of the comics medium to represent one moment in time" ("Shadow" 208). Artie's breakdown is identified with Anja's recent suicide, his childhood as the captive son of Holocaust survivors, the historical mass murder of his parents' generation, and his mother's "depression." Unlike in prose, photography, or film, comics can simultaneously juxtapose multiple scenes, discouraging a straightforward reading based on cause and effect. This "rhizomatic" strategy can be particularly effective when chronicling events or emotions not easily translated into a linear narrative.

Spiegelman decompresses the narrative in the next three frames, with a moment-to-moment progression. In panel thirty, Artie remains in the lower left of the frame, but he has now collapsed into a full fetal position. His mother towers over him, an Amazonian figure, and we realize that we have traveled yet again through time. The floating text states, "I remember the last time I saw her" (Spiegelman, *Maus* 123). The frame, and the two that follow, are drawn with the serrated borders of an old snapshot, imbuing the images with the testimonial power of a photograph and the fixed, "unassimilable" (Hirsch 16) quality of a traumatic memory. In this three-panel narrative, Anja slowly walks into Artie's room, "late at night," and asks him, ". . . Artie . . . you . . . still . . . love . . . me . . . don't you?" (Spiegelman, *Maus* 123). The floating text in the gutter reads, ". . . I turned away, resentful of the way she tightened the umbilical cord . . ." as the word balloon above Artie states, "sure, ma!" (123). The next frame, thirty-three, is only half serrated, denoting that the photographic recollection is fading, with Artie's final memory of her etched into the illustration, ". . . she walked out and closed the door!" (123). The white, block graphic "clik" and the bold, black, wavering "agh!" appear like icons in a Batman cartoon. Only the top three-quarters of Artie's distressed face appears, again illustrated in the rough style of an expressionistic woodcut etching. The straight ninety-degree angle that contains Artie's partially-obscured head at the bottom right of the frame, and the final three panels of the strip that follow, reveal that we have left behind Artie's last memory of Anja and have entered the present. Yet, in panel thirty-three, Artie straddles both temporalities, a prisoner of the present past.

The final floating caption of the strip, above panel thirty-four, states, "Well, mom, if you're listening . . ." with Artie's word balloon completing the thought, "Congratulations! . . . You have committed the perfect crime . . ." (Spiegelman, *Maus* 123). But the panel illustration shows Artie, not Anja, in jail. His hands clutch the bars, but his face is obscured, and the prison hat barely visible, in the darkness of the cell. The subsequent frame pans further out, until, in the last panel of the entire strip, we see a wide shot of seemingly countless penitentiary cells. This closing image metaphorically represents the traumatic reaction of a twenty-five-year-old Spiegelman to his mother's suicide five years earlier. As with the animals of *Maus*, Artie's imagined imprisonment does not make the story a fiction, but a creative rendering that employs the craft of comics to convey an actual psychological state within a nonfiction context.

Unlike in the final shot of movie, or with the last words of prose story, "Prisoner" does not necessarily end with the closing frame and text. As presented in *Maus*, the four-page strip unfolds in a successive two-leaf spread, so the reader can recursively scan the concurrent panels. The images remain individually frozen, but collectively dynamic. Spiegelman's choreography continues to compete for our attention. Past and present meld, perpetually alive, attesting to the magic of this distinctive medium that does not encourage closure. Creative nonfiction comics may still be young, and not yet universally appreciated, but "Prisoner" endures as an early testament to its potential and power.

Notes

1. As Hilary Chute notes: "Comics, like the term for any medium, requires a singular verb. Treating comics as a singular has become standard" ("Comics" 462). She cites McCloud (4) and Varnum and Gibbon (xiii), "among numerous others supporting this usage" (Chute, "Comics" 462).

2. In his chapter "Closure," McCloud offers five types of sequences: moment-to-moment, action-to-action, subject-to-subject, scene-to-scene, aspect-to-aspect, and non-sequitur (71–72).

3. In the original version of "Prisoner" from *Short Order Comix*, reprinted in *Breakdowns*, the first of the four pages appears alone, on the right-side leaf, followed by the next two pages, as a spread, with the last page, alone, on the left leaf. In *Maus*, the four pages are presented as two double-leaf spreads.

Works Cited

Bahr, David. "Labile Lines: Art Spiegelman's 'Prisoner on Hell Planet,' Darryl Cunningham's *Psychiatric Tales*, and the Graphic Memoir of Mental Illness." *Lifewriting Annual: Biographical and Autobiographical Studies*. New York: AMS Press, 2015.

Caruth, Cathy. "Trauma and Experience: Introduction," *Trauma: Explorations in Memory*. Baltimore, MD: Johns Hopkins UP, 1995.

Chute, Hillary. *Graphic Women: Life Narrative and Contemporary Comics*. New York: Columbia UP, 2010.

_____. "Comics as Literature? Reading Graphic Narrative." *PMLA* 123.2 (2008): 452–465.

_____. "'The Shadow of a Past Time': History and Graphic Representation in *Maus*." *Twentieth-Century Literature* 52.2 (2006): 199–230.

Cioffi, Frank L. "Disturbing Comics: The Disjunction of Word and Image in the Comics of Andrzej Mleczko, Ben Katchor, R. Crumb, and Art Spiegelman." *The Language of Comics: Word and Image*. Ed. Robin Varnum & Christina Gibbons. Jackson: UP of Mississippi, 2001. 97–122.

Groensteen, Thierry. *The System of Comics*. Trans. Bart Beaty & Nick Nguyen. Jackson: UP of Mississippi, 2007.

Hatfield, Charles. *Alternative Comics: An Emerging Literature*. Jackson: UP of Mississippi, 2005.

Hirsch, Marianne. "Editor's Column: Collateral Damage." *PMLA* 119.5 (2004): 1209–1215.

McCloud, Scott. *Understanding Comics: The Invisible Art*. New York: Kitchen Sink, 1993.

Nyberg, Amy Kiste. *Seal of Approval: The History of the Comics Code.* Jackson: UP of Mississippi, 1998.

Sabin, Roger. *Comics, Comix & Graphic Novels: A History of Comic Art.* New York: Phaidon Press, 1996.

Spiegelman, Art. *MetaMaus.* New York: Pantheon Books, 2011.

_____. *Breakdowns: Portrait of the Artist as a Young %@&*!* New York: Pantheon, 2008.

_____. *The Complete Maus.* New York: Pantheon, 1997.

Varnum, Robin & Christina T. Gibbons, eds. *The Language of Comics: Word and Image.* Jackson: UP of Mississippi, 2001.

Wolk, Douglas. *Reading Comics: How Graphic Novels Work and What They Mean.* Cambridge, MA: Da Capo Press, 2007.

RESOURCES

Additional Works of American Creative Nonfiction_____

Long Creative Nonfiction and Extended Essay

Notes of a Native Son by James Baldwin, 1963 (memoir)

Fun Home: A Family Tragicomic by Alison Bechdel, 2006 (graphic memoir)

Life Is a Miracle: An Essay Against Modern Superstition by Wendell Berry, 2001 (essay)

Silent Dancing: A Partial Remembrance of a Puerto Rican Childhood by Judith Ortiz Cofer, 1990 (memoir)

Pilgrim at Tinker Creek by Annie Dillard, 1974 (personal essay)

A Heartbreaking Work of Staggering Genius by Dave Eggers, 2000 (memoir)

Nickel and Dimed: On (Not) Getting By in America by Barbara Ehrenreich, 2001 (literary journalism/memoir)

Another Bullshit Night in Suck City by Nick Flynn, 2005 (memoir)

The Temple Bombing by Melissa Fay Greene, 1996 (literary history / memoir)

The Sweeter the Juice: A Family Memoir in Black and White by Shirlee Taylor Haizlip, 1995 (memoir)

Blood, Bones, and Butter: The Inadvertent Education of a Reluctant Chef by Gabrielle Hamilton, 2012 (memoir)

Liberty Street: Encounters at Ground Zero by Peter Josyph, 2012 (literary journalism)

The Liars' Club by Mary Karr, 2005 (memoir)

A Walker in the City by Alfred Kazin, 1951 (memoir)

The Soul of a New Machine by Tracy Kidder, 1981 (literary journalism)

The Woman Warrior: Memoirs of a Girlhood Among Ghosts by Maxine Hong Kingston, 1989 (memoir)

Arctic Dreams by Barry Lopez, 2001 (literary journalism / memoir)

Oranges by John McPhee, 1975 (literary journalism)

The American Way of Death by Jessica Mitford, 1963 (literary journalism)

The Way to Rainy Mountain by N. Scott Momaday, 1969 (literary history / memoir)

Out of My League by George Plimpton, 1961 (literary journalism / memoir)

Hunger of Memory: the Education of Richard Rodriguez: An Autobiography by Richard Rodriguez, 1981 (memoir)

Wanderlust: A History of Walking by Rebecca Solnit, 2000 (essay)

Half a Life: A Memoir by Darin Strauss, 2011 (memoir)

Hell's Angels: The Strange and Terrible Saga of the Outlaw Motorcycle Gangs by Hunter S. Thompson, 1966 (literary journalism)

Stalking Irish Madness: Searching for the Roots of My Family's Schizophrenia by Patrick Tracey, 2008 (literary history/medical memoir)

If You Knew Then What I Know Now by Ryan Van Meter, 2011 (personal essay)

The Chronology of Water by Lidia Yuknavich, 2011 (memoir)

Single-Author Essay Collections

Notes from No-Man's Land: American Essays by Eula Biss, 2009.

The Solace of Open Spaces by Gretel Ehrlich, 1985

The Immense Journey: An Imaginative Naturalist Explores the Mysteries of Man and Nature by Loren Eiseley, 1957

Ever Since Darwin: Reflections in Natural History by Stephen Jay Gould, 1977

Woman and Nature: The Roaring Inside Her by Susan Griffin, 1978

Writing a Woman's Life by Carolyn G. Heilbrun, 1988

Getting Personal: Selected Writings by Phillip Lopate, 2003

Dreaming of Hitler: Passions & Provocations by Daphne Merkin, 1997

Up in the Old Hotel and Other Stories by Joseph Mitchell, 1992

Days and Nights in Calcutta by Bharati Mukherjee and Clark Blais, 1977

My Kind of Place: Travel Stories from a Woman Who's Been Everywhere by Susan Orlean, 2004

Arts of the Possible, Adrienne Rich, 2001

The Death of Adam: Essays on Modern Thought by Marilynne Robinson, 1998

Talk Stories by Lillian Ross, 1966

How Literature Saved My Life by David Shields, 2013

The Gay Talese Reader: Portraits and Encounters by Gay Talese, 2003

Never Drank the Kool-Aid: Essays by Touré, 2006

Essays of E. B. White by E. B. White, 1977

Bibliography

Bak, John S. & Bill Reynolds, eds. *Literary Journalism Across the Globe: Journalistic Traditions and Transnational Influences*. Amherst: U Mass P. 2011.

Bishop, Wendy. "Crossing the Lines: On Creative Composition and Composing Creative Writing." *Colors of a Different Horse*. Ed. Wendy Bishop & Hans Ostrom. Urbana, IL: National Council of Teachers of English, 1994. 181–194. ERIC Online.

_____. "Suddenly Sexy: Creative Nonfiction Rear-ends Composition." *College English*. 65.3 (2003): 257–275.

Bizzaro, Patrick. "Writer's Self-Reports, (Com)positioning, and the Recent History of Academic Creative Writing." *Composing Ourselves as Writer-Teacher-Writers: Starting with Wendy Bishop*. Ed. Patrick Bizzaro, Alys Culhane, & Devan Cook. New York: Hampton Press, 2011. 119–132.

Boynton, Robert S. *The New Journalism: Conversations with America's Best Nonfiction Writers on Their Craft*. New York: Vintage, 2005.

Cheney, Theodore A. Rees. *Writing Creative Nonfiction: How To Use Fiction Techniques To Make Your Nonfiction More Interesting, Dramatic, and Vivid*. Berkeley, CA: Ten Speed Press, 1991.

Forché, Carolyn & Philip Gerard, eds. *Writing Creative Nonfiction: Instruction and Insights from the Teachers of the Associated Writing Programs*. Cincinnati, OH: Story Press, 2001.

Gammarino, Thomas. "Class Barriers: Creative Writing in Freshman Composition." *Currents in Teaching and Learning*. 1.2 (2009): 19–27.

Girard, Amanda & Carey Smitherman. "Creating Connection: Composition Theory and Creative Writing Craft in the First-Year Writing Classroom." *Currents in Teaching and Learning*. 3.2 (2011): 49–57.

Heilker, Paul. *The Essay: Theory and Pedagogy for an Active Form*. Urbana, IL: NCTE P., 1996.

_____. "The Place of Creative Writing in Composition Studies." *College Composition and Communication*. 62.1 (2010): 31–52.

_____. "Who Owns Creative Nonfiction?" *Beyond Postprocess and Postmodernism: Essays on the Spaciousness of Rhetoric*. Ed. Theresa

Enos & Keith Miller. Hillsdale, NJ: Lawrence Erlbaum Associates, 2003: 251–266.

Lardner, Ted. "Locating the Boundaries of Composition and Creative Writing." *College Composition and Communication.* 51.1 (1999): 72–77.

Mayers, Tim. *(Re)Writing Craft: Composition, Creative Writing, and the Future of English Studies.* Pittsburgh: U Pittsburgh P, 2005.

Newkirk, Thomas. *The Performance of Self in Student Writing.* Portsmouth, NH: Heinemann, 1997.

_____. *The School Essay Manifesto: Reclaiming the Essay for Students and Teachers.* Shoreham, VT: Discover Writing Press, 2005.

O'Connor, John S. *This Time It's Personal: Teaching Academic Writing Through Creative Nonfiction.* Urbana, IL: NCTE Press, 2011.

Singer, Margot & Nicole Walker. *Bending Genre: Essays on Creative Nonfiction.* New York: Bloomsbury Academic, 2013.

Talbot, Jill. *Metawritings: Toward a Theory of Nonfiction.* Iowa City, IA: 2012.

Talese, Gay & Barbara Lounsberry. *Writing Creative Nonfiction : The Literature of Reality.* New York: Harper Collins College Press, 1996.

Zinsser, William, ed. *Inventing the Truth: The Art and Craft of Memoir.* Boston: Houghton Mifflin, 1987.

About the Editor

Jay Ellis teaches at the University of Colorado at Boulder, where he is a fellow of the Center of the American West and the Program for Writing and Rhetoric's faculty advisor for *Journal Twenty Twenty*. When his students launched this journal in 2013, it was the country's only exclusively creative nonfiction publication to be written, edited, and produced by undergraduates, featuring undergraduate art, and appearing both online and in print. He has also taught literature and composition in the English and the Expository Writing Departments of New York University, where he completed a dissertation on Cormac McCarthy, and at the University of Texas Dallas.

Research interests include spatial configurations in American literature and culture and feminist aspects of post-World War II literature of the American West. Publications include another Critical Insights volume, *Southern Gothic Literature* (Salem, 2013); the essay "'Do you see?' Levels of Ellipsis in *No Country for Old Men*" in *Cormac McCarthy:* All the Pretty Horses, No Country for Old Men, The Road (Continuum, 2011); and chapters in *Rhetorical Democracy* and *Bloom's Modern Critical Views: Cormac McCarthy*. He has contributed to *The Rocky Mountain Review*, *Negations: An Interdisciplinary Journal of Social Thought*, *Concho River Review*, *Sulphur River*, and *Chelsea*. His first book, *No Place for Home: Spatial Constraint and Character Flight in the Novels of Cormac McCarthy* (Routledge, 2006), remains in print. He has recently completed a second novel, *Going Around*, and is working on a creative nonfiction essay, "My Dark Places: Southern Gothic, Texas," and *Don't Fence Me In: Reading, Watching, and Living in American Spaces*. A professional jazz drummer for many years, he has performed extensively in Boston, New York, his native Dallas, and Colorado's Front Range, including Red Rocks Amphiteatre outside Denver.

Contributors_____

David Bahr is an assistant professor of English at the Borough of Manhattan Community College, The City University of New York. He received his doctorate in post-war twentieth-century American literature and autobiography at The Graduate Center, The City University of New York. His journalism and creative writing have appeared in numerous publications, including the *New York Times*, the *New York Times Book Review*, *GQ*, *Poets & Writers*, *Publishers Weekly*, *The Village Voice*, *Prairie Schooner*, *Time Out New York*, *The Advocate,* and *Boys to Men: Gay Men Write About Growing Up*. His scholarship has been published in *Reconstruction: Studies in Contemporary Culture, Affective (Dis)order and the Writing Life: The Melancholic Muse, Graphic Pedagogy*, and *Lifewriting Annual: Biographical and Autobiographical Studies*. His work has been cited by The Best American Essays series and *The Missouri Review*, and he has been awarded writing fellowships at Yaddo and The Edward Albee Foundation. He thanks the PSC-CUNY 44 Grant and 2014 BMCC Faculty Development Grant for providing the time to research and write the essays for this collection.

Brandon Benevento works as a PhD student in the English Department at the University of Connecticut, where he teaches composition and class-focused literature courses and studies creative nonfiction, political economy, and twentieth-century American literature. His dissertation project employs memoir, reportage, and literary criticism to explore and portray class relationships occurring at locations of labor and leisure. In his spare time, he runs a property management company in the New Haven area, a job in which he excels at picking up lots of trash. He lives with his wife Amy in Branford, CT.

Kelly Clasen is an instructor of English at Hutchinson Community College in Kansas, where she teaches composition and literature. A native of rural south-central Kansas, she earned her master's and PhD in American literature from the University of North Texas. Kelly's research interests include regionalism, American women's fiction, gender studies, and environmental ethics. Her publications highlight environmental themes in works by Kate Chopin, Hamlin Garland, Charles Chesnutt, and Willa Cather, among others, and have appeared in *Southern Studies*, *The CEA Critic*, and *The South Carolina Review*.

G. Thomas Couser, a lifelong New Englander, graduated from Dartmouth College and got his doctorate in American civilization at Brown University. He then taught English and American studies at Connecticut College and Hofstra University. While at Hofstra, he founded and directed a disability studies program housed in the College of Liberal Arts and Sciences. His books include *Recovering Bodies: Illness, Disability, and Life Writing* (U of Wisconsin P, 1997); *Vulnerable Subjects: Ethics and Life Writing* (Cornell UP, 2004); *Signifying Bodies: Disability in Contemporary Life Writing* (U of Michigan P, 2009); and *Memoir: An Introduction* (Oxford UP, 2012). He has published personal essays in *The Hudson Review*, *New Haven Review*, and *Southwest Review*. He recently completed a memoir of his father, *Letter to My Father: Recognition and Reconciliation*. Now retired from teaching, he lives outside New London, Connecticut, where he enjoys sea kayaking and ice hockey in his spare time.

Jay Ellis teaches in the Program for Writing and Rhetoric at the University of Colorado, where he is also a fellow of the Center of the American West and faculty advisor for *Journal Twenty Twenty*, an all-undergraduate publication of creative nonfiction. Ellis began performing on drums in shopping malls, VFW (Veterans of Foreign Wars) halls, stock shows, and theaters at age eleven and studied performance and jazz composition and arranging at Berklee College. He earned his MA in interdisciplinary literary studies at the University of Texas Dallas and his PhD in American literature at New York University. He writes novels, creative nonfiction, and scholarship on Southern Gothic and Western American literature. Publications include *No Place for Home: Spatial Constraint and Character Flight in the Novels of Cormac McCarthy* (Routledge) and a previous *Critical Insights* volume, *Southern Gothic Literature*.

Ross Griffin is a PhD student at the University College Cork, Ireland. His research interests include, among others, creative nonfiction, war-writing, Orientalism, and the portrayal of American exceptionalism in literature and film. Having earned a bachelor of technology in information technology from the University of Limerick, Ross took a circuitous route through several golf courses and construction sites in the US and Ireland to return to college, where he earned his master's degree in modernities. Entering the final stages of his PhD, his doctoral research investigates the representation of American exceptionalism in creative nonfiction written by veterans and journalists of the Vietnam War.

Peter Kratzke was raised in the Great Pacific Northwest before venturing east to pursue his doctorate at the University of Kentucky, has since taught in Wisconsin, Texas, Michigan, and, at long last, Colorado. In 2015, he will once again be on the move, journeying from the University of Colorado's Program for Writing and Rhetoric to the University of Northern Colorado's English Department. Given his many figurative, as well as literal, miles, Kratzke could pen a travel novel, but instead chooses the more conventional scholarly route, publishing articles about such authors as Sarah Kemble Knight, Mark Twain, Edgar Wilson ("Bill") Nye, Ambrose Bierce, and Jack London. Kratzke also understands the other side of the academic publishing process: a long-time member of the College English Association, he serves as the associate editor for *The CEA Critic*. Finally, while not leading the life of a scholar-teacher, Kratzke enjoys writing about his adventures bicycle touring—taken from a creatively nonfictional point of view, of course.

Katherine Lashley is a PhD candidate in English at Morgan State University. Her dissertation analyzes the themes of gender, disability, and social class in young adult dystopias, including *The Hunger Games* by Suzanne Collins and *Divergent* by Veronica Roth. She also analyzes gender and disability in multicultural literature and has published an article, "Writing Body and Culture: Mohja Kahf's *The Girl in the Tangerine Scarf*" in the *Journal of American Studies of Turkey*, and she has published the book chapter, "Disability in Octavia Butler's Kindred: Dana, Alice, and Carrie" in *Critical Insights: The Slave Narrative*. In 2011, she published her memoir, *My Younger Older Sister: Growing Up With An Autistic Older Sister*. She teaches first-year writing courses at Towson University and Harford Community College in Bel Air, Maryland.

Shira Segal received her doctorate in film and media studies from Indiana University's Department of Communication and Culture and her master's in cultural memory from the University of London's Institute of Romance Studies. As a feminist film scholar with expertise in documentary and avant-garde cinema, her work spans gender studies, genre studies, film theory, and new media. Her dissertation *Home Movies and Home Birth: The Avant-garde Childbirth Film and Pregnancy in New Media* examines the aesthetic and cultural history of alternative film and media practices surrounding the maternal body over the past fifty years. Her new work, titled *First Person Fe/Male: The Gendered Self in First Person Cinema*, investigates the dynamic between gender, technology, and aesthetics in personal filmmaking practices across documentary, experimental, and home-movie history as well as by contemporary image-makers on the Internet.

Christopher Allen Varlack is a lecturer in the Department of English at the University of Maryland, Baltimore County where he teaches courses in composition and creative non-fiction. He received his BA in Communications from Loyola University Maryland and his MFA in Creative Writing from the University of Southern Maine. He is currently a PhD candidate at Morgan State University. His recent work has been published in *Critical Insights: Zora Neale Hurston, Critical Insights: The Slave Narrative,* and *Critical Insights: Virginia Woolf & 20ᵗʰ Century Women Writers*, among a number of other multi-authored reference works. His current research focuses on the alternative intellectual strategies of key Harlem Renaissance authors such as Langston Hughes and Claude McKay.

Beth Walker is a writing consultant at the University of Tennessee at Martin. Her creative work has been published in such journals as *Alaska Quarterly Review, Cream City Review, Yellow Medicine Review*, and *Homeworks: A Book of Tennessee Writers* (University of Tennessee Press). Her teaching essays appear in *Kansas English Journal, Pupil: A Journal of Rhetoric and Composition Pedagogy* (California State Fullerton), the anthology *Pass/Fail: 32 Stories about Teaching, from Inspiring to Hilarious* (Kleidon Press), and the college textbook *Practical Composition: Exercises for the English Classroom from Working*

Instructors (McFarland). Her current research is in revision, adaptation, and pop culture, especially focusing upon girls' detective series and *The Walking Dead*. A long-time student and practitioner of Natalie Goldberg's methods, she has presented workshops on *Writing Down the Bones* to high school students and to teachers and tutors at professional conferences, in addition to using *Bones* in the freshman composition classroom.

Christopher Walsh received his BA and PhD degrees from the University of Wales, Swansea; his PhD discussed Cormac McCarthy's novels in relation to ideas of Southern exceptionalism. He has lectured at Hull University in the UK and the University of Tennessee, Knoxville. He has published several articles, a couple of chapters and one book on McCarthy (*In the Wake of the Sun: Navigating the Southern Works of Cormac McCarthy*), as well as pieces on the Southern Gothic. He currently lives in Ely, Cambridgeshire with his wife Nikki and two children, Billy and Annabelle. He works in central London, where he's the head of e-learning for a medical college. Chris is also currently studying for an MSc in digital education at the University of Edinburgh.

Index

Burroughs, William S. 7
Butler, Benjamin 121

cancer 13, 126, 129, 130, 131, 135
capitalism xvi, 9
Capote, Truman 3, 10, 20, 24, 63
Carlson, Marla 144
Carson, Anne 29
Carson, Rachel 10
Caruth, Cathy 204
Cerf, Bennett 111
Césaire, Aimé 101
Charon, Rita 128
Chekhov, Anton 126
Chute, Hilary 197, 209
cinema 153, 154, 155, 157, 158,
    164, 165, 166, 197, 226
Cioffi, Frank 204
Civil War x, 8, 9, 96, 110, 120,
    123
Civil War trilogy 120
Cleaver, Eldridge 105
Clinton, Hillary 13
Cofer, Judith Ortiz xxvii, 215
Collins, John 70
Combs, Sean 77
Comics 196, 197, 199, 200, 202,
    209, 210, 211
Conway, Jill Ker 95, 97
Cook, Robin 126
Cooper, James Fenimore 6, 79, 86
Cooper, Susan Fenimore ix, 9, 79,
    92, 93
Cooper, Wayne F. 104
Crafts, Hannah 8
Crane, Stephen 10
Crawford, Matthew 186
Crayon, Geoffrey xxii, 6
Crichton, Michael 126

Cronin, A. J. 126
Crookman, Junius 107
Cruse, Harold 104
Cutter, Weston 40, 41

D'Agata, John xviii, 29, 30, 31,
    35, 40, 42, 45, 46, 47
Daisey, Mike 41, 47
Dargis, Manohla 164
Davis, Jefferson 110, 114
DeBaggio, Thomas 129
Defoe, Daniel 25, 27, 28
Defonseca, Misha 134
DeGeneres, Ellen 13
de Kruif, Paul 124
depression xiii, 11, 52, 130, 192,
    198, 199, 207
Deren, Maya 163
Derounian-Stodala, Kathryn 4
de Wael, Monique 135, 137
Dickinson, Emily vii, xiv
Didion, Joan 10, 23, 24, 181
Dillard, Annie 10, 215
Disney, Walt 198
Documentary Image 153
Dorris, Michael 135
Doubrovsky, Serge 56
Douglass, Frederick x, 8, 95, 105,
    108
Doyle, Arthur Conan 126
Drake, Clair 104
Dreiser, Theodore 11
Du Bois, William Edward
    Burghardt 96
Duplessis, Joseph-Siffred 77

Eakin, Paul John 15, 21, 58
Edwards, Jonathan 63
Eggers, Dave 31, 45, 215